YOUR SOUL AT WORK

Five Steps to a More Fulfilling Career and Life

YOUR SOUL AT WORK

*Five Steps to a More
Fulfilling Career and Life*

By
Nicholas W. Weiler
In collaboration with
Stephen C. Schoonover, M.D.

HiddenSpring

Acknowledgments The publisher gratefully acknowledges use of the following: Excerpt from *The Abolition of Man* by C. S. Lewis, copyright © C. S. Lewis Pte. Ltd. 1943, 1946, 1978. Extract reprinted by permission. Excerpts from *God and the Astronomers* by Robert Jastrow, copyright 1978 by Robert Jastrow. Reprinted by permission of the Carol Mann Agency. Excerpts from *Back to Virtue* by Peter Kreeft, copyright 1986, 1992 by Peter Kreeft. Reprinted by permission of Ignatius Press. Excerpts from *Pensées* by Blaise Pascal, translated by A J Krailsheimer (Penguin Classics, 1966), copyright © A J Krailsheimer, 1966. Reproduced by permission of Penguin Books Ltd. The poem "In Broken Image" from *Complete Poems* by Robert Graves, copyright 1961 by Robert Graves. Reprinted by permission of Carcanet Press Limited. Excerpts from the Leadership Education Program workbook, © copyright 1995 by The Foundation for Community Encouragement. Used by permission. Excerpt from *The New Jerusalem Bible*, copyright © 1985 by Darton, Longman & Todd, Ltd., les Editions du Cerf and Doubleday, a division of Random House, Inc. Reprinted by permission of the publishers. Excerpt from the *New American Bible*, copyright 1970, 1986, 1991 by the Confraternity of Christian Doctrine, Washington, D.C. Reprint permission granted by World Bible Publishers Inc., Iowa Falls, IA 51026, U.S.A. Scripture quotation marked "(TEV)" is taken from *Today's English Version*, Second Edition, © 1992, American Bible Society. Used by permission.

Cover design by Mark Horton

Book design by Saija Autrand, Faces Type & Design

Copyright © 2001 by Nicholas W. Weiler and Stephen C. Schoonover

Library of Congress Cataloging-in-Publication Data

Weiler, Nicholas W.
    Your soul at work : five steps to a more fulfilling career and life / by Nicholas W. Weiler in collaboration with Stephen C. Schoonover.
        p. cm.
    Includes bibliographical references (p.).
    ISBN 1-58768-006-8 (alk. paper)
    1. Work—Religious aspects.   2. Vocational guidance.   3. Self-actualization (Psychology)
    4. Vocation   I. Schoonover, Stephen C., 1947–   II. Title.
    BL65.W67 W45 2000
    650.14—dc21   00-063358

Published by
HiddenSpring
an imprint of Paulist Press
997 Macarthur Boulevard
Mahwah, New Jersey 07430

www.hiddenspringbooks.com

Printed and bound in the United States of America

To my wife, Claire, to our children, Tim, Ann, Chris, Kevin, and Maura, and to their spouses and our growing tribe of grandchildren. These are the people who have contributed most toward making my personal journey rewarding, unpredictable, and fun.

Claire and I have traveled the road as a team through good times and bad. We've learned together. She already knows what this book has to say.

I wrote this primarily for our children and their families—to share lessons learned over three decades of watching and experiencing what does and does not work for people who want to earn a living while still pursuing their deepest personal hopes and enjoying the trip.

Nicholas W. Weiler

Author's Note

This book is very much a joint effort between Steve Schoonover and me. We've been working together developing and teaching these concepts for over 15 years. The task of writing the book became mine only because Steve already had a full schedule managing a busy consulting organization.

Throughout the text I have used the pronoun **"I"** to express my more personal thoughts, and the pronoun **"we"** to express our joint ideas.

While various organizational incidents in the book are based on actual situations, all are composites of similar events that happened across several different companies. Names and details have been changed to protect confidentiality.

N.W.W.

ACKNOWLEDGMENTS

This book was in process for over three years. I can never give sufficient thanks to all the people who contributed to the content and clarification of my thinking as the manuscript evolved.

My first thanks go to Steve Schoonover, my collaborator, friend, teacher, and long-time partner. Without him there would be no competency research or personal self-assessment tools, both of which are major foundation stones for the book's content and credibility. We learned a great deal together in over 15 years of research and program development, first in the United States and then throughout the world. Next I want to thank our editor, Jan-Erik Guerth. His insight into what we wanted to say and his excellent editing suggestions added enormously to the structure, focus, and clarity of the final manuscript.

To mention only a few of the others, I want to thank the late Dr. Daniel J. Levinson, M. Scott Peck, M.D., and Fr. Benedict J. Groeschel, C.F.R., whose friendship, writings, suggestions, and counsel have contributed enormously to major portions of the text. And I want to give very special acknowledgment to the late Mary Ann Schmidt, former president of the Foundation for Community Encouragement (FCE), who told me not to revise my earlier career book, but instead to write something completely new integrating our latest research and insight gained during the 17 years the first book was in publication.

My thanks also go to my friends, children, and colleagues who read and critiqued various sections; to Marian S. Kellogg, my boss and early mentor during her years as vice-president at GE; to Mary Nell Schoonover and Kevin Perrotta whose patience, professionalism, and multiple editings kept me motivated and on track throughout a series of earlier drafts; and to Richard Gerace, whose word-processing expertise turned my amateur typing into something readable.

Finally, I want to express my gratitude to our many organizational advocates, from first-line supervisors to senior vice-presidents and CEOs throughout GE and Steve's numerous client organizations—those who were willing to break old mindsets, take risks, and try new things, especially in the earlier days when competency-based performance and leadership development programs were much less known and proven than they are today

Nicholas W. Weiler

TABLE OF CONTENTS

CAREER AND LIFE WORKBOOK

PREFACE

Loss of morale, burnout, and attrition, especially among professional and managerial employees, have become issues of increasing concern for individuals and the organizations they serve. Many in the work force are experiencing a difficult-to-pinpoint frustration—a growing sense of being too driven, with no time for family, important relationships, or other personal values. They are asking, but finding little opportunity to answer, the question, "Is this really what I want to be doing with my life?"

Defining what we really want in life isn't easy in today's time-pressured world. It requires filtering out an ongoing barrage of seemingly important, but often ultimately irrelevant external influences. Only then can we tune in and really hear our own internal voices and needs. Somehow we have to quiet down and pay serious attention to the much more important, really life-defining realities of habitually neglected core values. We need to acknowledge what are often intellectually suppressed but desperately felt longings for genuine meaning—for a greater sense of fulfillment and even spiritual growth in what we do.

Feeling this need, many are drawn to books by popular spiritually oriented writers. However, afterward they don't know how to apply what they've read to their time-pressured, work-dominated lives. On the other hand, the "how to" business-oriented career-development books they read tend to shy away from much discussion of an individual's more spiritual concerns. This leaves them frustrated and not knowing how to put it all together.

We sense a need for a different kind of book that bridges the gap between straight spiritual and straight business writers. Our intent is to present a number of concepts agreed to by some of the great spiritual giants of history in a language and context people can relate to their daily work activities. We follow this up with some very practical, research-based "how to" tools and techniques to help you better integrate your personal, spiritual, and work endeavors. We think this combination in a single book can have significant impact.

The tools and techniques presented are based on lessons learned from more than 15 years of interviewing and observing people who have—and have not—found personal fulfillment and satisfaction in their lives and careers. Our research team has interviewed over 4,000 individuals, conducted over 400 group/focus group sessions, and developed over 200 competency models, identifying critical success behaviors and job experiences in a broad spectrum of career specialties across the United States, Europe, Asia, the Near East, Mexico, and South America. The people we've interviewed and observed have included both managers and nonmanagers in over 60 organizations.

The self-diagnosis instruments and tools we present are currently being used by a wide variety of organizations, including top multinational manufacturing companies, small private businesses, banks, and not-for-profit social service institutions. They have been successfully tested for many years over multiple career fields, national cultures, and organization sizes.

Listening to and observing people across many different careers and organizational cultures have taught us a great deal about how people build successful careers. One of the things we've learned is that we need to integrate our strongly felt life values and spiritual longings into our careers. If we neglect these—if we keep them separate from our work lives—our careers will not produce much real satisfaction.

We think this book is unique in two ways. **First**, it puts the process of career planning into a larger perspective and recommends ways to put your work at the service of a deeper and more spiritually satisfying personal life journey—a journey that transcends career success and keeps it in perspective as merely one, and never *the* ultimate criterion for success in life.

We'll describe how people's basic life perspectives or *mindsets* tend to drive the career choices they make, often unconsciously. Specific career values and choices typically vary and change as individuals progress through predictable life stages. However, people who build satisfying lives also tend to have a broader, clearly defined personal life philosophy with more enduring overarching values that dictate the direction of choices they make. We'll encourage you to identify what these overarching values are for you.

In earlier chapters we'll recommend ways to break through old disempowering myths and mindsets so you can look with greater clarity at the realities of your life and career today. With improved clarity you can separate your own from society's or others' imposed expectations. Then, with a clearer head, you can define your unique, deeply felt, personal values and needs. These then become your personal criteria for building career goals that can have lasting meaning.

Second, we'll present a very structured and proven process, including a *Career and Life Workbook*, for defining your uniquely personal success criteria, integrating these into concrete life goals and negotiating a career path to achieve them.

Throughout the book we stress the need for a continuous dual focus—first, a focus on defining *what* you really want and need to find fulfillment in *your* life, and second, a focus on specific *how to's*. Our experience shows that clarity on the *what* is essential before people can make satisfying use of any *how to's*.

Our goal is to provide a balance between the big picture and the little picture—between our frequently unacknowledged internal need for personal, spiritual growth and our external need for success and survival in the workplace.

Our intent is to help you notice and continually keep your eye on both your deepest personal needs and the practicalities of earning a living. It *is* possible to integrate both into a life you find rewarding. It isn't always easy, and there inevitably will be setbacks. However, our experience in watching those who do it shows it can be exciting, great fun, and extremely gratifying.

"The mass of men lead lives of quiet desperation."

Henry David Thoreau

"The above may be true but we've discovered it definitely isn't necessary— for men or women. There is a better way and many are pursuing it."

The Authors

INTRODUCTION

In our journey through life we need to know our mission. We need some clear sense of why we are on the road. To see our joys and our inevitable sorrows in some meaningful context, we yearn to know the objective of our voyage—our ultimate reason to be. This leads us to spiritual questions that are seldom asked, much less answered, in materialistic contemporary society. We pay a hidden but severe price for ignoring them.

MY BRIEF WINDOW OF TIME

Why was I born? Why am I living? In what should I invest my hopes, my energies, and my love? Who and what do I want to become during my brief window of time on this earth? What is my purpose? Can it be a lasting purpose that provides direction and hope for a meaningful destination beyond this life? Is the enormous effort I am putting into my work moving me toward or away from the real meaning I seek? If I want something different, how do I change?

Many are finding these questions difficult to answer. Few work organizations are providing an effective process or set of tools to help answer them. In an era of global competition and leaner, more demanding work environments many organizations are dangerously borrowing on human capital by creating what are often profitable but inhumane conditions of overstressed, overworked, and burned-out employees. People are longing for a greater sense of purpose in their work. To survive in a highly competitive workplace, many become so responsive to their organizations' demands that they lose their sense of self. They yearn for more personal autonomy in managing their own lives but don't know how to achieve it.

The more enlightened organizational leaders dislike the situation as much as those they lead. At some level they realize they need, and are desperately looking for, new ways of thinking and operating that can better meet the deeper, more human needs of the business, the individual, and the society they both serve.

The chief executive officer (CEO) of a major computer software institution demonstrated his feeling of helplessness in the current environment when he spoke at a training session for his company's top young leaders. One participant spoke of his difficulty finding any time to spend with his family or pursue any nonwork related personal values. The CEO said he understood but had no answers and cited his own divorce as a symptom of the problem. Then, unpleasantly but candidly, he made what he said was a *politically incorrect* but honest observation. He said the truth was that there were probably six or seven people waiting in line to replace anyone, including himself, who could not (or would not) keep up the pace. He meant well but it was a discouraging and not very hopeful answer. Very likely it was also an answer based on some unchallenged but questionable implied organizational values and assumptions we will explore later.

A BETTER WAY

What can be done to improve things? We've discovered a lot can be done. You don't have to accept the assumptions and boxed-in mindset evidenced in the CEO's answer. And you don't have to wait for your boss or organization to get its act together. You can start now. There are people who are already overcoming the chaos of an unstable and unpredictable career marketplace. They are doing it today. They haven't eliminated all frustration and stress from their workplaces. No jobs are trouble-free. However, they have learned how to seek out and identify their own more enduring personal truths and values and how to pursue them on the job. They're even having fun doing it. They've discovered there are some reliable techniques they can use—and competencies they can develop—to help them survive, grow, and prosper whether or not their organizations ever improve.

SOME RESEARCH-BASED SOLUTIONS

This book is designed to help people find their own answers despite the chaotic career realities that may surround them. We've spent a lot of time looking beyond the surface clichés. We've conducted extensive studies of what works and does not work in developing and implementing personal career strategies. We wrote this book to share what we've discovered.

We won't answer your questions for you. You should beware of anyone who tries to do that. It's your life and the answers will not be meaningful unless they are specifically yours. Instead, we'll present a systematic process with concrete tools and techniques to help you answer the questions for yourself. We'll also describe a common set of generic core skills (or competencies) people demonstrate in successfully negotiating the accomplishment of their chosen career objectives no matter what those objectives might be. The process, tools, and competencies we present were derived from research conducted over 15 years and throughout the United States, Canada, Europe, Asia, the Near East, Mexico, and South America.

A VARIETY OF ORGANIZATION SIZES

In the research, we interviewed people pursuing careers in a broad spectrum of organizations. Whenever we use the word *organization*, therefore, we will be referring to enterprises ranging in size from very small two or three person private business or social service endeavors to major international companies.

Most of our research has been with college-educated people working in these organizations. Our findings apply primarily to this population. Others, however, have participated in our workshops and said many of the tools and techniques we'll be describing were also useful to them—particularly the process presented for deciding personal values and identifying future career and life goals.

FORGOTTEN WISDOM

We have also studied the accumulated wisdom of many current and ancient spiritual writers, philosophers, religious leaders, and psychologists to factor in and compare their recommendations with the results of our own observations. Over the years great spiritual leaders of both the Eastern and Western traditions have given us enormous insight into what does, and does not, constitute enduring life satisfaction. While this insight is sometimes given lip service, it's too often overlooked. It ends up being forgotten in the day-to-day busyness of today's short term, materialistically oriented society. We hear a faint voice of dissonance trying to break into our consciousness, but we don't heed it. We wonder why we are nagged by a vague sense of incongruity and dissatisfaction, but we don't know what to do about it. We need a road map for stepping off the treadmill to explore and resolve the incongruities. We will present a road map that has helped others step off the treadmill long enough to think through and plot a more satisfying future.

A PROVEN PROCESS

The approach we will describe works. The materials have been carefully crafted and fine-tuned in a series of seminars and workshops conducted over several years with professionals in many different specialties and at multiple career levels throughout the world.

AUTONOMY NEEDN'T WAIT

The research shows you don't have to wait for the environment to improve or the organization to get its act together. There are people who are finding meaningful careers within organizations today. We spoke with them. They have learned that autonomy and potency are possible despite chaotic organizational environments. Many learned this the hard way when faced with survival, as global competition forced massive downsizing in their businesses.

Many talented professionals, who faced the disruption of what they had believed were enduring career trajectories, realized for the first time that they had never really taken much personal control over their work lives. They had been running too fast to notice where they were going. They had been so busy responding to external demands they had never taken time to listen to their own internal voices and define clear expectations of their own. Now their organizations were derailing or even rejecting them. Did that mean they should reject themselves? That subtle but essential question became even more critical than the loss of income.

Most, eventually, if painfully, found new career paths and grew from the experience. Many established a new, more secure self-esteem based on internal self-sufficiency rather than on organizational recognition and reward. They developed better-defined, more fulfilling priorities in life and an improved contact with themselves, their personal life journeys, their families, and even their God.

In retrospect, career disruption proved a good thing for many. We began to feel that they were in subtle ways better off than those who have never faced an economic or career disruption. A lot of us are still running mindlessly with no time or necessity to stop and notice, to become aware of ourselves and our needs as persons, to define our personal values and beliefs and learn how both can be realized or destroyed in a society focused on external expectations and rewards.

Watching autonomous people across many career specialties, we discovered that what they do is not mysterious. It is, however, relatively rare. Few people in our culture understand the techniques of autonomy—the basic fundamentals of how to develop and maintain the personal empowerment needed to achieve personal values in a depersonalized environment. We believe that when you finish this book you will understand a number of techniques others have used successfully. We hope you'll decide to use them for yourself.

As authors we're optimistic. We believe work organizations can and will gradually improve their career environments. We've spent our professional lives helping organizations do that. Some of the biggest improvements any organization can make are to help their employees become more autonomous and less dependent. Organizations should be candid about the fact that no organization can offer any truthful guarantees or predict the future. They should provide methodologies to help the individuals grow in directions they want to grow no matter what happens in the organization. Paradoxically, individuals who take charge of themselves, defining and pursuing their own career goals, also usually end up being an organization's most productive employees and most likely to remain on the payroll.

AUTONOMY REQUIRES AWARENESS

Personal autonomy comes from developing a clear awareness of how most work organizations *really* operate. This can keep us from being blinded by naive expectations about how they are *supposed* to operate. This knowledge then allows us to design personal programs to deal with the observed realities. Becoming autonomous also involves examining the often unconscious assumptions (or myths) behind the way organizations and people behave. Becoming autonomous means bringing these assumptions into clear conscious awareness and deciding which you do and do not agree with.

BALANCING SELF-FULFILLMENT WITH A SENSE OF CONTRIBUTION

What many feel has become an excessive emphasis on *Selfism*—almost to the exclusion of the needs of society or other people—seems to be slowly but distinctly subsiding, primarily because it simply has not worked. It's made people feel worse rather than better about themselves. It's created a sense of isolation, estrangement, and lack of community that many find distressing. Self-fulfillment will always and rightfully be a high priority in life and career planning. Increasingly, however, we find people expressing a need for something more than the often excessively competitive and self-centered focus on personal satisfaction we have seen in recent years. Many now feel a strong need to balance individual self-fulfillment with a more altruistic and spiritual dimension in their work. They yearn for the sense of contribution that comes from feeling we are also accomplishing things that are of significant service to others.

CAREER AND VOCATION

In recent times the word *career* has been used most frequently to describe a person's life work. A person with a career is usually seen as engaged in work that brings personal satisfaction and continuous skills growth. The opposite would be having a job you simply must do to earn a living. A different word may better describe what our research shows people long to have in their work life. That word is *vocation*.

Vocation includes everything we find in a career plus something more—an almost spiritual sense of one's work as a *calling*, an opportunity to do something you were uniquely created or called to do, something that has meaning beyond the self. To hear a calling, however, one has to silence a lot of external noise. One has to sort through a number of difficult-to-ignore but illusionary myths that scream at us in our multimedia society and block the inner voice that leads us to our calling.

We'll devote a complete chapter to some of these more dangerous myths. Then we'll present a process and tools designed to help you turn your work life into both a career *and* a vocation.

FIVE STEPS

This book is divided into five sections. Each deals with an essential step in a five-part sequence that we believe successful people follow in effective career and life planning. Together these steps and their accompa-

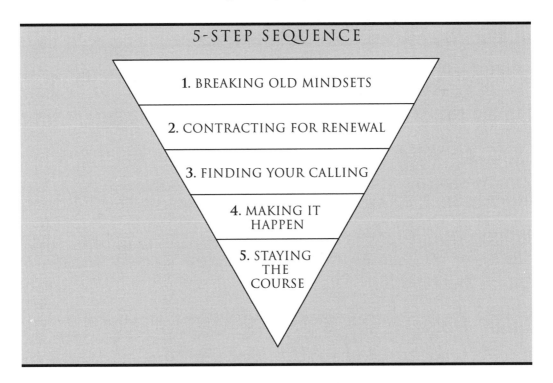

5-STEP SEQUENCE

1. BREAKING OLD MINDSETS

2. CONTRACTING FOR RENEWAL

3. FINDING YOUR CALLING

4. MAKING IT HAPPEN

5. STAYING THE COURSE

nying tools form a progressive sequence you can follow to identify, negotiate, and pursue your own unique career goals.

One of the problems with career planning is that while everyone
agrees it must be done, few actually do it. What's wrong? We find that
many career planning programs—personal and organizational—flounder
because people overlook or skip one or more of these five steps, often in a
rush to save time. The most negative consequence is that they typically fail
to identify and explore the deeper, more spiritual consequences of the
choices and decisions they are making. Also, when skipping steps causes
their efforts to break down over the long run, they waste much more time
recycling through repetitive and frustrating false starts.

In presenting these steps we will follow a sequence that ultimately
ties the separate parts into a unified whole. Individual sections are meant
to raise questions before they discuss potential answers.

A New Mindset—a Disciplined Process—Tools to Implement

The early sections of the book ask you to diverge—to break mindsets and question some contemporary beliefs that can seriously hamper
people in their career planning pursuits. The later parts of the book outline a step-by-step process with recommended tools to help you develop
specific future career plans that meet your own, not someone else's needs.
Examples of the tools we'll present include:

A *CAREER AND LIFE WORKBOOK* for use after you have
completed reading the book. This workbook helps you synthesize
and personalize lessons learned from the research and techniques
presented throughout the text. It contains a series of exercises you
can use to define your personal life-value priorities, and identify
what career path can best achieve them. If you need more space
for some entries just use notebook paper and follow the workbook
formats.

COMPETENCY SELF-ASSESSMENT TOOLS that define a
set of core competencies which research shows are critical for success in almost any career field you select. These tools are *included in*

the workbook to help you identify and address your most important current and future personal competency improvement needs.

AN INVESTIGATIVE INTERVIEW FORM including a recommended procedure for identifying and interviewing people who are successfully pursuing whatever career path the workbook has helped you choose.

Throughout the book we will also present a series of short reflections (shaded in gray), each with a few questions you can use to help you personalize the ideas being presented and relate them to your own life and career.

The detailed workbook exercises and tools, however, have deliberately been placed in the workbook rather than in the text. You can complete the exercises much more effectively when you have a better idea of how each fits into the larger picture. With this in mind, we recommend you not do any of the workbook exercises or make any workbook entries until after you completed reading the text. This is what people do in our Career and Life Workshops.

A LIFELONG PROCESS

The process we'll be describing is lifelong, and the tools are designed for you to keep on your shelf for continued use as specific new challenges and situations occur.

In the end, the search for relevance to your career and life will naturally be your own. The sequence we'll describe relies a great deal on your ability to assess what parts of the process will be useful to you, to choose which tools and techniques will be most relevant, and to tailor them to your needs.

1. BREAKING OLD MINDSETS

2. CONTRACTING FOR RENEWAL

3. FINDING YOUR CALLING

4. MAKING IT HAPPEN

5. STAYING THE COURSE

STEP 1

BREAKING OLD MINDSETS

In **Step 1** we focus on breaking old mindsets in two areas.

First, we'll look at some older thinking many feel is behind the loss of spirit felt so frequently in today's workplace. We'll also look at how a variety of contemporary thought leaders feel you can begin a new journey toward the recovery of purpose and meaning.

Second, we'll examine several pervasive but self-defeating myths or false assumptions that can be serious roadblocks on your life journey.

Reversing a Loss of Spirit

In working with both small and large organizations across multiple countries, we've observed a widespread malaise. We see very busy people who are often more harried than animated or excited about what they do. They use various vague, culturally acceptable words to express a certain loss of soul in their work. They put up a good front, but underneath their attitudes and moods are not very upbeat.

What's wrong? Why aren't they more enthusiastic? Why aren't they feeling that sense of meaningful contribution we all need to make our work satisfying and fun?

A lack of spiritual values and fulfillment in their work is the most frequent complaint we hear from highly educated and articulate people in today's organizations. But they tend to mention these complaints only in off-the-record conversations. On the job there is reluctance to speak of soft concepts such as *spirit* or *soul*, or of the desire for an increased sense of community with others in what we do. If we speak of these things, people might think we've gone soft or are not realistic. These ideas may get occasional lip service in our dwindling leisure hours, but they are frequently pushed to the background in our career endeavors. Calling it realistic, we keep our noses to the grindstone at work and focus instead on meeting the hard, highly quantifiable, but not always highly meaningful production or output measurements expected in our pragmatic culture. Quantity of output overrules quality of life, often because it's easier to measure and talk about. Is this truly realistic, or even pragmatic? Or does it show a tendency to bury our heads in the sand?

It is a split and frustrating existence if you have to leave your soul at home when you go to work and return home tired and overworked with no energy left for the soul.

AN OVERARCHING MEANING

There are multiple reasons why complex, intelligent human beings go to work. Earning a living is important. Recognition is important. But neither is the total explanation for human endeavors. Profit and production output are essential, but they can never be the total solution to our human need for finding an overarching meaning in life. This is so obvious we hesitate to write it. But in a tense and overdemanding workplace these obvious truths too often go unnoticed and unaddressed. We cite the obvious because, over many years of observing highly intelligent people in very sophisticated organizations, we have repeatedly seen the obvious being suppressed or ignored by people who, in their hearts, know better.

UPDATING OUR MINDSETS

Talk of spiritual things, such as an overarching meaning in life, is unfashionable in the workplace. Such talk is all right off the job, but at work discussion of anything not visible and measurable is looked on as impractical and unrealistic. At work, people rely on rational, scientific thinking to answer all questions, solve all problems, and satisfy their needs.

A great many of our business, organizational, and university leaders are rooted in this separation, this splitting off of people's souls and their need for meaning from the workplace. A teacher from a large university told us he meets periodically with a group of professors from many different universities to discuss their spiritual concerns. They meet privately and away from their schools because it's embarrassing (possibly even threatening to their careers) to discuss these things on their campuses. At least they're conscious of the split and are taking action to compensate for the missing spiritual elements. Many simply block out their spiritual needs, even off the job, and wonder what's wrong.

Paradoxically, many of our most advanced scientists have become increasingly open to the unknown spiritual dimensions of their work. As leading-edge technologists they know the limitations of their methods. They have learned that the more questions their sciences answer the more new questions are generated. The questions don't diminish. They expand endlessly and the scientists find that exciting.

In his book, *God and the Astronomers*, Dr. Robert Jastrow explains how the discoveries of Albert Einstein, Edwin Hubble, and other major scientific geniuses of the nineteenth and twentieth centuries established the big bang theory of the creation of the universe. They then realized—somewhat to the initial surprise of several—that this theory proved very consistent with the Bible's affirmation of creation from nothing in the book of Genesis. In a brief biographical chapter on Einstein Jastrow tells us:

> For Einstein, the existence of God was proven by the laws of nature; that is, the fact that there was order in the Universe and man could discover it.[1]

Jastrow, an internationally known astronomer and authority on life in the cosmos, founded NASA's Goddard Institute for Space Studies and held professorships at Columbia University and Dartmouth College. After an exhaustive review of discoveries by Einstein, Hubble, and their scientific peers and successors, Jastrow concluded that the scientist:

> has scaled the mountains of ignorance; he is about to conquer the highest peak; as he pulls himself over the final rock, he is greeted by a band of theologians who have been sitting there for centuries.[2]

Interestingly, it's been our experience that scientists in *hard* technologies like mathematics and physics are often more open to the spiritual dimensions of reality than those in the *soft* social, psychological, and business sciences. In some ways many eminent soft scientists and business leaders—and many of us—may be viewing our work with an older mind-set that the more aware leading-edge hard scientists have moved beyond.

BEYOND THE "ISMS"

The modern age has produced many "isms," a long chronology of materialistic ideologies that one after the other have promised to provide *the* answer—*the* solution to humankind's search for happiness and fulfillment. Each has produced some good, but none has produced the totality of what many ardent followers were led (or led themselves) to expect. Marxism, Liberalism, Socialism, Capitalism, Rationalism, Empiricism, and Utilitarianism are only a few examples of ideologies that ultimately failed to meet the overstated expectations they generated.

Materialistic "isms" have been crumbling all around us—few gracefully and some with bloodshed. As ideologies they have become tarnished. The glow is gone. In different ways the developers of these ideologies probably thought too simplistically and promised overly simplistic solutions that are running out of steam as followers become more aware of the world's true complexity. There are other reasons, of course. One may be that materialistic ideologies often focus our eyes on the wrong ball or even the wrong ball field.

The "isms" have catered to our more than human desire for short-term final solutions to our problems. Materialistic "isms" tend to imply, if not promise, that humankind can find some sort of heaven on earth, a quick or at least certain arrival at an ultimate and satisfying destination. In contradiction, most wise spiritual leaders (across many centuries, creeds, and cultures) have told us life is a *journey*, not a *destination*. They say that while the journey can be highly rewarding, it will seldom be easy and can never be considered completed in this life because our ultimate destination lies beyond this life.

A career (especially when we can also make it a vocation) is something that we hope will be an endless journey through progressively higher stages of insight, learning, and personal growth. Steve and I are fellow travelers who, by watching others wiser than we, have discovered many things they can teach us about making the journey more exciting and rewarding—but never trouble-free.

More Than Just "Nature"

The long-held belief that technology and the scientific method alone can bring us fulfillment and universal progress has faltered. It's still popular in some circles but it's disproved and no longer very realistic or even practical. We have learned over many decades of actual experience that what Francis Bacon once called humankind's supreme good, the progressive "conquest of nature," has brought, not only such wonders as space travel and modern medicine but also such horrors as genocide and the possibility of nuclear holocaust. After great initial optimism the sophistication, the arrogance, and the pride of our so-called enlightened modern age has ushered in much distressing confusion, disillusion, and disappointment in unfulfilled promises. Something is missing. Something has been lost.

We certainly don't want a return to technological ignorance. However, C. S. Lewis gives real insight into where some of our current uneasiness and sense of loss come from when he says:

> For the wise men of old, the cardinal problem (*of human life*) had been how to conform the soul to reality, and the solution had been knowledge, self-discipline, and virtue. For (*the modern*), the problem is how to subdue reality to the wishes of men, (*and*) the solution is a technique.[3]

Philosopher Peter Kreeft tells us that along with modernity's so-called practical philosophy of the *conquest of nature* comes:

> . . . a new theoretical philosophy that objective reality *is* only nature, that nature is all there is. This is Naturalism, the reduction of objective reality to matter, time, space and motion. The alternative to this philosophy is Supernaturalism, the belief that objective reality includes something more than nature. . . .[4]

By something more than nature Kreeft means a spiritual reality above and beyond the material and observable, including "something like God." He then concludes that:

> If "objective reality" means God, then we had better conform to him, and it is silly to try to make him conform to us.[5]

True Pragmatism

Many of us, however, lead our lives as though we were, for all practical purposes, atheists (or at least reluctant agnostics). *Naturalism*, as defined by Kreeft, is an insidious phenomenon. It sneaks up on us and we confine ourselves to its narrow views without noticing what we are doing. Though most of us believe in a reality beyond observable nature, we act as if we do not. We give spiritual considerations no meaningful time. We don't factor them into our daily lives—especially our frantic and distracted working lives. We exhaust ourselves pursuing Naturalism's short range, transitory, and ultimately unsatisfying goals. This frantic pursuit blocks our vision of the longer-range, more satisfying realities. We ignore spiritual goals that are more difficult to visualize with our limited, short-sighted human faculties but for which we long—and without which we feel disenchanted and know we will find no ultimate fulfillment. Not a practical way of life, but a pervasive one. I know. I have spent a lot of time running on this frustrating and unconscious treadmill accompanied by many of my most respected colleagues. If you are like me, you need constant vigilance to step outside the race periodically and consciously plot where you want to go. It isn't easy but it can be done and it's critically important.

Two World Views—Both Built on Faith

All journeys have a starting point, a basic foundation point from which we plot our subsequent course. Whatever ultimate goal we have, the directions we choose to get there will differ depending on where we started. As we navigate our individual journeys through life, we base all our decisions, every choice we make at every fork in the road, on one of two very different fundamental starting points or world views about the nature of reality. We can build our lives and our fates on the choice that Kreeft describes as *Naturalism* based on the assumption that human reason is supreme and this world (*i.e.*, nature) is all there is. Or we can choose *Supernaturalism* based on the assumption that there is more—that beyond nature as we know it there is an intelligence far surpassing our puny human intellects and we are charting our courses to a higher place where we can ultimately know:

> what eye has not seen and ear has not heard and it has not entered into the human heart to think.[6]

Both these world views are based on faith. Neither can be proven rationally or scientifically. Valuable as they are, reason and the scientific method can never prove or disprove anything that is beyond our ability to observe—and modern scientific advances continually reveal that, even with our most advanced instrumentation, the greater part of reality seems to lie beyond, rather than within, our observation capabilities.

However, most of our best thinkers seem to conclude that even limited human logic points to a higher intelligence—rather than mere chance—behind the clearly visible precision, complexity, order, and beauty of the universe we can observe. Our wisest spiritual leaders have recommended faith in a higher reality derived from Revelation. To us this seems a more sensible faith; more in tune with what we intuitively sense to be true from even the limited observations we can make. It also seems to be far less of a blind leap into the dark than the arrogance and hubris of those who would recommend a far riskier (*i.e.*, less pragmatic) faith in ultimate nothingness—a belief that we humans are the highest intelligence and our course should be plotted on the assumption that this is the only existence we will ever have.

One of history's greatest scientific minds, Blaise Pascal, spoke eloquently about the absurdity of people who busy themselves in the ultimately petty concerns of this life while giving no thought to—and making no preparations for—the next life. Pascal is the mathematician and physicist who founded the theory of probabilities on which most modern scientific experimentation is based. He writes:

How can such an argument occur to a reasonable man? . . . "I know that I must soon die but . . . I will go without fear or foresight to face so momentous an event". . . . Who would wish to have as a friend a man who argues like that? . . . Who would choose him from among others as a confidant in his affairs? . . .

The same man who spends so many days and nights in fury and despair at losing some office or at some imaginary affront to his honor is the very one who knows that he is going to lose everything through death but feels neither anxiety nor emotion. It is a monstrous thing to see one and the same heart at once so sensitive to minor things and so strangely insensitive to the greatest. It is an incomprehensible spell, a supernatural torpor. . . .[7]

Pascal, who wrote some 300 years ago, developed the precursor to modern calculus and was one of the founders of today's scientific methodology. His language is a bit antiquated, but his thoughts are contemporary. He could be describing our society's often-narrow view of life, which allows little time for the bigger picture realities.

OUR CHOICE AND OUR CONSEQUENCES

The choice is ours. Which world view will it be? One thing almost all spiritual leaders agree on is that we humans have the gift of free will—and the choices we make with this free will have consequences that we bring on ourselves.

Much of this book will be about choices—choices we recommend you choose to make from a world view with an empowered hope that says you can significantly influence the directions you take in your life's journey—a hope that believes the choices you make have real meaning. The goal is not merely success and recognition in this world, but an unimaginably better life beyond this world. This more than justifies some very thoughtful navigation and hope.

THE FORGOTTEN VIRTUE

Kreeft, who has an ability to distill ancient wisdom agreed to by many spiritual writers in concise and contemporary terms, has some interesting things to say about hope:

Hope is the forgotten virtue in our time, for hope means hope for heaven, and modernity's nose-to-the-grindstone this-worldliness dares not lift up its eyes to the open skies. Hope means that our heads do not bump up against the low ceiling of this world; hope means that the exhilarating, wonderful, and terrifying winds of heaven blow in our ears. . . . Hope means that my deepest values, wants, demands, longings, and ideals are not meaningless blips on my inner mental sea but are like radar, an indication of objective reality. Hope means that when I must choose life, the reason is that at the heart of reality, life is chosen. Hope means that when I say that it is better to be than not to be, my very existence and the existence of everything that is joins me in a great universal chorus of approval. Hope ultimately means that my implicit desire for God is God's own trace in my being. Hope means that my agony and ecstasy of longing for a joy this world can never give is a sure sign that I was made for him who is Joy.[8]

Somehow this hope described by Kreeft seems more exciting—and worthy of the effort we put into our vocations and lives—than limiting ourselves to hope for a mere decade or so of comfortable retirement in Palm Springs, Phoenix, or Miami. It's more fun and positively energizing to think bigger.

A Journey with a Guide

I once heard about a poet who wrote some of his best poetry during a time when he was in prison. I have never forgotten the lifetime impact his story had on my world view. Later, someone asked how he could write with such positive imagery and hope in the filth of his prison cell. He said he had to make a choice. When he gazed out beyond his cell window he could look down "at the mud"—or look up "at the heavens." He described it as "a simple turn of the head." Many of our best mystical writers would also suggest that when he looked up he found not only the heavens but a guide he could hear only when he quieted his internal turmoil enough to listen.

Modern society rightly puts great emphasis on using logic and reason to analyze observable facts, a process that has produced much material progress. But an overemphasis on this world's nitty-gritty observable realities can have a negative effect. It can keep us looking down "at the mud." How often do we turn our gaze upward?

A journey in pursuit of overarching meaning—a journey seeking satisfaction of the personal, community, and spiritual needs that people privately complain are missing in their lives—inevitably leads to a realm of reality many find uncomfortable to contemplate. It brings us, eventually, to mystery and invites us to acknowledge the limitations as well as the strengths of our rational, human thought processes.

Such ideas are difficult and often embarrassing to talk about in modern work cultures. It is easier to talk about things we know and can explain. One of the most damaging phenomenons our technological age has produced is a pervasive, seemingly overwhelming utilitarian perspective. That perspective finds meaning not in internal, personal, or spiritual realities, but almost exclusively in quantifiable external things, in the outputs (especially financial results) we produce. Intuitively, we know better but we behave as if we don't. We blindly assess our personal value and career options on the material measurements of what we can earn or produce, rather than on who we are and who we are becoming. Our avoidance of the fact that we intuitively know better produces much modern angst. Even when we try to ignore it, some inescapable internal voice or intuition nags us with the sense that something is wrong.

Where does this voice come from? Is it our foe or ally? Some of the best ancient and contemporary spiritual writers tell us it is our ally and they even suggest where it comes from. They stress the importance of getting in touch with and listening to the internal voice of a Spirit beyond ourselves, a Spirit that imparts a wisdom greater than our own. Such listening is especially important when we listen for our calling or vocation in life. Those of us who are strong believers in the Christian tradition would speak of the Holy Spirit. To make the point that listening is important and practiced worldwide in most non-Christian traditions M. Scott Peck, M.D., author of the bestseller *The Road Less Traveled*, deliberately uses only the word *spirit* written with a small *s*.

Psychoanalyst Carl G. Jung, who built on Freud's foundations and brought brilliant new insight to modern psychology, concluded the human race has a "collective unconscious." To Jung, the collective unconscious is an enormous source of wisdom available to all, but only if we silence the external din enough to tune in. Jung's collective unconscious may be analogous to the Spirit described by our theologians and spiritual writers—and it tends to be drowned out in a utilitarian culture too exclusively focused on the external measurables.

We need to listen to this Spirit but it is difficult. Often we really don't want to hear what it has to say because it sometimes suggests change and most of us mightily resist change. However . . .

"Freezing" Our Design Gets Us Stuck

When our intuition and inner voices make us uneasy or give us the feeling that something is wrong, we often block the message. We think it means we have failed or made some irrevocably wrong turn in the road. Often, however, it means just the opposite. It means we have succeeded. We have made good progress so far but we've reached a plateau in our growth—a way station in our journey. We're lingering or stuck and it's time to move on. It's time to take a look at our life map, congratulate ourselves on our progress, and plot new directions. The uneasiness can be our ally, not our enemy. It can be a beneficial red light telling us it's time to stop a moment and think about the next stage in our journey. It's time to "listen for the Spirit." Listening can bring important new insight, warning us that staying too long in the same way station will hinder our growth—or even start us slipping backward.

New insight, even when it contradicts or corrects old insight, does not mean we are failing or have been stupid. It means we have stayed intelligent and alert to new data. We're still alive and growing. When we reach the point where we can't let new insight correct our old insight we have, in industrial terms, "frozen" our design. If Ford had frozen his automotive design with what was then the outstanding Model-T, the Ford company would not be doing well today. Instead, Ford updates its designs every year based on new lessons learned. Even in our sixties and seventies we are too young to freeze our design. Winston Churchill was voted out as prime minister in his seventies but he returned to office and continued to grow as writer and artist for years.

Often the new directions don't have to be dramatic or involve a significant job change. Research shows that acknowledging emotional pain when we are experiencing it and getting in touch with the causes are usually major steps forward in themselves. These steps can bring reenergizing new insight that moves us in more satisfying internal directions, sometimes with a relatively minor external course change.

STAGES OF THE JOURNEY

While some psychiatrists and psychologists tend to shy away from addressing the more spiritual dimensions of their clients' distress, some of the most outstanding of them in the twentieth century have concluded that a meaningful spiritual journey is the essential foundation for a psychologically healthy life journey. The two can't be separated. The split between them is unhealthy and causes much of the modern malaise we cited earlier.

A number of highly regarded contemporary social scientists have studied how people journey through life and identified specific stages of development, which we pass through from birth to old age. If you carefully study modern psychological research and the wisdom found in centuries of older spiritual writers, you will find it enlightening to discover how much the modern mirrors the old work.

Two individuals have particularly influenced our research on career stages. Both, through extensive empirical research, identified a series of predictable life stages healthy people go through in their journeys. Both tell us that arresting our growth or freezing our design at any intermediate stage inevitably leads to stagnation and distress.

A pioneer in this work was Erik Erikson, a psychiatrist from Harvard. In *Childhood and Society*[9] and a series of subsequent books reporting over three decades of research, he identified predictable patterns of progressively more sophisticated life stages that people grow through from birth to death across multiple cultures worldwide. Building on both Erikson and Jung, Yale psychologist Daniel J. Levinson focused on the stages of adult development. He spoke of the myth in our Western culture that people are supposed to be mature at age twenty-one. He studied both men[10] and women[11] in multiple careers—including hourly workers, CEOs, novelists, and homemakers—over several decades of their lives and found clear patterns in the stages, and transitions between stages, that all went through. Looking at this pattern he concluded that a successful life involved growth through these stages in a continuous journey toward higher and higher levels of maturity.

Many other contemporary social scientists have conducted research and identified specific developmental stages humans pass through as they evolve and grow in life (*e.g.*, Lawrence Kohlberg,[12] Margaret Mahler,[13] James W. Fowler,[14] and Fr. Benedict J. Groeschel, C.F.R.[15]).

While the wording and specific focus may differ, the stages described by the various life stage experts tend to be congruent with each other and with those described by other developmental psychologists.[16] In most available models, the experts emphasize the inevitability of conflicts and uncertainty, as well as the need for ongoing change if we are to grow.

In a later chapter, we will describe a synthesized set of career-related life stages that we have developed by integrating our own career specific research with insight gained from the authors mentioned and others as well.

At each successive stage of our career journeys we tend to revisit, reassess, and usually rebalance our priorities in the life values we are pursuing—sometimes switching emphasis from those we have already achieved to some we may have neglected. We reenergize ourselves, often by taking on some new and different challenges in areas we decide we have neglected.

We'll talk about this in some detail because much of the research indicates that successful growth through these stages determines how much satisfaction and fulfillment we feel in our lives and work. In fact, successful growth seems to be much more important than what specific career specialty we choose—or even whether or not we achieve much worldly recognition and reward in our career endeavors.

First, however, it is important to look at some myths, which can significantly block our personal and spiritual growth if we don't rid ourselves of their false assumptions.

Deconstructing Myths that Lead to Self-defeat

Life journeys typically are not smooth. If we want our work lives to further our emotional and spiritual as well as material growth there are roadblocks to be overcome. Some are obvious and some are not. Some can be predicted and are faced by most of us. Many are surprises and unique to the individual. We can't predict them all. However, armed with the right attitude and some tools, we can probably identify and overcome most of them. It can be very helpful and efficient to know the more predictable roadblocks and how others have overcome them. Then we don't have to reinvent every wheel.

This chapter will address what we feel is an important and pretty ubiquitous category of roadblocks—a number of myths or false assumptions that are so pervasive in our society they often drown out the inner voice that is trying to communicate our real needs and calling. They confuse our thinking and, when unevaluated, they can cause serious trouble. These myths are predictable enough that most would recognize them. However, the falsity of their assumptions is not always obvious. We sometimes accept these myths because others around us act as if they accept them. It's fashionable. We probably wouldn't accept most of them if we thought them through. But we don't take the time and, often unconsciously, go along with others in thinking and behaving as if they were true.

We need to bring these myths into clear awareness. We need to deconstruct them and assess the erroneous thinking they lead to. We need to take an unflinching look at how accepting them can disempower us and lead to a loss of spirit in our life journeys.

The following are some examples of self-defeating myths that dis-empower people.

MYTH 1

I am not responsible for my behavior.

It's fashionable today to blame—to deny personal responsibility for our own lives and spiritual journeys. The media help us believe we are overwhelmed by our environments. Any day's news provides scapegoats we can hold accountable for anything bad that happens to us—even for the undesirable things we do to others. We can blame stress, economic competition, social inequities, our parents, our bosses, drugs, organizational chaos, etc. Anything but ourselves.

These difficulties exist. They are real and they are difficult. But, contrary to much prevailing belief, almost none is insurmountable. They are obstacles to be overcome and, if we use them as excuses, we will not overcome them to build a rewarding life and career. In smaller print, many less visible media stories tell us case after case of people who decided to empower themselves, who overcame almost any imaginable obstacle and went on to lead fulfilling lives.

Helen Keller is only one example of many people who took responsibility for their careers despite overwhelming obstacles. She was blind and deaf, but she was also smart enough to decide she had options. Only she could choose among her options and no one in the world could save her from the consequences of her choices. Rather than giving in to her devastating disabilities, she made the best of her situation and became a world-renowned twentieth-century author and social reformer. No one would have blamed her if she had given in. Everyone would have been sympathetic and understanding. However, no one, no matter how guilty they felt about their inability to help, could have saved her from the consequences of choosing to give in. She could not have it both ways. She could not quit, blaming her justifiable circumstances, and still have all the advantages of the life she led by going on.

All choices have consequences, often predictable consequences.

There is a truism we too frequently overlook in the heat of emotional decisions. The people or circumstances we blame for our dilemmas in life usually don't have to face the consequences of the choices we make. We have to face those consequences—essentially alone.

I once had to point this out very painfully to a teenage son. Realizing how difficult the teen years can be, I had promised not to relocate again once my children were in high school. Then I reneged and made one last move after our oldest son finished his freshman year. Things did not go well for him, socially or academically, and he let me know continually that I was to blame. His honor-student grades slipped until we worried whether he would get accepted by a decent college. My lecturing about his diminishing college prospects only made things worse. It was my fault. He was right. What to do?

Finally, in desperation, I took a calculated risk. I gave up and admitted I was helpless. I went to his room one night and said I had accepted the fact that he would never go to college. He would hear no more about it from me. It was his life, not mine. When he was ready we could start making alternate plans. He was stunned. He said that couldn't be. All his friends were going to college. I said yes, but they were getting better grades. He said they hadn't been forced to move. I admitted that was true. He said it was my fault, not his. I was to blame. I said that was true also, but, unfortunately, I was not going to be the one to suffer the consequences. He would be the one to miss college. He stuck to his blame. It was my problem. I told him he was right and I felt very guilty. If his goal was to punish me and make me feel guilty, he had succeeded. I would probably feel guilty the rest of my life but that would not get him into college. There wasn't a college admissions officer in the world who cared at all about my feeling guilty. All they cared about were the grades he wasn't getting. No magic and no solution would come from my feeling guilty. It was out of my hands.

It was a painful awakening. I don't think he slept much that night. I didn't. But he got the message. He put the choice and the responsibility for action in the hands of the only person in the world who had the power to do anything—himself. Satisfying as my guilt was to him, he decided his own best interests lay in going to college. His grades, even his social life began to improve. He got into a good college and today he has finished graduate school.

It could easily have gone the other way. It takes courage and maturity to admit no one else out there, not the culprit who caused your problem—not even your own father—has any power to save you from the consequences of the free choices you make. He could have chosen to leave responsibility for action in my guilty, helpless hands. If he had, I'd still be suffering, but he'd be suffering more. He doesn't remember the incident very well, but his actions still show he remembers the lesson learned.

I learned a lesson too. I straightened out my priorities. I kept my promises after that. We made no further moves despite some tempting possibilities. My son's younger brothers and sisters have finished college and we still live in the same house.

We may seldom be responsible for the difficult circumstances we face, but we can always assume responsibility for the choices we make in response to those circumstances. We can *take charge* and our free choices, inevitably, will dictate our consequences. We will devote a significant part of this book to a tested and proven methodology you can use to take very positive charge of your own life choices and career.

If parents or society overdo protecting children from the consequences of their own choices, the children can feel helpless. They may never discover the powerful results, positive and negative, that their own very willful choices can bring.

MYTH 2

Someone else has the answers for my life.

In defining our personal life values and goals we too often look outside ourselves for answers. The key word here is *answers*. It's good to look outside ourselves for information about lessons others have learned by pursuing life and career paths we may be considering. But we want to look inside ourselves for answers, for clear data-based decisions and choices that reflect our unique and personal criteria for a successful life.

Too often we plan our lives based on other people's success criteria. We try to figure out what others expect of us and then attempt to meet their expectations. Somehow we think this will bring us satisfaction. We're surprised and we feel cheated when it doesn't. This is a natural approach. From kindergarten through college we're taught to figure out what the teachers want and give it to them. This brings success, or at least decent grades. This is not all bad when we're students. It's a smart way to get through the school system. The problem comes when we graduate, move out into the world, and discover that the expectations are not that clear anymore. When someone then asks what we want to do with our lives the question seems unfair. Whoever taught us to answer that? We've been taught to ask what the establishment (society or our teachers, organizations, and peers) expects and then mold ourselves to conform.

But the establishment is not a living, thinking being. The establishment is an *it* made up of thousands (or even hundreds of thousands) of *them's*, all struggling with limited success to communicate with each other. Establishments (particularly if they are work organizations or large groups of people) rush forward blindly, changing course unpredictably and at dizzying speed. In terms of career or skill expectations, one year the demand is all for engineers and technologists. A few years later engineers can't find jobs. The demand switches to M.B.A.s. Later it turns out that so many switched to M.B.A.s that they have become a glut on the market.

The establishment has no enduring expectations. It's fickle and blind. What it expects depends on unpredictable economic cycles, on what tyrant is threatening whom in the third world, on the unknown outcome of national elections and so on. Who can predict all that? Who can plot a life or career journey on such shifting sands?

In the end, with an unpredictable establishment, the only predictable reality is inside the self. What is my inner voice telling me? Where does my energy flow naturally and easily? That's where I'll have a competitive edge and do best. That's where I'll find personal meaning and growth in dimensions that are important to me.

People who don't listen to their internal voices, who go into engineering, for instance, only because that's where the money is, often end up being mediocre engineers. If engineering is not intrinsically interesting to them, they tend to get behind in the state of the art. They waste energy forcing themselves to go to work. Natural engineers, those whose energy flows freely to the technical, pass them by.

Natural engineers and technologists who force themselves to go into management against their will (often for reasons of status or money) usually don't make good managers. They don't like managing. Natural managers pass them by. The frustrated engineer gets behind in technology and does not perform well in management. He or she ends up being neither—or gets smart and switches back—even if it means a cut in pay.

Listening to your inner voice has very pragmatic as well as spiritual and emotional rewards. It energizes you and makes you good at what you do. The career marketplace supports people in things they're not good at only when the skill involved is a fad or in short supply. When the fad passes, the demand drops. Then the work force in a given skill (like accounting or engineering) tends to fall back to the level of people who are really good at it. If you're a recognized top talent in your field and it is natural to you, you can usually find a job whether the fad is running up or down. On the other hand, if you're forcing yourself to perform, you may find a more exciting job, increased satisfaction, and more security in another field you like better. Many delighted people tell us that, in retrospect, being fired was the best thing that ever happened to them. It forced them to think, to change, to reassess their priorities and decide if their current paths were meeting those priorities. They saw their work lives and their organizations more realistically—with a new awareness of what actually was important to them.

Often these people had worked for years in jobs they disliked or in organizational cultures that didn't support their values. They stayed through habit or because they were afraid there was nothing else they could do. When their organizations were downsized and forced them out they were initially depressed. Then they discovered, to their surprise, that they could do very well and were much happier in their own businesses, or in different organizations more in tune with their needs and aspirations. Outplacement specialists, who help people that have been downsized find new jobs, tell us this is a very common pattern.

In the end, the only real fulfillment and security comes from being true to ourselves and from being one of the best at what we do. It is far easier, and lots more fun, to be the best if we like what we do, and if not only the work but also the output has meaning and significance for us. If this doesn't result in a lot of money, so what? If you can earn a decent living and spend your hours at work feeling that what you do has meaning for you, you're ahead. How many rich people look back and wish they'd made less money and had more soul in their work? Money can't buy back the loss of spirit many experience on the job.

MYTH 3

Meeting the organization's success criteria will fulfill my needs.

We also hope you're smart enough not to base your self-esteem on—or measure your personal worth by:

- the same criteria your organization uses to measure its success (*e.g.*, beating all competition at any cost)
- other criteria your organizational (or peer) culture may suggest you measure yourself by (*e.g.*, assumed top priority placed on fast-track mobility up the hierarchy).

Your personal values and success criteria might be very different, but you may be too busy to notice the discrepancy, even for years, if you don't stop periodically and really think about it. Organization success criteria have a seductive habit of becoming group norms (and unconsciously assumed personal success criteria) by which individuals in the organization measure themselves.

The young man in our introduction, who asked his CEO about how to balance his work and family, could easily have fallen into this trap. The CEO who answered his question placed high value on his company's organization success criteria. These included impressing Wall Street by doing whatever it took to outperform all competitors. While his values represent success for him, they may not represent success for you or me. However, we may march blindly ahead and not notice the discrepancy for years. If we deliberately and consciously take time to analyze the situation, we may discover we define success for ourselves with very different priorities.

The CEO was apparently willing to sacrifice a number of personal values, such as time with family—even his marriage—to meet his organizational goals. He didn't like the sacrifices but, consciously or unconsciously, he made a personal choice to give being the CEO top priority. He probably assumed others would make the same value choice. Wrong assumption, but one many in the organization undoubtedly went along with—and were equally driven by—because they didn't stop to think it through. The young man's question indicated the CEO's priorities were not his. He felt trapped and distressed in a job that seemed to allow him no mental or spiritual space to do anything but work. He didn't like it. I wouldn't like it either.

It's OK for him to have very different priorities from the CEO's—and he doesn't have to change the CEO's to make his own right for him. He simply has to become clearly aware of the discrepancies, even if it's temporarily painful, and quietly take that into account in his life and career planning.

It isn't easy to resist internalizing your organization's external success criteria to the point where they drown out your own inner voice that is trying to tell you who you are, what you personally value, and what you want to become. However, resistance is not necessarily disastrous. And it doesn't always mean you have to leave the organization. Resistance doesn't have to be public. It can be very private. You just have to stay conscious of who you are and continually remind yourself that your values and success criteria differ from the organization's.

The men and women in the company where the CEO spoke were boxed in by his values and lifestyle only if they chose to share his choice of putting top priority on fast-track upward mobility in his company. Others were willing to quietly negotiate different, more balanced life and career tracks without leaving the company. That wasn't always easy, but it was courageous and it put more soul back into their work and lives. For example, one excellent performer we know gently deferred when his organization recommended he move to a career path that would prepare him for rapid growth to high-level management assignments. He felt administrative management wouldn't allow time for the technical challenges he found more creative and wanted to pursue. He eventually grew into a series of well-paying technical jobs where he could do the work he loved, travel less, spend more time with his family, and mentor, but not manage, younger technical talents.

If people perform well in what they want to do, and the work is needed, most organizations will try to accommodate their preferences. Those who can't negotiate the career paths they want where they are should begin a quiet search for another organization that better meets their needs. We know many who have successfully done that. To us they seemed happier and more successful as human beings than the multimillionaire executive we knew who flew in on a private jet to attend his son's wedding but was so driven by his company's priorities he had no time to stay for the reception.

MYTH 4

As my organization improves, my personal needs will be met.

Even where there is no conflict in values, autonomous people know they can't rely on any managerial hierarchy or human resource system to define or meet their needs. Some organization leaders will be interested in their employees' personal growth and satisfaction. Others will be self-centered people, inclined to keep better performers on their projects long after they have outgrown the work. Even the best-intentioned organizational leaders usually don't have very sophisticated career counseling skills. Their efforts often do more harm than good. Typically, the most beneficial thing people in leadership positions feel they can do is develop others as clones of their own self-images. They assume that what is good for them is good for you. That probably isn't what you have, or should have, in mind.

While it is true that developing subordinates is one of any leader's prime responsibilities, this process must be kept in perspective. If you want to explore career tracks other than the ones your immediate superiors followed their help can only be very limited.

Here's why.

Your boss knows how to get one step ahead of you in his or her own specialized organizational function—period. If that is your final ambition you may be safe to depend on your boss as at least one expert on that career track.

Your boss usually knows little or nothing about how to perform in other functions or specialties. A boss in engineering probably knows little more than you do about how people pursue careers in finance, social services, marketing, or human resources.

Unless your boss is a broad, multifunctional business manager, odds are he or she doesn't know how to become one and probably doesn't even know in any detail what people like that really do. The boss may learn, but how long can you wait?

As an antidote to depending unrealistically on your boss for help, you must somehow broaden your data base and implement a plan for broadening yourself. Such a plan requires direct contact with people who are currently pursuing the type of life values and career tracks you aspire to five or more years from now. Only people who have done the work can accurately tell you what the work consists of and what performance it takes to get there.

Even the best human resource systems are better at promoting already-developed people than at developing new talent. The top talents cited in most organizations' staffing inventories are typically people who became visible by developing themselves. They looked at the human resources system, warts and all, figured out where it would help and hinder them, and worked around it (or negotiated proactively within it) to get the experience, training, and skills development they needed.

The change to more modern, less hierarchical organizations doesn't do much to meet individuals' needs either. Organization evolutions (deconstructing and reengineering organizational structures and systems) are not new and they will always be with us. The good ones help assure the organization's survival by adapting it to changing client or market needs, but they don't guarantee any increased satisfaction or personal value achievement for individual employees.

Don't put an organizational *it* in the driver's seat of your life unless you really don't care where you're going. Don't wait for your work organization to get its act, or its human resources systems, together. Autonomous people don't wait. They steer their own course through ceaseless change with their antennae on and with their brain and senses always alert. They develop enduring take-charge-of-themselves competencies that help them not only survive, but also prevail and contribute in dimensions they value no matter which way the organization evolves. If your organization doesn't provide a good process and tools to help you do this, consider this book a starter driver's manual.

MYTH 5

There is a right answer to every problem—and I should have it.

Much to the surprise of many, particularly younger recent college graduates, the right answer to most any work or career question (or problem) is also—like life—not a destination but a journey. The highly technical president (himself a Ph.D. in engineering) of a major corporation made this point very forcibly one day when I heard him address a gathering of deans from top engineering schools across the United States. He was the last speaker at the conference. The already-tired deans had settled into their seats expecting a predictable presentation saying why they should send their best graduates to the president's company. His opening comment brought the sleepy group instantly to attention. He said he wanted them to know that if they believed they were developing technical leaders they were kidding themselves.

When they asked why they were not, he said their graduates usually had excellent technical skills but they were naive in that they defined success as finding *the* right answer to technical problems. He told the deans that getting the students to break that mindset was very difficult and they could never succeed if they continued to think that way.

A university, he said, especially an undergraduate school, is typically an unreal world where students are told which problems to work on and are then rewarded for finding the right answers as defined in the professor's head or the back of the book. That was fine in school but not in the real world. In the real world technical leaders have to decide which one of many problems to work on. Once they have decided, they usually have to build consensus among a group of colleagues who often don't agree with them and want to pursue other problems. Once the leaders have consensus they have to negotiate resources, often competing with other groups seeking the same resources to pursue other problems. Even when they have negotiated consensus and the resources they never reach *the* answers. They never have more than tentative solutions (*i.e.*, way stations) that require endless testing and correction as they implement their answers and learn from their mistakes. The president used the example of the spaceship that never flies in a straight line journey to the moon. It continually zigzags in wrong directions and has its course adjusted as electronic surveillance corrects errors and continually redirects it toward its ultimate goal.

His message was that schools and industry have to teach students to look on problem-solving and life as a journey of continuous improvement, as never-ending progress toward better and better answers. If they ever think they have the final answer they've probably frozen their design and started downhill.

New college graduates are not the only people who need to think this way. A top human resources staffing executive in a Fortune 500 company explained the same point to me. His job was to assess candidates and make a final selection recommendation when any general manager or higher position was filled. His track record in predicting people's future performance was legendary. I asked him what single characteristic he felt most reliably predicted success in a leadership job. "Intellectual integrity," he answered. When I asked what that meant, he said more simply, "They have enough self-confidence that they don't have to be right."

He said effective leaders, even effective individual performers, in any endeavor are usually the first ones to notice and communicate their mistakes. The executives who sought his selection advice knew that anyone they put in these leadership positions would make mistakes. What they couldn't tolerate was the insecurity of not knowing whether mistakes had been made, of having someone work for them who wouldn't admit mistakes, who would waste valuable time covering up. The best security they could hope for was someone they trusted to quickly and continuously bring mistakes to their attention and recommend ongoing course corrections.

Robert Graves wrote the following poem. I keep it in my office to remind me how counterproductive it would be ever to think I'm really *enlightened* or have *the* final answers to anything.

In Broken Images
by Robert Graves

He is quick, thinking in clear images;
I am slow, thinking in broken images.

He becomes dull, trusting to his clear images;
I become sharp, mistrusting my broken images.

Trusting his images, he assumes their relevance;
Mistrusting my images, I question their relevance.

Assuming their relevance, he assumes the fact;
Questioning their relevance, I question the fact.

When the fact fails him, he questions his senses;
When the fact fails me, I approve my senses.

He continues quick and dull in his clear images;
I continue slow and sharp in my broken images.

He in a new confusion of his understanding;
I in a new understanding of my confusion.[17]

Graves's poem reminds me how unreasonable it is for me to think I have the final answers to anything. Once I decide I really know what I am doing, I'm afraid I'll turn off my antennae. My senses will be dulled and I'll miss the clues that tell me when it is time for course correction. I don't want to get stuck in a way station where I won't hear my internal voice pointing out new, more rewarding directions.

This is true in my spiritual as well as my work endeavors. I don't want to miss the internal course guidance that the Spirit can give me. Centuries ago St. Augustine wrote about the folly of finite humans believing that they can find final answers to the infinite mysteries of creation. He said:

Truly you are a hidden god, the Savior.
If you find a god you understand, you have built an idol.

These two writers also remind me to be wary of others (including peers, bosses, or other influential people in my life) who think they have *the* answers—especially if they try to impose their career or life values on me. I'm more trusting and comfortable with others who are strong enough to avoid the comfortable but dulling way stations of imagined rational or materialistic certainties. I would rather journey forward with others who are also searching tentatively and in broken images for the elusive but also very real mystery beyond the material realities. I have come to believe that journey alone can bring any truly lasting satisfaction and meaning.

I want to watch and learn from people who are daily fighting the good fight against insidious, and debilitating pride—that perhaps most disastrous of human flaws described by centuries of spiritual leaders as humanity's prime barrier to a successful life journey. I want to overcome my very human but unrealistic need to be right—or, as theologian Paul Tillich once described it, my need to *be* God rather than to *seek* God. I want to work at developing a real, not phony humility, which is never weak but can be my most powerful strength and teacher. As our case histories demonstrate, a humility that keeps people searching for feedback and course correction can be an enormous advantage in just about any career field.

In terms of my career I learned from Dan Levinson (see page 24) that I will probably never, in this life, reach a full or final answer to the question of what I want to be when I grow up. Before meeting Dan, I thought fifty-year-olds who came to my office still wondering what they wanted to be should have known long ago. After hearing Dan's research, I decided it was the healthier fifty-year-olds who were still searching and had not frozen their designs. I now want to continually evaluate and redetermine who I want to be from the ever-increasing maturity of each successive life stage. I want to keep learning. Fortunately, this ties in nicely with the external realities of today's career marketplace where things change so fast that predictions are most people will pass through several different careers in their work lifetimes.

MYTH 6

My behavior and actions are immediately understandable to others.

While most universities are good at teaching the important rational, scientific processes for solving problems, most schools, especially the highly technical ones, spend far too little time on teaching their students to communicate their ideas. The students are not taught to build understanding and consensus among people with different personalities, work specialties, and agendas (*e.g.*, sales, finance, and engineering) whose cooperation is required if their ideas are to be implemented. As the president who spoke to the engineering school deans said, in school the excellence of our solutions is often self-evident (*e.g.*, matches the instructor's preexisting answer). Our answers stand on their own and sell themselves. This is not typical in real situations where we have to work with and through other people.

Several years ago I saw a classic example of how important communications and interpersonal skills are for anyone who wants to accomplish something—or negotiate a career—in organizations. I was reading a report about an unusually bright individual who had attended a large corporation's talent-assessment program. During the program participants worked in group problem-solving exercises while a staff of psychologists and operational managers observed them. Afterward participants received written feedback on their performance.

The feedback on this individual said he was so intelligent that he frequently had reasonable answers before the rest of the group had even defined the problem. Then the report made a statement I'll never forget. It said that his "being right was irrelevant." How could his "being right" be "irrelevant"? It was irrelevant because he could never communicate his being right to the rest of the group, and all the problem solutions required their cooperation. At the end of each exercise he watched the others move off in the wrong direction because they never listened to him.

Why didn't they listen? Because he didn't listen to them. He didn't notice that they simply did not understand him. He didn't ask questions to test what they did and did not understand about what he was saying. He didn't notice the obvious fact that he was ramming final solutions down their throats while they were still disagreeing on what the problems were. He would not stand back, analyze where they were in their progress, help them diagnose, lead them through the thinking process he had gone through in arriving at a solution, and help them contribute to and develop personal ownership in the solution.

He had plenty of clues. The group asked him questions that would have shown him where they were. But he wouldn't respond at their level. He continually blocked out the data that would have told him where they were. Instead, he interpreted their questions as resistance to or criticism of his ideas. When he didn't answer the questions they asked, but each time launched into another repetitive hard sell of his own solutions, they concluded he was a little slow and not bright enough to understand them. His responses were indeed "irrelevant" to the specific questions they were asking. They began to ignore him, and the more his frustration built, the more he began to sound like an ineffective broken record. What a frustrating fate for the most intelligent person in the group!

When we point out the importance of interpersonal communications, especially to younger technically oriented people, they often tell us they don't want to get involved in organizational politics. They prefer to stay above that. They'd rather concentrate on their technical work and leave politics to others.

People who get what they want—who sell their ideas or negotiate rewarding career paths in complex organizations—are frequently accused of using politics as though that were automatically something bad. It needn't be.

If we define politics negatively as unethical compromise, copping out, manipulating destructively, and making closet deals that would stink in the sunlight, then it is definitely bad practice. This is the common definition when the word is used derisively.

If we define politics as an astute awareness of the human dimensions, as reality orientation and sensitivity to the unspoken needs and feelings of others' values, anxieties, and interpersonal styles, as concern for the best possible solutions incorporating the best of everyone's ideas, and as a carefully developed set of interpersonal competencies for taking all of the above into account when we want to accomplish change or improvement—politics can be very positive.

We tend to confuse positive and negative politics. We should be careful to keep negative and positive politicians separate in our thinking. We can learn a lot from positive politicians. Not accepting or understanding the critical realities of positive interpersonal communications is perhaps the most common roadblock to negotiating and accomplishing career goals.

Our behavior and actions are immediately understandable only to people who think like we do, who share our same values, priorities, and biases, and who have thought through a given problem or situation in the same sequence and depth we have. That may be a small audience. Communicating with the rest takes time, sensitivity, and a willingness to hear and respect others' viewpoints. It requires interpersonal skills developed through practice. It also requires the humility to modify our opinions based on different perspectives others have developed. If we don't notice the need, take the time, develop the skills, and stay open to new perspectives we will probably have a hard time getting our ideas heard or negotiating what we need for career or life satisfaction anywhere.

A MORE ACCURATE PARADIGM

These myths are a sampling of the barriers we often unconsciously erect to block our progress in finding career and life satisfaction. Once we see the falsity of these and similar myths—once we see the dead ends their erroneous assumptions lead to—we can look at reality with clearer heads. Then we can begin to identify and take action to overcome the barriers and move our lives in the directions that we want to go. To do this we need to make new, more reality-oriented career contracts with our organizations and ourselves.

1. BREAKING OLD MINDSETS

2. CONTRACTING FOR RENEWAL

3. FINDING YOUR CALLING

4. MAKING IT HAPPEN

5. STAYING THE COURSE

STEP 2

CONTRACTING FOR RENEWAL

Here we will start the process of applying insight gained in Step 1 to our day-to-day lives and work settings.

In the introduction we said there are five critical steps we have discovered that successful people follow for effective life and career planning. Up to now we have been discussing the first step that asks you to *diverge*. It invites you to break out of some misleading older mindsets—to deconstruct several of contemporary society's most dangerously disempowering myths and erroneous thinking. Once you have broken through any old and faulty thinking, you can develop new, clearer perceptions of reality. You can see additional possibilities. You can develop a new mindset more likely to help you achieve what you decide are your most important life values.

45

Then you need to *converge*. You need to start focusing on the development and implementation of very specific future career action plans that meet your personal success criteria. In later chapters we will present a *Taking Charge Process* and set of tools many others have found very helpful in accomplishing this.

We spoke first of mindsets because people often have to clear away the baggage of old myths before they can use *any* career planning tools very successfully.

Next, in **Step 2**, we will look at key ingredients in the career contracts we need to empower ourselves for realizing our true life values and for navigating our progression through the critical learning of each life stage.

Negotiating Agreements with Yourself and Others

Contracts Are Based on Expectations

When we speak of career contracts between individuals and organizations, we are not suggesting written legal documents. We refer rather to the too-often unarticulated psychological contract between an employee and an employer, to the frequently implied but seldom clearly defined set of mutual expectations that arise concerning who can be relied on to do what, and when, to further the mutual interests of both the individual and the organization. The myths discussed earlier are examples of how dangerous and misleading any ill-defined expectations can be, particularly when they imply that an individual can rely on an organization to do more than any organization can realistically promise.

Expectations Must Be Articulated

If they are to form the base for a clear contract, expectations must be articulated, realistic, and understood by all concerned. Understanding who is expected to do what is critical to the success of any activity, even something as apparently passive as reading a book or hearing a lecture.

For instance, what is your contract with us as you read this book? It should not be one-sided. Think about it. You expect us to write something that is informative and useful. What do you expect of yourself? Shouldn't you contribute too? We can illustrate this with a brief reflection.

BRIEF REFLECTION

Before reading further, sit back and get as comfortable as you can. Empty your mind of distractions. Think about what you are feeling and wanting right now.

Ask yourself the following questions. Close your eyes and think quietly about the answer after reading each question.

1. **What do you really want to get out of this book?** What would the best of all outcomes be for you personally?

2. **What can you do personally to make sure this happens?** What actions, energy, or attitude can you personally contribute as opposed to remaining passive and expecting the book to do it alone?

3. **Based on past experiences** (books, workshops, discussions, abortive career planning attempts) where you did not get what you wanted, **what might you have done personally to foul it up?** What are you likely to think, assume, or do to prevent your best of all outcomes from happening? Relax and be honest. You don't have to show this to anyone.

4. **Attach a feeling to this, a one-word feeling** (angry, hostile, disappointed, confused, fearful, etc.) **that usually comes to you when your hoped-for expectations are not met.** This will probably be a very familiar feeling you experience often. **Remember it.** This feeling can become an ally, a **built-in warning signal** that you need to make a contract with yourself for change.

BRIEF REFLECTION *(continued)*

5. **What can you do to prevent future foul-ups?** How can you learn from past experience? How can you avoid things you might do to prevent your best possible outcome? What can you do differently this time to help you get what you want?

Looking at your answers to these questions, **develop a brief personal action plan** in your mind. Decide what you will do and not do as you read the rest of this book. **How can you now avoid doing the things you typically have done to foul things up? How can you start doing the things you need to do** to get what you want from this book and from life?

BEGIN THE REST OF YOUR LIFE WITH A CHALLENGE

We use this reflection to make several useful points at the beginning of our career workshops. It's a new experience for most people to begin a workshop (or a book) by being challenged. Unexpectedly they have to look at themselves. They have to make a commitment to themselves about what they will do to make the experience meaningful for them. They have to admit there are ways to prevent themselves from realizing their expectations and look at ways to avoid doing that.

Most of us begin a lecture, book, or workshop with a passive show-me attitude. We assume the detached role of critic. We expect to be entertained or improved. The burden and responsibility for results are on the teacher or author.

Being challenged is important. You should begin planning the rest of your life by being challenged. You should be personally committed to getting your desired results. It's your life. Most enter a work organization with a tell-me attitude. You expect to be told what to do. You will work hard. You expect the organization to make certain it's worth your while. If it doesn't lead to your satisfaction the system went wrong. The system didn't meet your needs.

The contract is unspoken and unspecified. When we really think about it we know it's a naive, unreal contract. But how often do we take time to think about it?

It's safe to blame the system. Systems are always imperfect. No one will contradict us on this. Systems are nonpersonal *its*.

Unspecified contracts with *its* provide a safe outlet for blame, but they don't make you feel much better if you're not happy with what you're doing, or if you're not contributing in dimensions you believe are helping you to grow and contribute in meaningful ways to others. It's more productive and fun to negotiate specific contracts that help you achieve your desired outcomes in workshops, in books, and in life.

There are two types of contracts involved in the process of planning your life and career. These are:

- *contracts you make with other people* when meeting your goals requires cooperative action with someone else.
- *contracts you make with yourself* to do specific things that are required to meet your goals.

Contracts with organizations are examples of the first type. They involve other people.

CONTRACTS WITH AN ORGANIZATION

In planning the rest of your career in an organization, you should carefully identify:

- what you need to contribute.
- what your superiors can be expected to contribute.
- what the organization can be expected to contribute.
- what the ground rules are going to be.

Career planning and contracting within an organization are forms of cooperative problem-solving. Problem-solving without valid data is an exercise in frustration.

What you want, need, expect, and value are valid data in any career planning contract. Negotiating effectively to include these issues in a psychological contract with an employer requires that you first define them for yourself. You must decide what you really want for you (as distinct from what your boss, the organization, or your peers think you should want) before you can begin negotiating to get what you want.

The values you want to realize in each life stage along with the personal interests, skills (or competencies), and abilities you want to pursue on the job become your personal criteria for success in choosing a specific career path. Pursuing a career that meets your unique personal criteria is success in your terms. You should contract for this.

An organization can try to create a proper climate and provide tools and techniques to help you develop your criteria, but no superior or human resources department can ethically tell you what you should want (though many try and, unfortunately, many people listen).

An organization can help you collect data to decide which career paths meet your criteria. An organization can make incumbents and experts in different career paths available to give you information. An organization can help you become aware of openings that may meet your criteria (if you identify and communicate them). In short, the organization can and should supply information and data to help you decide, but you must learn to seek out this data. The organization can answer questions. You must learn to develop and ask questions to generate specific data that are relevant to your unique decisions. Organizations don't have ESP.

Once you've defined the *what*, the organization can assist on the *how* (training programs, current job enrichment, new job opportunities, tuition refund, location choices, etc.). The possibilities are endless. You must sort out and select those that are uniquely relevant to you and negotiate for them. Otherwise, you may spend years in confusion and indecision.

The supermarket supplies an enormous variety of foods, but it does not design your diet, force-feed you, determine whether you are to be heavy or thin, low or high in cholesterol. You do that. The supermarket may try to program what you eat through aggressive advertising. If you have any sense, you ignore the advertising and decide for yourself.

If you identify and develop some skills of value you want to pursue, organizations can become your job supermarkets. If you become really good at something and one organization doesn't carry your preferred job brand or work environment, there are other organizations, none of which has enough really good people. You can shop or, as many have done, set yourself up in business selling your skills to organization clients that need part-time consulting in your field.

The foregoing is so obvious that it may sound condescending, even trite. As you read on, however, you may discover that your part of the career planning contract is not obvious at all. Avoiding tough decisions on contradictory values (*e.g.*, location versus opportunity) may have you at a career impasse. You may be avoiding the decision so skillfully you're not even aware of the conflict or the impasse. You may require a contract with yourself to break the impasse and get your life moving in directions you want to go.

CONTRACTS WITH YOURSELF

We believe organizations have a clear obligation to help employees define their own unique criteria for success and pursue career paths that meet these criteria. However, the reality is that most organizations don't do this very well.

Successful people we interviewed said they had to find ways to do this on their own. Intuitively, they realized they could not wait or depend on any system. They took charge, made a contract with themselves, and acted. One young woman we interviewed, for instance, did some personal career planning and discovered she needed several critical job experiences not available at the small location of her company where she worked. When her plant manager refused to let her pursue a transfer to a larger company location, and the human resources organization couldn't get him to change his mind, she persisted on her own. After several months of unpopular negotiations, she convinced the plant manager herself. Then it took another several months of self-initiated search to find an opening at a company location that could provide the needed experience. Eventually she achieved her career goal. She moved into a very high level management position that would never have been available to her if she hadn't found a way to get the critical experiences.

Making a contract with yourself to get your life moving in directions you want to go begins with accepting the fact that you are a prime contributor to just about everything that happens to you. Good things seldom happen without your taking some action to make them happen.

Likewise—aside from earthquakes, disease, unanticipated corporate restructuring, or other dramatic events beyond your control—you are usually an active contributor when things don't go your way. If you're failing to meet one of your important career goals, and you think about the facts objectively, you will usually discover that you are influencing the situation. There are many ways you can do this. To list just a few examples:

Not doing something that's required to meet the goal. You may not be pursuing the needed training (*e.g.,* full time or after hours) to qualify for something you want to do, not investigating what self-generated action steps are required to get what you want (*e.g.,* how did people who hold these jobs qualify themselves?), or not taking the first known action step required (perhaps suggesting and negotiating a new job enriching assignment in your current position) for fear of failure or rejection. You may simply not be defining what you want even to yourself.

Meeting a contradictory goal that's more important to you, and not admitting to yourself that you've actually made the trade-off. The sense of contribution you get in your current social service job may really be more important to you than the higher salary some of your contemporaries receive in more commercial endeavors. You can't have both and you've really made the choice, but you won't accept it. You vacillate, punish yourself by feeling frustrated and angry, agonize in bogus indecision, and complain that social service people should make more money. As a result, even though you've made the right trade-off for you, you end up getting no personal satisfaction from either value (social service or money).

Doing something that prevents you from meeting your goal. You may be resisting the effort required for purposefully seeking out new opportunities more in line with your needs, even though you find your current job frustrating and unsatisfying. On your current job, for fear of making mistakes or potential failure, you may avoid taking on new challenges, hold back your ideas for work process improvements, or not recommend new projects you think would benefit both you and your organization. Research shows that successful people tend to take more risks, experience more real failure, and build their knowledge and competence by learning from mistakes made. People who risk no failures have a slower learning curve.

Once you learn to notice what you're doing—or not doing—to help or hinder your career growth you can develop a conscious contract with yourself to improve things. You can decide what has to be done, in what sequence, and assume ongoing personal responsibility for assuring things happen as planned. The rest of the book will show you how to do this.

Later, you can document a contract with yourself, define specific career goals, and develop a practical action plan for achieving them by completing the exercises in the *Career and Life Workbook* we present at the end of this book.

ESSENTIAL CONTRACT INGREDIENTS

The specifics of contracts like this will differ with each person. Generically, ingredients essential to any contract with yourself to meet your personal criteria for success should include:

Value Analysis—Determining your most important current values (*e.g.*, money, location, service to others, time with family), rank ordering them, and deciding which you will trade off if faced with a contradiction (*e.g.*, the job you want not being available in the location you want). As we said earlier, many people keep themselves in a state of continual agitation by refusing to make focused value decisions.

Establishing Job-content Objectives—Identifying what specific combination of skills or competencies (*e.g.*, intellectual, technical, interpersonal, physical, artistic, mathematical, etc.) you want to develop and exercise in your future on-the-job activities. These objectives become your criteria for judging the content of potential future jobs. If a potential opening involves doing a lot of financial or technical analysis by yourself with no opportunity for interacting with others—and interacting with others is important to you—you will avoid that job even if it is a promotion. You can't assess potential future career paths effectively until you have some standard or criteria for judging whether or not what you find is for you.

Collecting Real (Not Stereotyped) Data to Determine What Types of Jobs Really Meet Your Personal Success Criteria—You can't decide whether or not you want to be a business manager, a high school teacher, a technologist, a salesperson, a priest, or a college professor until you've talked to several people who have done these things and found out specifically how they spend their day. You need data to measure against your criteria. This sounds obvious but we deal regularly with grown-ups, some of them at very high levels, who have never collected this type of data for themselves. Many are beating themselves to death because they're dissatisfied with what they're doing and can't decide where they want to go next. Who can decide with no data, or with superficial speculations about what other people do, or with stereotyped position-guide descriptions? These same people wouldn't make business decisions with such limited data. It's only their lives for which they have no time.

Establishing an Objective and a Plan—Identifying a specific career path you want to follow—one that represents the best possible match to your criteria, one that lets you achieve your most important values and exercise/develop skills or competencies you really enjoy and want to grow. This requires collecting information to find out precisely what it takes to achieve your career goals, matching that data to your current qualifications, and building skill development into your current job or generating next job options to fill in the gaps.

Negotiating Continuously—Maintaining an ongoing series of formal and informal negotiations between you and your organization on a quid-pro-quo basis so that you can contribute to organization goals and at the same time continue to grow toward your own goals on some reasonable timetable. Our interviews show that successful people seldom wait for an organization to suggest job enrichment or change to them. They tend to be very squeaky wheels about negotiating work they can believe in and find rewarding. If a job is not meaningful to them, or if it's moving them in directions they don't want to go, they find a way to change without waiting to be asked.

Developing Interpersonal Competence—Few people are intuitive interpersonal process experts. Most successful people have worked hard and consciously at developing their interpersonal sensitivities, awareness, and persuasive techniques. Lack of interpersonal competence is a major barrier (in our opinion *the* major barrier) to negotiating self-fulfilling and personal growth-oriented work in organizational environments.

Updating Regularly—A good career (or life) plan involves a series of conscious decisions over time. It's a flexible, rolling forecast that you update regularly to incorporate such things as new data assimilated, temporary setbacks, and new value insight. Effective career planning is not a one-shot effort.

Continually Checking Your Spiritual Compass—Regularly reviewing your short-term career goals, criteria, and decisions to make certain they will support your broader, longer-term life goals—to be sure the shorter-term gains you seek won't lead to longer-term loss of spirit, that they won't derail you onto what become unfulfilling sidetracks that divert from the more meaningful, and satisfying ultimate goals you want your life journey to accomplish.

A ROADMAP TO SAVE TIME

At first glance, an approach like the above may appear to be time consuming but it doesn't have to be. Done right, it can end up conserving time.

In Step 3, we will outline a disciplined, step-by-step *Taking Charge Process* for fulfilling each of the essential contract ingredients described above. The tools and exercises presented in the workbook will show you how to complete each step in minimum time.

THE EFFICIENCY OF FOCUS

There is a common misconception that the only way people can achieve career goals is to devote so much time and energy to them that all other values are traded off. This is not necessarily so. Some achieve career goals that way. Others focus their energies in an intelligent, data-based fashion that enables them to concentrate on high-impact (as opposed to make-work) efforts and leaves plenty of time for other things.

With better focus, you may discover you can achieve more that is relevant to you with significantly less effort than you're expending now. You may be wasting a great deal of energy and time on nonproductive activities because you lack focus. Many people dissipate enormous amounts of nonproductive energy coping with anxieties generated by lack of personal goal clarity.

A CLEAR GOAL CONSERVES ENERGY

Goal clarity and motivation are two key interrelating variables in the process of getting what you want in life and on the job. If we think in terms of an economy of energy model, goal clarity and motivation interact to influence how effectively we generate and use energy.

Fuzzy or ill-defined goals don't invite much self-generated motivation to achieve them. With unclear goals, energy is dissipated in confusion and anxiety. By clarifying goals, you can liberate this dissipated energy and make it available for productive achievement. Goal clarity makes it possible to concentrate your energies on activities that are directly relevant to accomplishing career goals. With focus, you can work smarter instead of longer.

Hopefully, you're already in the position of having clear goals and active self-fulfilling programs for achieving them. However, it's our observation that relatively few people working in impersonal organizations (even at very high levels) are already in that position. The most noticeable symptom that all is not well is anxiety.

WHEN TO CONTRACT FOR CHANGE

If anxiety is the symptom, anxiety is also the clue. Anxiety is your internal, automatic-warning signal that all is not right and it's time for a contract with yourself to analyze why and make a course correction. In this sense, anxiety can be a positive, beneficial experience. Most of us try to suppress anxiety. We deny it, blot it out, or try to force it to go away. We see it as a negative reflection on our worth, a sign that something is wrong with us.

Everyone has anxieties. Anxiety doesn't necessarily mean something is wrong with us. It's often merely a signal that something may be wrong in our lives, or perhaps simply that something could be better.

Anxiety can be a very positive motivator for change. Many of the world's most significant accomplishments would never have happened without people becoming anxious about the way things were to the point where they wanted to improve them.

We shouldn't deny anxiety. It's more productive to let ourselves experience it and analyze what's causing it. We should look for what it is we're reacting to in the situation, and for what it is we ourselves are doing, or not doing, to maintain the difficulty.

Dealing with the known is easier than suppressing the unknown, and it's less fatiguing. When we know what is causing anxiety we can develop a plan for improving things. If we've made a mistake, we can learn from it and begin corrective action. All of us make a lot of mistakes. That's also a natural trait that needn't be blotted out. Action is the prescription for a building anxiety, and past mistakes are the basic building blocks for future growth.

ANXIETY MAY MEAN YOU HAVE SUCCEEDED

There is a form of restlessness or anxiety common in our work lives that has nothing to do with mistakes. It has to do with boredom and reaching plateaus.

In looking at my own life I have found a clear cyclical pattern. Each period of excitement, energy, and growth has been followed by a leveling off and then a plateau. The plateau often meant I had mastered what there was to learn in a given job or challenge, or I had worked through key concerns of my current life stage. I was feeling safe where I was and resisting movement on to the next stage. My learning had stopped. I rested on the plateau for a while and then went into a satisfaction slump. I got bored, tired, and very anxious. When the slump dropped low enough that I became acutely uncomfortable, this roused me enough that I forced myself into new challenges where I could start up the growth and learning curve again. Understanding this cyclical pattern gave me new perceptions and insight. Before, I always got depressed when I felt anxious or bored. I assumed all my anxieties were signs I had taken a wrong turn, failed, or been wasting my life on the wrong thing. When I felt this way I fought change. I felt that acknowledging I needed change was acknowledging failure.

Seeing the cyclical pattern gave me a different perspective. It showed anxiety and boredom could be signs I had succeeded, signs I had mastered something and was ready to build on that, to move on to a new and higher growth plateau. As the life stages research shows, this is what life in this world is about—overcoming barriers, mastering things, learning, growing, and moving on to new plateaus—progressing daily closer to our goal of becoming ever more complete human beings. That tied in with what I had always heard in my spiritual and religious training. I was glad to see these different areas of my life beginning to integrate and coalesce. I felt good about it. I began to feel progressively more and more satisfied and fulfilled. Anxiety is not quite so scary anymore. It is another *on* button for forward movement.

Right now you may have no pressing desire to use this book's techniques for changing anything. One reason may be that you are in the middle of a satisfying growth curve, or resting on a plateau consolidating your energies for the next climb. When you finish the book, keep it on your shelf. When (or if) you start on the down slope, get it out again and do some of the exercises in the workbook.

If you are avoiding thinking about change for fear that would be acknowledging past mistakes, stop doing that. Only losers believe they can't make mistakes. Winners expect to make lots of mistakes, learn from them, and move on.

There may not be any mistakes involved at all. You may simply be at the end of a firm and successfully built plateau. That's a strong signal you're ready to look higher.

Those of us with families and financial obligations can't relieve anxiety by quitting our jobs tomorrow and taking up fishing in Hawaii, skiing in the Yukon, or working full time with the poor in the ghetto. Nevertheless we can almost always, at any age, and without jeopardizing our incomes, find ways to negotiate for new challenges and growth in our current situations, on and off the job. Also, most of us—if we sit down, use our brains, and make a contract with ourselves to generate a strategy—can develop many more options than we realize for maintaining our incomes and pursuing more life-fulfilling meaning in our work (inside or outside our current organizations).

In our next section we will describe the *Taking Charge Process*. This contains twelve critical tasks that together complete steps 3 and 4 of the five-part sequence we've found people follow for success in career and life planning.

1. BREAKING OLD MINDSETS

2. CONTRACTING FOR RENEWAL

3. FINDING YOUR CALLING

4. MAKING IT HAPPEN

5. STAYING THE COURSE

STEP 3

FINDING YOUR CALLING

Here you continue the process of *converging* and begin to focus on concrete goals and action plans. In **Step 3** we give you a roadmap with specific tools you can use to develop each of the essential contract ingredients and find your unique calling in life.

First, we'll introduce a step-by-step process for *Taking Charge* of your career and developing your own personal criteria for success.

Second, we'll talk about identifying your personal life value priorities as you pass through some very predictable life and growth stages.

Third, we'll show you how to decide what you want to do on the job (*i.e.,* what types of skills or competencies you most enjoy exercising and want to grow day-to-day at work).

61

Fourth, we'll discuss how to combine the above into your own special criteria for success and identify future career paths most likely to meet them.

Fifth, we'll give you a procedure and format for conducting *Investigative Interviews* with people ahead of you on the career paths you choose. We'll also give you a tool for assessing whether or not careers like theirs meet your personal success criteria. This will help you eliminate false starts and focus on career goals with the highest potential payoff.

Sixth, we'll present some research-based self-assessment tools to help you define specific personal improvement goals focused on developing key competencies our research shows people need for success in almost any career specialty.

Taking Charge Process
Introduction

It isn't enough to long for a more meaningful work life. We have to plot a better path and then take action. We have to clearly define what we are looking for and then persistently seek it.

Fulfilling careers seldom happen by chance. With few exceptions people who find personally meaningful vocations do so because they assume responsibility for their journeys. They define clear goals (including their proposed routes, important way stations on the road, and final destinations). They develop plans and schedules for achieving these goals. They implement and follow their plans, correcting course as they learn new things about themselves along the way. They monitor their progress and persevere in facing frequent setbacks until their goals are achieved.

Persistence

Winston Churchill was once invited to speak to the young men at his alma mater, Harrow. Before he spoke the head of the school described him to the students as "the greatest orator of our time—perhaps of all time." They expected a long speech. Instead, Winston gave them a very short speech. After acknowledging his introduction, he said:

> Young men, never give up. Never give up! Never give up!
> Never, never, never, never.

Then he left the podium. It was a simple but powerful message. Those who knew his life knew he lived his message. He wasn't just being clever.

He believed that what he had to say was important and that making his point simply might help it sink in. He was right. Churchill was a master dramatist who knew his audiences. People have been quoting that speech for decades and, for many, I am sure it's been life changing.

FINDING OUR MISSION IN WHATEVER HAPPENS

When we speak of persistence it's important to reemphasize we are not talking about inflexibility—about the stubborn pursuit of specific career goals we establish early in life and refuse to change no matter what new lessons we learn in their pursuit. Rather we are talking about benefiting as much from our failures as our successes—about a never-ending process of making continuous life choices that maintain our moral integrity and reflect a humble openness to new insight as we progress through each life stage. We're talking about never losing hope—and never giving up—despite the fact that, like Churchill, we can't always predict and control the outcomes of what we do.

A DISCIPLINED APPROACH

Churchill was painfully aware that success is not a barrier-free life. Finding personal meaning and life fulfillment comes from defining what we want and persisting despite barriers. That's easy to say and obvious if we take time to think about it. But who has time? Accepting responsibility for our own lives and persistently charting our own courses are nice thoughts but how do we follow through on them? Is all this practical? Can anyone really do these things in the pressures of today's work climate?

The answer to these questions is yes. It is practical and there is a way. You can do it. And there is a disciplined methodology to help you with the charting. Steve and I haven't invented the steps in this process. We've merely documented them after years of interviewing and observing other people who were successfully charting their courses and finding it very rewarding.

The *Taking Charge Process* we'll describe next will help you accomplish two of the five critical steps for effective career planning. It will help you *Find Your Calling* in life (Step 3) and develop a practical plan to *Make It Happen* (Step 4). It will give you a systematic way to identify what type of career path you want to pursue and what it actually takes to pursue it successfully. By using the process, you can save a great deal of time by crossing off unproductive doors and misleading sidetracks. This is how you begin transforming your *career* into a *vocation* or *calling* that can give real meaning to your work endeavors.

Don't skip this process. Read through it now. Then, when you finish the book and have the full perspective, use the *Career and Life Workbook*. It will lead you through a series of exercises that address and complete each important task.

THE *TAKING CHARGE PROCESS*

Figure 1 outlines the first few tasks in the process. These are devoted to defining your own personal criteria for success. You do this by first identifying your most important life values and noticing where you are and what issues you need to address next in some very predictable stages of adult life development. Then you use past experience to help identify what skills and abilities you most enjoy exercising and want to develop in your future work. The combination of the top *life values* you want to achieve and the *skills or competencies* you want to exercise and develop then becomes your list of *personal criteria for success*.

FIGURE 1   TAKING CHARGE PROCESS

Finding Your Calling

1. **Determining Your True Life Values**
2. **Tracking Your Life Stage Progression**
3. **Deciding What You Want to Do**
4. **Establishing Your Personal Criteria for Success**

Now let's start to look at each of the tasks shown in Figure 1.

DETERMINING YOUR TRUE LIFE VALUES

If you don't like your job, you probably can't afford to just quit. Few people can. First you have to identify new opportunities you will like. Before you can do that, you have to make some careful choices among many possibilities. People sometimes get stuck in way stations on their career and life journeys because they think they have no other possibilities. They feel sidetracked or on a plateau, and they don't know how to identify,

FIGURE 2 WHICH DOOR?

develop, and pursue different, more rewarding career options. This brings us to an interesting career and life planning paradox. Often we fail to develop and pursue more productive career possibilities not because we can imagine too few, but because we fantasize too many and become immobilized by our inability to make choices.

A Parable

A friend of mine once gave me the following homily. It illustrates how many smart people never develop more productive career options, but instead invest their energies in downgrading others' success.

> Dumb people frequently get what they want through focus and energy. They have narrow perspective. They pick one door, beat on it until they're bloody, and get through. Then they pick the next door behind it and do the same thing. This can eventually, though sometimes painfully, lead to significant satisfaction and accomplishment.
>
> Bright people, on the other hand, have broader perspective. They see many doors and frequently immobilize themselves, saying "Which door . . . which door . . . which door?" They can't seem to focus. This can go on for years or lifetimes. It's often accomplished by complaints of feeling underutilized and/or trapped.
>
> Bright people who get immobilized by the "which door" phenomenon often end up working for dumb people in jobs they don't like. They find this very frustrating.
>
> Dumb people know they're dumb. They don't try to hide it. Not being sophisticated, they don't mind asking what might be seen as stupid questions. And they will ask these questions of anyone who might have the answers. Even when they are in high level positions they'll approach people at all levels, including the lowest in the organization, and ask a lot of questions to collect information.
>
> Bright people don't like to be seen asking dumb questions. They're sophisticated and want to keep up their images. Often, rather than look stupid or admit they don't know something, they will avoid asking questions and pretend they know the answers. The result is that bright people often end up working for dumb people who know more than they do. They find this even more frustrating.

Dumb People Are Smarter than We Think

The bottom line, of course, is that the dumb people in this homily are not so dumb. In reality they are very bright and often very honest—particularly with themselves. They've learned to ask questions, acknowledge and learn from others' expertise, and collect needed information. They've developed the personal discipline to focus their energy, make informed decisions, cross off some doors, and move ahead through the doors they choose.

Typically it's lack of information that prevents bright people from choosing doors and moving on. They get immobilized because they don't know what's behind the doors. Without this information they can't make decisions. Bright people usually claim to care what's behind doors that interest them, but frequently they don't get around to investigating and finding out. It's as though they prefer to wait for automatic doors that open by themselves.

We have counseled many very bright and talented middle-age professionals who were agonizing over whether or not to pursue specific career moves (*e.g.*, from technical work to sales, marketing, or project management) when they had no more than speculative or stereotyped ideas about what people on the career paths they were considering actually did or what skills were required. They had never done any real investigating by talking to a sampling of people who were already performing successfully in the type of positions they aspired to. These same people would never make a decision in their technical specialties (*e.g.*, engineering or finance) without collecting and evaluating the facts first. It was only their lives they were trying to plan in uninformed, seat-of-the-pants fashion.

Bright people who get immobilized need to end their impasses by doing some very basic research in the job marketplace. They need to spend some time systematically asking questions, collecting data, and investigating what's really behind the doors they fantasize. This is the only way bright people can eliminate doors they don't want and focus energy effectively on doors they do want.

MARKET RESEARCH, GOOD AND BAD

After spending several years managing the selection of job candidates for a market research organization I concluded there were two types of market researchers—those who do their homework before they start collecting information and those who don't. Those who do their homework think through precisely what it is they want to find out in advance, and they decide how they will evaluate the information before they collect it. Prior to gathering data, they develop clear criteria for what it is they are looking for (*e.g.*, is geographical location an important personal consideration in their choice of work). Defining their criteria helps them determine what questions to ask and from whom to seek information. They can then focus their research and conserve energy. Criteria also become the standards against which they can assess the information after they collect it (*e.g.*, how many of their personal criteria can be met in a career path they've looked into). Those who don't develop their criteria in advance rush out and collect random information, usually from too many or the wrong people. Then they end up being confused by the mounds of information they have gathered because they have no standards against which to evaluate the information—no criteria to tell them whether or not the career options they have been researching meet their needs.

CRITERIA BEGIN WITH LIFE VALUES

Some of the most important criteria we need to define before doing market research or looking behind any career doors are our life values. It's important to know what personal values we want to achieve in life, on and off the job. Then we can research and strategize a career to help us meet the most possible of these values. Making an initial list of our values is usually the easy part. Most of us can come up with a long list. The real challenge—the tough part of determining values—comes in the choices we have to make in setting our priorities, in deciding which values we will give up or trade off when we face inevitable contradictions.

I don't know about you, but I want everything. I don't want any contradictions or forced choices. I want to eat and drink all I like and never gain weight. I want the freedom and flexibility of a single life and all the rewards of a loving spouse and children. I want to live in a small, intimate, low pressure, academic town and have all the challenges, money, and status of a job that may only be available in places like New York or Chicago. I want Santa Claus to come along and let me have it all. And I don't think I'm unusual in this. I think most people, reasonable or not, want just about everything.

If I let myself think about it, however—if I face the unpleasant reality that there are contradictions and I can't have everything—I'll probably discover I do have some preferences. Each of us wants some things more than others. Precisely what we want and in what rank order is distinctively different for each individual. Accepting someone else's—organization's, peer's, or teacher's—rank order is not a very adult decision. Accepting someone else's rank order for me is laziness, unwillingness to do my own tough thinking, or excessively conforming behavior.

If I wait for Santa Claus to give me everything, Santa will not come. Blind chance or someone else will make the trade-offs for me. Both are really nondecision options, and both are dangerous. Letting chance or someone else make the trade-offs for me will rob me of many things I want most and substitute things I don't want nearly as much.

DECIDING OUR OWN VALUES

We help people start identifying their most important personal values by asking them to prioritize 20 typical career-related life values. We do this by giving them a set of 20 cards, each of which defines one of the values. Then we have them practice identifying contradictions and making trade-offs by giving up the cards two at a time until they get down to the top five they would be least willing to trade off. Most find this a tough but enlightening process. Of course, most will achieve more than five of the values, but forcing themselves to focus down on only five introduces a valuable discipline.

The process of looking carefully at your life values and establishing clear priorities may force you to make some conscious trade-offs you've been avoiding, particularly when you compare what your top value priorities are with the values you are actually spending most of your time pursuing today.

Figure 3 shows 20 typical life values people want to pursue. Some will realize more than others. It's unlikely anyone will realize them all, however, because several are likely to contradict each other. This is not because the establishment or system is plotting mean things, but simply because that's the way the world is. You can complain that this is not fair, get angry, and refuse to accept the fact that you have to trade off anything. Or you can simply refuse to look at reality and wait for fate, Santa, or someone else to eliminate the contradictions for you so you don't have to choose. If you do either of those things you'll probably get and stay stuck in a way station, very likely an angry and disgruntled way station. It's easier to become your own Santa Claus by making choices, ending the impasse and moving on.

FIGURE 3 TYPICAL CAREER-RELATED LIFE VALUES[18]

- **Friendship**   To work with people I respect and to be respected by them.

- **Location**   To be able to live where I want to live.

- **Enjoyment**   To enjoy my work. To have fun doing it.

- **Loyalty**   To be committed to the goals of a group of people who share my beliefs, values, and ethical principles.

- **Family**   To have time with my family.

- **Leadership**   To motivate and energize other people. To feel responsible for identifying and accomplishing needed group tasks.

- **Personal Development**   To learn and to do challenging work that will help me grow, that will allow me to utilize my best talents and mature as a human being.

- **Security**   To have a steady income that fully meets my family's basic needs.

- **Wisdom**   To grow in understanding of myself, my personal calling, and life's real purpose. To grow in knowledge and practice my religious beliefs. To discern and do the will of God and find lasting meaning in what I do.

- **Community**

  To be deeply involved with a group that has a larger purpose beyond one's self. To perform in effective and caring team-work.

- **Wealth**

  To earn a great deal of money (*i.e.*, well beyond my family's basic needs). To be financially independent.

- **Expertness**

  To become a known and respected authority in what I do.

- **Service**

  To contribute to the well-being and satisfaction of others. To help people who need help and improve society.

- **Personal Accomplishment**

  To achieve significant goals. To be involved in undertakings I believe personally are significant—whether or not they bring me recognition from others.

- **Prestige**

  To be seen by others as successful. To become well-known. To obtain recognition and status in my chosen field.

- **Power**

  To have the authority to approve or disapprove proposed courses of action. To make assignments and control allocation of people and resources.

- **Independence**

  To have freedom of thought and action. To be able to act in terms of my own time schedules and priorities.

- **Integrity**

  To live and work in compliance with my personal moral standards. To be honest and acknowledge/stand up for my personal beliefs.

- **Health**

  To be physically and mentally fit.

- **Creativity**

  To be innovative. To create new and better ways of doing things.

-

-

-

You don't, of course, have to limit yourself to these 20 typical values. The blank bullets at the end of the list are meant to indicate you can add any other values that might be really important to you.

PARENTS, MENTORS, ORGANIZATIONS, AND OTHERS

When people prioritize their life values we suggest they sort out any voices they might carry in their heads from other people telling them what they should value. There are four categories of voices each of us should particularly monitor. These are the voices of our parents, mentors, organizations, and others.

Many values come from our parents. Most are probably very worthwhile. We share and want to retain them. It's important to look at values transmitted from our parents. However, we must make certain we are not unduly influenced by those we may not share. We might be putting an inflated emphasis on wealth as the answer to all our problems, for instance, if our parents faced economic deprivations we don't face, and more money had an urgency for them it needn't have for us (or if our parents were very wealthy and prized that). Perhaps a parent put great emphasis on independence while we'd prefer to trade off some of that for an increased sense of service or community with others. Wanting something different from our parents doesn't mean they were wrong. It just means we're different and probably living in different circumstances.

Most professionals have one or more significant mentors during their 20s and 30s. Mentors are usually people 8 to 15 years older than we are—teachers, bosses, or experienced co-workers who take us under their wings and teach us the tricks of the trade in our occupational specialties. They help us establish ourselves as members of our trades or professions. Mentors are valued and essential contributors to our learning. A mentor serves in a role similar to that of master in the old master-apprentice system.

To become masters themselves, however, apprentices must finally break from masters, become their own persons, and steer their own courses. This often happens when people are between the ages of 35–40 and realize they have been too subject to influence by those who have authority over them. They then stand on their mentor's shoulders, build in new directions from that firm foundation, and extend their capabilities beyond their mentor's. A transition takes place. The mentors cease to be authorities and instead become valued friends and peers. If apprentices don't graduate to become their own masters the mentors have failed. The transition may be temporarily traumatic for both mentor and mentee. However, good mentors eventually learn to brag about their graduates and find new apprentices. If mentors refuse friendship to you in other than an apprentice role, that's their decision and problem, not yours. You needn't get angry. You can continue to be understanding and grateful, but still firmly independent.

Identify and think about your mentors. Sort out what they have said you should and should not value. Decide where you do and do not agree today. You may still be associated with a mentor or you may be carrying some strong value messages from mentors you haven't worked with for years. If so, assess them and pursue only those you still agree with.

Many companies are attempting to better align individual employee behavior with the organization's vision and mission. They often do this by communicating various organization values employees are expected to acknowledge and commit themselves to. This is basically a good trend. If you know what your organization's values are you can better understand what's expected of you. And you can better decide if your personal values are compatible. This doesn't have to be an all or nothing decision. It's better to look at each specific organizational value, articulated or implied, and decide whether or not it conflicts with what is important to you. You will probably find it's easy to agree with the majority (*e.g.*, quality or customer service). There may be some, however, like "working whatever after hours or weekend time it takes to get the job done" in a significantly downsized and overloaded operation—or "always exceeding the previous quarter's sales figures"—that you need to put into better perspective or even resist.

Another potential contaminating influence on our choice of values can often be found in relationships with our "others"—in our own competitive instincts and need to be one-up on our friends, siblings, or peers. I learned the concept of others from a very pragmatic compensation manager I worked with years ago. A dispute arose about a top employee's dissatisfaction with a raise. Fresh from graduate school, I gave the compensation manager volumes of statistical data proving the individual's raise was correct. After listening he said: "I know that. So does he, but he's still unhappy. What raise did his 'other' get? It must have been more."

He then explained his personal theory that everyone has "others"—usually people close to them in age—against whom they compare their progress. The other may be a sibling, a college classmate, a friend, or a peer in the same organization. There may be more than one other, and there is usually at least one in the individual's current organization. If the person is doing better than the other, he or she is happy and satisfied even if both are low paid. If a person does less well than he/she perceives the other is doing (and others do tend to exaggerate their progress), he or she is unhappy even if both are overpaid.

I can't prove this theory but I believe it. I immediately identified a few others and realized how much it hurt when I thought they were getting ahead of me. I knew that wasn't rational but it still hurt. Hopefully, competition with my others is not making me trade off any top priority values just to keep up. Their values are probably and legitimately very different from mine. They may be paying a high price in some dimension (*e.g.*, time with family) that is more important than power or money to me. It's even possible they're trading off their own key values to stay ahead in a nonconstructive competition with me if I'm their other. Both of us may be sacrificing important values in a race neither even wants to be in. What a way to waste time and lose spirit.

Where does it end? It ends when I call a halt for me. The others must determine how it will end for them. Think about who your others are. What price might you be paying for the competition? Clearly see that in your mind. Do you really want to race? If not, plan what you will do differently in the future to avoid these useless competitions.

STAYING ANCHORED IN LIFE VALUES THAT BRING PERSONAL MEANING TO *YOU*

If you don't know who you are, you will probably become for other people (*e.g.*, superiors, peers, or society) what they need or want you to be. There will be no self. Being what others expect you to be may even bring high recognition and material rewards, but if there is no self there will probably be little true meaning. You life will drift away from you unanchored and in directions you don't really want to go.

Even when we believe our life values reflect our own inner preferences it's important to test this assumption regularly. Life values are frequently influenced—often unconsciously—by our evolving life environments (*e.g.*, faddish cultural or organizational norms). It's important to identify these influences periodically, make certain they are conscious, and test how they are supporting or impairing pursuit of our important life and spiritual goals.

We need to know and stay anchored in who we are, in what we personally value and stand for. Our actions probably won't always reflect our deepest beliefs. There will be gaps between our values and our behaviors. Filling those gaps is a constant struggle for everyone. If we don't notice the gaps—if we don't strive continually to fill the gaps by better matching our values and behaviors—chances are we will find sparse meaning in what we do no matter how great the external rewards.

The following brief reflection will help you make a quick assessment of what *your* value priorities are today. Later, you can take a more in-depth look when you do the exercises in the workbook. Before you do the reflection sit quietly a moment and get in touch with your own thought process. Monitor any voices you carry around in your head from other people (*e.g.*, society, the media, peers, former teachers, your organization) telling you what it is popular to value. Put them aside and get in touch with what *you* want. Then ask the Spirit for guidance and listen to your inner voice. Hear what it tells you about what values you really want and need to pursue if you are to put more meaning in your life and career.

Because this is a book about career planning, we have presented a list of career or vocation-related values. It is not a list of moral principles. We can't make a complete list of those in a book like this. You've probably already learned much of what you need to know about those from a long list of spiritual writers and leaders who are much wiser than we. What we show in Figure 3 is merely a list of fairly typical day-to-day value concerns (only some of which involve moral principles in themselves) that most of us need to track and assess continually throughout our life journeys.

BRIEF REFLECTION

Look at the 20 Life Values in Figure 3. Then take an erasable pencil and make a few temporary marks on Figure 3 following the instructions below. Don't take a lot of time to do this. Just record what comes to your mind quickly. See what initial response comes to mind first. You can do a much more thorough Life Values exercise later, when you complete the workbook.

Bottom 3

Put a **"B"** in front of your **bottom 3** values (*i.e.*, those you would be most willing to give up).

Top 3

Put a **"T"** after your **top 3** (*i.e.*, those you would be least willing to give up).

Least Important Value

Review your bottom 3 values and circle the **"B"** after the single value you would be most willing to give up (*i.e.*, the value that has the lowest priority for you personally).

Most Important Value

Review your top 3 values and circle the **"T"** after the single value you would be least willing to give up (*i.e.*, the value that has top priority for you personally).

Compare your top values with those you spend most time pursuing today.

Principle-based *Decisions* vs. Evasive Value *Clarifications*

When we prioritize our life values it is important, however, that we make what Stephen Covey and many of our modern behavioral experts call *principle-based* value *decisions*. That requires a lot more than the typically evasive value *clarification* exercises that are so popular in today's value avoiding society.

Unfortunately, many contemporary values clarification exercises tend to foster not tough decision-making, but a currently popular form of easy-out escapism. They provide a way to pretend we are making meaningful choices while avoiding any hard decisions. They give us a tool to play what Peter Kreeft describes as "moral ping pong." He tells us that questions addressed by facilitators in many modern values *clarification* exercises are:

> . . . never about the roots or grounds of values, about *principles*. Instead, they are about feelings and reasoning, *calculations*.
>
> They never ask questions about virtues and vices, about character, but ask only about what you would do or rather what you would "feel comfortable" doing.
>
> The one moral absolute in (*typical*) values clarification is that there are no moral absolutes, and the only thing forbidden is for the facilitator to suggest that . . . there *is* objective truth in the realm of values, for that would mean some of the students are wrong, and that would be "judgmental," the only sin. In fact the very procedure itself teaches a nearly irresistible lesson: values are all up for grabs, are matters of individual or social taste; no one has the right to teach another here; values are "my" values or "your" values, never simply true values; values, in short, are not facts but feelings.[19]

This approach to deciding and living our values is obviously ridiculous—at least when someone like Kreeft takes an objective look and tells it like it is in nonevasive language. If you are like me, somewhere deep down you have always known it was ridiculous. But if you're like me you've also not always been as courageous as Kreeft in owning up to it—or expressing it.

While we do have to choose our own values, we shouldn't do that in a moral vacuum. Clearly there are some objective moral principles we have to consider. I don't believe values, especially moral and spiritual values, are all relative. I have never believed that. But I haven't always been willing to be clear about—and consistently practice—what I really do believe. That kind of behavior might challenge people. In much of modern society it's not considered politically correct and I don't want to be unpopular. I want to be sophisticated, urbane, and well-liked even by people I know are behaving in direct contradiction to what I believe— even when they are subtly pressuring me to behave the same way. What a way to waste a life! I don't have to get on a soapbox and convert the world. However, I do have to be certain I at least really know where I stand and that my behavior and language are *always* consistent with that.

If we have a difference in values, I have to make certain my behaviors are not slipping into compliance with my audience's rather than my own moral beliefs. I don't have to berate or lecture everyone I disagree with. That would often be a waste of time anyway. However, I do have to make certain that my actions (*i.e.*, everything I do) are consistent with what I really want (*i.e.*, personal morality, integrity, and self-respect) and not with what I can easily deceive myself into thinking I want (*i.e.*, more recognition and personal popularity). And while I don't always have to say everything I believe, I do have to be very careful never to say anything I don't believe.

SOME VERY AVAILABLE ROAD SIGNS

Steve and I are not theologians. It isn't our job in this book to teach the details of moral values. You don't need us to do that anyway. You already know them. They have been spelled out for you by much more learned and spiritually advanced people than we. They are as obvious as the Ten Commandments and the Sermon on the Mount with its eight magnificent Beatitudes. I don't think many of our readers will deny the validity of those two documents as roadmaps for a more fulfilling journey—not only through this life but far beyond to a much higher realm. If you do disagree with them, you are an unusual person. Kreeft points out the simplicity and universal acceptance of the Sermon on the Mount when he says:

> The greatest sermon ever preached takes only fifteen minutes to read and can be printed on a single page; yet it has changed the world more than any other speech ever made. Even Gandhi found nothing in his rich, six thousand-year-old Hindu tradition to equal it. Even atheists, agnostics, and humanists testify to its greatness. The whole world stares in ecumenical orgy of agreement at it; yet the whole world fails to *follow* it, exactly as the man in Jesus' parable at the end of the sermon (Matt. 7:24–27) who built his house on the sand of hearing instead of on the rock of heeding.[20]

Are we mapping our lives and energy-consuming vocational pursuits on the drifting sands of transient and cyclical contemporary fads? Or are we using the solid life anchors provided by this great sermon, by the commandments, and by the great spiritual writers of Islam, Buddhism, Hinduism, and other major religious traditions? Are we deafened by the noise of the media, or by organization and peer pressure? Or are we listening to centuries of Eastern and Western spiritual giants who have provided us with the time-tested, enduring, very public principles and values we've always had available to us as road signs for plotting and pursuing more fulfilling journeys?

Most of us are doing a little of each. The trick is to keep moving relentlessly toward firmer ground. It isn't easy, but it brings the only true satisfaction and the stakes are high. The real graduation prize, the only satisfying destination is not a short, if physically comfortable, retirement in the sun, not fifteen minutes of fame, but an eternity of much more fulfilling light in an infinitely higher realm. What is a practical person to do? A practical person will pay attention and make the effort to keep his or her value choices on track. One individual I know, for instance, prioritized his values and concluded he was unhappily and excessively pursuing both wealth and personal recognition. He left a *career* that provided high visibility and material rewards for a less lucrative *vocation* that gave him more opportunity to pursue important social service, family, and spiritual values he'd been neglecting. He never regretted the decision.

Steve and I have each spent our share of time lost in the self-generated fog of value confusion and indecision. We know it's only human. But we have also discovered that it isn't necessary.

There are people who discipline themselves to penetrate the fog. They make the tough decision to take off their blinders and see the markers. Then they work hard at clearing the air whenever new mists inevitably form. This gives them a noticeable serenity despite a chaotic and unpredictable environment. It provides them with a calming surety of direction when many around them are circling blindly in a foggy refusal to make value decisions, or in failing to act when they discover their values and day-to-day activities are in conflict.

We've said that many of the values we define in Figure 3 are not moral principles in themselves. However, there is a morality implicit in how and to what extent we pursue any given value on the list. There is a proper balance. We know that intuitively even when we don't allow this clear knowledge into our consciousness. Some values are definitely more important than others in light of our journey's ultimate destination. And an excessive pursuit of several can easily lead to an imbalance that we know, if we clear the fog, is *not* moral. Paraphrasing Kreeft, we *know*, but we do not always *heed*. And we are geniuses at not noticing we are not heeding.

Kept in appropriate perspective, none of the values on the list is right or wrong in itself. However, pursued out of balance, many can become debilitating and road-fogging false gods. We tend to think of false gods as antique and currently nonexistent phenomena. No one has worshiped Zeus or a golden calf for millennia. In truth, however, we have not eliminated false gods; we have renamed them. If you don't know the names, our values list can give you several clues.

When you compare your value priorities with what values are actually taking your time these days, are there any discrepancies or gaps? You are very unusual, or untruthful, if you see no discrepancies. Are there a few imbalances that have, for all practical purposes, become unacknowledged false gods that are leading you off course? If so, what will you do about that?

It's up to each of us to make our own tough values choices. Recognizing this can be scary for even the bravest of us. But there is good news to go with that. We can empower ourselves and get back on course. The hardest part is tracking the many times we drift off course, admitting what's happening, and taking corrective action. As our tough-minded CEO said earlier, the spaceship would never get to the moon if it didn't constantly correct course.

PERSONAL GROWTH AND SATISFACTION

If we track our progress and stay on course, our values will evolve and mature. We will grow and the growth will be satisfying. Being clear on our values can keep us anchored when the situation around us is falling apart. It can keep us in touch with our authentic selves, with who we are and, most important of all, with who we want to become in our ongoing development as both human and spiritual beings.

Being clear about and tracking our values can help us heal the split between our spiritual and material aspirations. Most people, whether or not they recognize and acknowledge it, find little meaning in material progress without some accompanying sense of personal growth toward a more spiritual maturity. Those who deny this are often smug, but seldom very happy. What self-satisfaction they project to the world is often fragile and based on sad, self-deceiving hubris.

Most contemporary life stages research demonstrates that spiritual, as opposed to strictly material, evolution is essential for meaning and personal peace. In addition, our wisest prophets and sages have regularly told us that spiritual growth is the most powerful and enduring path to meaning in an otherwise difficult-to-understand world. To keep our life value choices and overall spiritual pursuits compatible with each other, it helps to do periodic reviews of where we are now and how we're progressing through the various adult life stages contemporary psychology has discovered.

Tracking Your
Life Stage Progression

Earlier we mentioned the work of people such as Erik Erikson and Daniel Levinson, who conducted extensive research and identified a series of very predictable life stages healthy people go through in their journeys through life. At each stage we tend to reassess and rebalance our life values priorities. It's helpful to know what some of these stages are so that when we pass through them we can be aware of what's happening and know that it's normal. Since our focus here is on careers, we will briefly summarize six stages of adult career development that we have synthesized from the work of many who have studied the adult growth process. For a more in-depth understanding we recommend the writings of Erikson, Levinson, Groeschel, Fowler, and others (see bibliography) who describe the process in more detail.

Stages of Growth

Addressed with the right mindset these are stages of personal growth. The movement through the stages is a progression. As we pass from one stage to the next, often with some difficult periods of transition, we learn and mature in the process. If we acknowledge and work through the issues of each successive stage we become better human *and* spiritual beings.

These following stages carry us from our late teens to postretirement. The ages shown for each stage are only rough estimates. People may pass through the stages several years earlier or later than the estimates shown. Individuals vary widely in their progression through the stages.

85

STAGE 1

Autonomy and Tentative Choices *(Approximately 18–26)*

In this stage we are typically developing personal autonomy and leaving the family to establish an independent home, finances, etc. We're developing our own sense of personhood as separate from parents and childhood peer groups. We try out new relationships (*e.g.*, romantic interests, professional associates, peer groups, and friends). This is typically a period of tentative or provisional commitments. We're comfortable there is plenty of time ahead to change our minds on provisional decisions concerning things like location, occupation, plans to marry or not marry, friends, key life values, etc. Our focus is on defining ourselves as individuals and establishing an initial life structure.

STAGE 2

Young Adult Transition *(Approximately 27–31)*

This is usually a period of significant turmoil—of looking at who we are becoming and asking if we're really journeying in directions we want to go. We question most of our earlier tentative choices. Have we made the right decisions? Are we running out of time for changing our decisions? Are our decisions becoming permanent before we want them to? Do we really want to make this location, career path, or romantic relationship permanent? Will we or will we not settle down and have a family? Is time running out? Often with considerable angst similar to the better known mid-life crisis we rethink our provisional decisions and maintain them or change them in the process of making more permanent choices.

STAGE 3

Making Commitments *(Approximately 32–40)*

This is typically a period of relative order and stability where we implement and live the choices made in the young adult transition. We settle down into deeper commitments involving work, family, our community ties, etc. We focus on accomplishment, becoming our own persons, and generating an inner sense of expertise and mastery of our professions. By now we have a better developed and fairly well defined, though not usually final, dream of what we want to achieve in life. We put significant energy into achieving the dream.

STAGE 4
Mid-Life Transition *(Approximately 41–48)*

This is the stage of mid-life questioning that's been discussed so much in the popular press. Here we tend to question everything again. If we have not achieved our dreams we wonder why not. Were they really the right dreams? If we have achieved our dreams we look at what values we might have neglected in their pursuit. Was it worth it? Either way we're probably disillusioned. A period of reassessment and realignment usually takes place, including recognition and rebalancing of key polarities,[21] such as:

Immortality vs. Mortality—While young people know better intellectually, emotionally they seem to feel they are immortal. In mid-life we start to realize it may be half over and we want to make the best of what remains. This typically requires some revision of priorities and values—perhaps less emphasis on values already achieved and more emphasis on those we have neglected.

Constructive vs. Destructive—Up to mid-life, most of us fool ourselves that our behavior has been constructive while we had to deal with others' destructive behavior. In mid-life we get the uncomfortable insight that we have also engaged in our share of destructive as well as constructive behavior. This insight is painful but essential if we want to continue growing intellectually and spiritually.

Nurturing vs. Aggressive—Whether we have focused on aggressive (*e.g.*, fast-track corporate careers) or nurturing (*e.g.*, teaching, social work, or homemaking) behavior to date, in mid-life we often want to rebalance. Some aggressive corporate people want to spend more time nurturing with their families or in socially oriented work, and some who have been in more service-oriented nurturing careers want to pursue something more aggressive or financially rewarding.

The experts stress that acknowledging the turmoil, experiencing the pain, and facing and resolving the polarities are essential for continued growth and satisfaction. Refusing to acknowledge or experience mid-life anxieties and questions—or at some unconscious level trying to go back and be 20 again—is usually a sure way to get stuck and disgruntled in a way station.

STAGE 5

Leaving a Legacy *(Approximately 49–65)*

The period after completion of the mid-life transition can be one of the most productive of all stages. We are usually at the peak of our mature abilities here. If the issues of the mid-life transition have been acknowledged and addressed we can make our greatest possible contributions to others and society. Here we can be less driven, less ego-centered, less compelled to compete with and impress others. Instead we can focus on what really matters to us, on developing younger people, on community with others, on leaving some personal legacy that really makes things better for people (whether it's recognized as our personal legacy or not), and on accomplishing values that our maturity and greater spirituality tell us have the most true meaning in the overall scheme of life.

STAGE 6

Spiritual Denouement *(Approximately 66 and Beyond)*

This is the stage of tying things up, of completing the design of what we want to become, of finalizing our growth and assessing/fine-tuning the persons we have made of ourselves. This stage can go on for many years. It can be hopeful or cynical depending on how realistically, humbly, and effectively we have resolved (or now finally resolve) the issues faced in earlier stages. We may move into this stage sooner or later depending on how rapidly we have developed in earlier stages—how much we have moved beyond our narrow selves. Here we come to grips with the ultimate limitations of life, ourselves, and mortality. We can look hopefully and unflinchingly at the ultimate meaning of our life and the life of others in the larger context. We do the best we can to pass whatever wisdom we have gained on to others. We accept others for what they are, seeing them as growing like we are and part of humankind's diversity. Our sense of community continually expands as we prepare for survival of the spirit beyond our mortality.

A REASON TO BE

What ultimately is career and life success? What are we striving for? Why? What is our reason to be? The answer to these questions, and the significance we find in each of the life stages, will be very different depending on which world view we take.

If *Naturalism* is our world view, much of this life, including the life stages, doesn't make much sense. There is no ultimate goal. We perfect ourselves more every step of the way in life and then, at the height of our growth, we cease to exist. Not a very motivating scenario. Also a risky scenario. If we were betting on the wrong world view the negative consequences are far more severe and lasting than anything that happens to us in this life.

Naturalism's idea that we humans represent the ultimate intelligence can seem—at least momentarily—very sophisticated and flattering to our egos. Many very intelligent people have been seduced by this idea and spent their entire lives stuck in this rut. However, inevitably, those who have tried to replace God with human reason (especially when it has been their own reason they decided to revere) have done more harm than good. They have usually also ended up disillusioned and unhappy. However well meaning their original intentions were, the seduction of power—the idea of "being" rather than "serving" God—got them, and us, in trouble. The result has been much suffering, pain, unequal justice, and bad things happening to good people in this world. Hitler and Stalin occur to us as two extreme examples of people who took this path. Naturalism has not given us much to celebrate. The reality of Naturalism is that, when we get beyond its original seductions, it tends to keep our gaze focused down, on the mud. Most of us from the depths of our too often neglected souls ache for more. Something in our innermost being cries out for a higher purpose—real meaning and goals that can be more satisfying and enduring than the transient successes, the "vanities" of this life. We long to make that all-important simple turn of the head. We don't want this troubled existence to be all there is. We want to lift up our eyes beyond the restricted ceiling of earth and hope for heaven.

Supernaturalism gives us that hope. Supernaturalism goes substantively beyond Naturalism and provides meaning, even to our sufferings. Supernaturalism makes life a positive journey toward a higher place, with rewards far surpassing anything Naturalism can promise. Also, not only our spiritual, but even our finest scientific leaders tell us the "faith" of Supernaturalism is much more consistent with the universe's observed logic and order than Naturalism's faith in the chaos of nothingness built solely on chance. Supernaturalism gives us an overarching reason to be, an ultimate destination. Fortunately, it turns out that the most advanced modern research on life stages helps outline a path to that destination with defined way stations that can help us map our progress during the journey.

They tell us the purpose of each stage is to further our growth—to increase our learning and give us new, more mature insights. Our primary purpose in life is not business, money, recognition, professional expertise, or career progression. Our primary purpose is to become complete human beings and to help others become complete human beings as we work together in cooperative community on resolving the issues of each life stage. How open we stay to this never-ending learning, and how effectively we assimilate and grow from the often painful insight of each stage, seem to be critical determining factors in how far we progress—and in whether or not we experience satisfaction and the peace that can only come from movement toward an ultimately meaningful goal.

Effective progression through the stages is congruent with what generations of spiritual writers have defined as the real purpose of life, spiritual growth—the process of purifying and preparing ourselves for a higher life. This is much more important than what specific career field or profession we choose, or how much material recognition and reward we receive for what we do. A successful career is one that enhances our spiritual growth. Our occupational choice should be one that can best enhance that growth. In later chapters we will present some proven techniques for helping us make that important choice.

If you continually track your progress, as we recommend, you may find you even want to change career fields occasionally as you progress over the years, reach plateaus, and need new challenges to start you toward the next stage.

There are many who have received very high levels of material recognition and reward, but appear to be frozen and unhappily stagnated at one of the lower-level life stage way stations. Likewise, there are people who are wise and at peace in very high level developmental stages who have never sought or received much material recognition and reward. Which group would you consider more successful?

There is nothing wrong with material success and recognition, if they don't distract us from more enduring realities and endeavors. If material success and recognition become ends in themselves, if they define the ultimate destination in our career and life journeys—there has been a great deal of social, psychological, and spiritual wisdom accumulated over the centuries—that tells us we will find arrival at that ultimate destination terribly disappointing.

The rich man in the parables, who ignored the beggar Lazarus at his gate, discovered too late that Lazarus and not he found his final destination in heaven. In recent times we've all read about case after case of wealthy, renowned media, literary, and financial personalities who ended their days in very public alcohol or drug ridden despair. Like the poet we cited earlier, most of these probably needed to lift their eyes and discover a higher reality.

Figure 4 outlines some key issues contemporary research tells us must be addressed and resolved at each life stage if we want a happier and more rewarding destination at the end of our journeys.

FIGURE 4 ADULT LIFE STAGES

Stage	Key Issues	Self-image	Goal Focus	Relationships	Community
Autonomy and Tentative Choices (18–26)	Autonomy vs. Dependence, Tentative vs. Lasting Choices	Developing sense of personhood as separate from parents and childhood peer groups	Defining self as an individual and establishing an initial lifestyle	Testing out new relationships (*e.g.*, love interests, peer groups, and friends)	Realigning focus from family of origin to new peers and groups
Young Adult Transition (27–31)	Turmoil vs. Certainty, Settling Down vs. Keeping Things Open	Questioning sense of self and who/what we want to become	Reassessing initial lifestyle and making more permanent choices/ commitments	Sorting out and deciding which relationships will become more permanent	Rethinking and evaluating commitments and connections
Making Commitments (32–40)	Master vs. Apprentice, Permanent vs. Tentative Choices	Firming up/ establishing a more permanent sense of self and who/what we want to become	Deciding a life direction and defining/aggres- sively pursuing a dream of what we want to accomplish in life	Making more permanent commitments to love relation- ships, friends, and peers	Establishing more permanent connections and community ties/ responsibilities
Mid-Life Transition (41–48)	Resolving Key Polarities— Immortality vs. Mortality, Constructive vs. Destructive, Nurturing vs. Aggressive	Reexamining realities of pro- jected ego and image vs. true self and strug- gling to define/ accept true self	Questioning the dream whether or not it was achieved and developing a more mature sense of what is really important	Recognizing/ acknowledging one's own nega- tive, as well as positive, impact on relationships and correcting course for deeper, more authentic connections	Disengaging from group and cultural pressures/norms to reevaluate and restructure priorities
Leaving a Legacy (49–65)	Contribution vs. Personal Bene- fit, Other vs. Self-Centered, Social vs. Inde- pendent Accom- plishments	Letting go of earlier inaccu- rate ego images and accepting oneself as a worthwhile being with weaknesses as well as strengths	Making the best of the time one has left to help others and leave a positive legacy	Settling into more realistic and rewarding relationships based on recog- nizing/forgiving each other's imperfections as human and helping each other grow	Re-engagement on a deeper, more objective, less driven, and more productive level with family, friends, and society
Spiritual Denouement (66 and Beyond)	Hope vs. Despair, Survival of Spirit vs. Mortality, Surrender vs. Control	Accepting self as dependent on a wisdom greater than one's own, recognizing that wisdom as benevolent, and submitting one's self and life to that wisdom's will	Tying things up and completing the development of the person/ spiritual being we want to become	Accepting others and recognizing/ respecting humankind's diversity as part of a greater wisdom's plan	Recognizing that life is only part of a larger, more enduring spiritual com- munity and helping others understand that

WHERE ARE YOU NOW?

We do not, of course, move in simple linear fashion from one stage to another with no going back. It isn't that simple. Instead we move through the stages in cyclical fashion, hopefully with a longer-term forward momentum, but inevitably cycling back and reworking concerns of earlier stages as we face unpredicted events, traumas, and fluctuating career, family, or interpersonal situations.

As you review these life stages think about where you are now. What stages have you passed through and which do you face next? What might that mean in terms of what you're thinking and feeling about your work and life today—and about your choice of life values to focus on at this point in time? As you look through Figure 4 how are you progressing? Which of the key issues have you resolved and which are you working on now? Where do you stand today in terms of the key issues and other categories listed across the top of Figure 4? Where do you want or need to concentrate your efforts next? The following brief reflection can help you consider these questions.

BRIEF REFLECTION

Read down each column under the categories listed across the top of Figure 4 (Key Issues, Self-image, Relationships, etc). Using an erasable pencil, put a check mark (✔) in the one box in each column that best defines where you think you are today. It may not be a perfect fit, but pick the one that comes closest. Then look at the boxes above the one you checked and put a question mark (?) in any you feel may still need some attention.

Look at your check marks and question marks as clues to where you currently are in your progression through the stages. What does this tell you? What impact might it have on the life values you feel are most important to you right now—or on your sense of changing if you are in a transitional situation between stages?

If you are part of a couple, you're not assessing your values or passing through the life stages alone. Two of you are making value choices and trade-offs. It's helpful to know and share where you both are now in your life stage progression and where each wants to go next in your individual and joint journeys. There will probably be differences that you need to accommodate while also respecting each other's individual growth needs. Then important future career decisions (*e.g.*, a job offer for one of you at another location) can be made with full awareness of what values each is trading off, and plans can be made to maximize growth for both of you after the decision.

It's important that we continually revisit, reevaluate, and link our life values to our deeper, more spiritual aspirations and growth as we pass through each life stage. It's important that we recognize and accept the fact that the values we are spending our time pursuing might have to change, sometimes dramatically, as we grow and mature. This doesn't necessarily mean we've taken a wrong turn. However, most of us do take wrong turns along the way, and recognizing that gives important insight that helps get us back on course. Correcting course and continually rebalancing are not signs of failure. They are simply signs we haven't frozen our designs. We're still moving ahead and improving the final product of what we want to become. We're still focusing on the stars and lifting our gaze out of the mud.

Prioritizing your life values and tracking your life stage progression are the first two tasks in the *Taking Charge Process*. The next task is deciding what kind of work will best achieve your values and advance your progression in directions you choose.

DECIDING WHAT
YOU WANT TO DO

Life values form one critical set of the criteria you want to meet in a career. Another important set of criteria involves the skills or *competencies* you want to exercise and develop. What do you want to be spending your time doing day-to-day at work?

A competency, in our use of the term, is something you do—a skill you exercise with a specific set of activities or behaviors required to demonstrate the competency. A *preferred competency*, which we describe as follows, is one you personally find satisfying. You enjoy doing the things required to demonstrate the competency.

A *preferred competency* is a set of behaviors or skills you enjoy exercising and want to develop or grow further in the future. It can also be something you want to learn in the future.

Do you want to develop increased technical or financial analysis skills using sophisticated computer programs, for instance, or do you not enjoy computer analysis? Would you rather develop some different negotiation, interpersonal, or conflict resolution skills in another type of non-computer-oriented work? Maybe you would like some combination of both technical and negotiation challenges.

We said it's important to identify where your energy flows naturally with no forcing. That's where you will do best. Economically, that's where you'll have the strongest competitive edge. Spiritually, that's where you'll have the best chance of negotiating assignments that help you achieve important life values.

PAST SATISFACTIONS

One of the best ways to identify what type of competencies you want to exercise in the future is to look at your past history. What types of activities have proved most satisfying for you? You can start to determine this by looking at your past peak accomplishments. We define a peak accomplishment this way:

A *peak accomplishment* is something you personally enjoyed doing and found highly satisfying whether or not others (*e.g.*, boss, peers, mentors, teachers) recognized and rewarded the accomplishment as significant. It energized you, made you feel good, and had real meaning for you.

Your peak accomplishments may or may not have anything to do with your current field of work. They may have been in school, in athletic or artistic endeavors, in social activities, in community or local volunteer government work, in crafts, or in other part-time hobbies.

In our workshops we ask people to identify their top 5 most personally rewarding past peak accomplishments, on or off the job. Examples they have given include:

Presented a technical paper	Built a deck on my house
Coached a children's soccer team	Succeeded in a significant
Closed a significant sale	leadership assignment
Developed a new computer program	Completed an academic degree
Taught a Sunday school class	Mentored a disadvantaged child

After people have identified their top past peak accomplishments, we ask them to use these as clues to what types of competencies they most enjoy exercising. Before you move on to that, however, we suggest you take just a moment to do the following brief reflection.

BRIEF REFLECTION

Think about what you feel might be the most satisfying accomplishment or activity of your life to date. You'll have more time to think about this later when you do the exercises in the workbook. For now though, see if anything comes to mind as your most personally satisfying accomplishment, on or off the job, whether or not anyone else rewarded or even recognized it.

Don't spend a lot of time on this and don't worry if nothing comes immediately to mind. Sometimes it takes a little longer to rediscover these things. If you think of a peak accomplishment, keep it in mind as you read the next pages.

REWARDING ACTIVITIES

Of course, your peak accomplishments are only a starting point. You can't just repeat past achievements. You can't graduate from college again or build the same deck again. You can, however, look at your past accomplishments for clues to what you want to do in the future. Determining what you did to achieve your top 5 peak accomplishments can help identify those competencies whose exercise has given you the most satisfaction in the past.

We've found that individuals can identify their most important types of preferred competencies by looking back and identifying what they actually did to achieve their peak accomplishments. We call these competency *types* (or categories) because this short exercise doesn't attempt to define all the specific behaviors that comprise each competency. It merely identifies general areas of competencies that people like to perform and feel most satisfaction using in their work settings. Later, we'll present specific behaviors for a set of core competencies research shows are important for effective performance in almost all career specialties. At this point, however, it's more useful to concentrate first on identifying what types of competencies were exercised in each peak accomplishment. We tell people not to be modest about competency strengths they've used in their peak accomplishments. Career success is a function of strength management.

Figure 5 shows a sample page from the format we use to help people identify what their preferred competencies are. The complete format is in the workbook. You can use that later when you complete the workbook exercises.

As Figure 5 shows, for each peak accomplishment listed on the left side of the page, types of competencies exercised are listed on the right side of the page opposite the accomplishment. If one of the peak accomplishments on the left side of the page is "coaching a children's soccer team," typical competencies used might be:

- Interpersonal communications
- Planning
- Organization
- Team-building
- Counseling

- Motivation/influence
- Performance feedback
- Conflict resolution
- Selection/talent assessment

These would be the types of competencies you might exercise on several different career paths, such as management, community relations, school administration, or other work activities requiring various interpersonal and organizational abilities. Clues to which career path would be best for you come from the pattern of these and other competencies derived from your other four peak accomplishments.

If a peak accomplishment was making a breakthrough in some technology and presenting a well-received technical paper, the types of competencies that could surface from looking at that might be:

- Technical comprehension
- Computer analysis
- Writing
- Organization

- Presentation
- Creativity
- Perseverance

These would be the types of competencies you might exercise in career paths such as research and development, or teaching in a technical graduate school. If your accomplishments included technical papers and

FIGURE 5   PEAK ACCOMPLISHMENTS . . .   . . . AND PREFERRED COMPETENCIES

PART ONE

List in column one below the five most significant (to you) accomplishments of your life to date (on or off the job) based on the criteria of what was most meaningful to you (not necessarily to a manager, an organization, or anyone else). What achievement gave you the most personal satisfaction, whether or not someone else shared (or recognized/rewarded) your enthusiasm for them? Use a separate block for each accomplishment.

PART TWO (To be completed separately and later)

After you have completed part one, complete column two below. Looking at each of your peak accomplishments, list the types of competencies (or skills) you had to use for successful completion of the accomplishment.

Your Peak Accomplishments (Describe in some detail. What happened? Who was involved? What did you do?)	*Your Preferred Competencies* (List skills in each accomplishment, even if you repeat some of the same skills on more than one accomplishment)
1. Coached a soccer team	• Interpersonal communications • Planning • Organizing • Team-building • Conflict resolution • Etc.
2. Presented a technical paper	• Technical understanding • Computer analysis • Writing • Organization • Presentation • Creativity • Etc.

coaching a soccer team, you might consider looking for a leadership role involving technical projects and people. On the other hand, if your prime accomplishments combined coaching a soccer team (people interaction skills) and fulfilling a passion for architecture and remodeling old houses, one possibility to explore might be real-estate development.

When you later do this exercise in the workbook, we suggest you do it with someone else, perhaps your partner if you are part of a couple. By yourself you might overlook several important competencies that occur to someone else when you describe each accomplishment. For instance, when workshop participants brainstorm competencies exercised in coaching a soccer team, many individuals overlook several important competencies (*e.g.*, conflict resolution or talent assessment). Others help bring these to their attention.

Figure 6 shows just a few examples of competencies people typically list when doing this exercise. We suggest people use this as a starter list but not limit themselves to the types of competencies shown. The possibilities are endless and no list can include them all.

FIGURE 6 SAMPLE COMPETENCIES

- Analytical Thinking
- Numerical Aptitude
- Interpersonal Sensitivity
- Technical Acumen
- Persuasiveness
- Integration
- Artistic Ability
- Graphic Arts
- Research Skills
- Clerical Aptitude
- Administrative Ability
- Financial Analysis
- Interpersonal Assessment

- Planning and Organization
- Creativity and Innovation
- Oral Communications
- Writing Skills
- Selling Relationships
- Presentation Skills
- Decision-making
- Teaching Aptitude
- Team-building
- Delegation
- Negotiation
- Problem-solving
- Carpentry Ability

The following brief reflection will give you a quick feel for how this brainstorming process works. Again, don't spend much time on this here. You can complete this task in much greater detail when you later work through the workbook.

BRIEF REFLECTION

If you identified at least one peak accomplishment in the previous meditation, think a moment here about what one or two preferred skills or competencies you might have been exercising in that accomplishment. Are these skills you generally like to exercise and would like to exercise more? Is your current job providing sufficient opportunity to do this?

PATTERNS OF SATISFACTION

When people we work with finish brainstorming all the competencies exercised in their peak accomplishments, they next look for patterns, eliminate overlaps, and consolidate their lists. When they complete these consolidations, the work they have done up to this point has identified and documented the two basic categories of information required for the next task.

ESTABLISHING YOUR PERSONAL CRITERIA FOR SUCCESS

The two categories of information you identify in the early tasks of the *Taking Charge Process* are your highest priority *life values* and the patterns of *preferred competencies* that made you successful in your peak accomplishments. Next you put these two things together and the combination then becomes your own unique set of *personal criteria* for a successful career (see Figure 7).

FIGURE 7 PERSONAL CRITERIA FOR SUCCESS

(The combination of your top *life values* and *preferred competencies*)

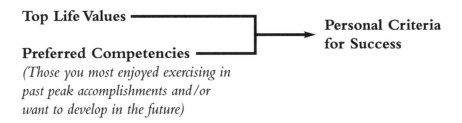

Top Life Values

Preferred Competencies
(Those you most enjoyed exercising in past peak accomplishments and/or want to develop in the future)

Personal Criteria for Success

A WAY TO FOCUS

You can use these criteria to:

- help focus on which doors you want to look behind
- develop questions to ask people you interview on career paths behind those doors
- evaluate the information you collect
- cross off doors that don't meet your criteria and decide which doors represent career paths that come closest to meeting them.

The next task in the *Taking Charge Process* (see Figure 8) focuses on identifying potential future career paths most likely to meet the success criteria you've identified as especially important to you.

FIGURE 8   TAKING CHARGE PROCESS

Finding Your Calling

1. **Determining Your True Life Values**
2. **Tracking Your Life Stage Progression**
3. **Deciding What You Want to Do**
4. **Establishing Your Personal Criteria for Success**
5. **Identifying Potential Career Paths**

Identifying Potential Career Paths

Reducing the Smorgasbord to a Practical Size

With the personal success criteria you have defined you can eliminate time-wasting indecision and false starts by being a more efficient market researcher. You can narrow down the endless smorgasbord of possibilities to a manageable few. You do this by using your criteria to make much more focused best guesses (*i.e.*, hypotheses) about which career paths (or doors) might best allow you to achieve the most possible of your important life values and exercise/develop your motivated competencies.

One of the best ways to select a future career path is to think beyond the next job and hypothesize positions you might like to be in five to ten years from now. This gives you a framework for pursuing interim positions that will take you toward (as opposed to away from) your desired longer-range goals. You hypothesize in two steps—brainstorming and consolidating.

You start with a brainstorming exercise by hypothesizing all future career paths you think might meet your success criteria. At this point, you can broaden your own thinking by showing your criteria to others and asking them what future career paths they think might meet your criteria. People usually find it easier to help when you have done your homework on the criteria and can give them a clear focus. They find it more difficult to respond when you use the smorgasbord approach of asking what careers they might recommend when you haven't defined your criteria and can't really outline what you're looking for.

Right now you've simply been reading about the *Taking Charge Process* in this book. You haven't yet done the detailed workbook exercises to define your own complete list of personal success criteria. However, to give you a feel for how the process goes, take just a minute and do the following reflection.

BRIEF REFLECTION

Consider the top life values you contemplated in the brief life values meditation on page 78. Then, consider the one or two most important preferred competencies that came to mind in your meditation on page 101. Are these two sets of criteria being met in your current job? Think of at least one different future career path that might better meet them.

When people brainstorm a complete list of future job hypotheses, we next ask them to look for duplications or overlaps and consolidate their lists down to the top 3 to 5 possibilities for further exploration.

When we brainstorm future career paths in workshops, we find the choices people make tend to fall into natural constellations that go together.

Working with people in industrial organizations we usually get one constellation that centers around an ultimate goal of higher level multifunctional leadership and corporate executive positions. By multifunctional we mean positions leading the cooperative integration of different functions such as design, manufacturing, finance, human resources, marketing, and sales. Examples would be general manager of a business segment in a large company or president of a smaller business.

We have other people who want to concentrate on being individual experts in engineering, human resources, research, or other special skills areas. These people are often dedicated to keeping up with the very latest state-of-the-art technology in their specialties. Some see multifunctional leadership as administrative work too distant from personal technical creativity or the end product. Multifunctional leadership requires transition into a different constellation of organizing, staffing, financial, and negotiating competencies that don't appeal to them.

A Variety of Gifts

No one in our workshops makes judgments, positive or negative, about someone else's career preferences. By this time in the workshop everyone understands we each have our own unique talents, desires, and success criteria. If we all had the same interests, it would be a boring and not very effective world. Many essential skills would be neglected and missing. As both the spiritual and psychological life stage experts tell us, ultimate worth comes not from any position or type of career path but from who you are and who you are becoming as a human being. Worth comes not from any specific talent but rather from how and for what purpose you apply the talents you are given. None of us can take credit for our unique talents. They are all God-given and for God's purpose.

John Henry Newman once said that he was certain God had created him for some definite service. In his long and often difficult personal career Newman concluded that God had given him some work to do, a mission that he might never know in this life but which would be revealed to him in the next.[22] The recognition Newman's writings received after his death, and the enormous good his work has since achieved would certainly verify the reality of his mission. However, most of his recognition has been posthumous.

Newman raised no false hopes. He admitted we may never completely know our full missions in this life, but he also believed that God created no one "for naught." If we pay attention and do our best to hear God's voice, Newman says we will "do good." Most spiritual writers tell us that, whatever work we do, the common good of the community and not the glory of the individual should be the overall standard for success in utilizing whatever talents we are given.

A BROAD SPECTRUM OF CHOICES

In our workshops we have people whose interests cluster around artistic pursuits, around teaching, counseling, and social-service work, around small entrepreneurial business interests, and so forth.

We've worked with individuals who developed highly ethical career strategies and achieved top level positions in major corporations where they had a very positive influence not only on the organization's business success, but also on how the organizations conducted business and treated their employees. We've had people decide they wanted to give top priority to investigating possibilities completely outside large organizations. Their interests have included interior decorating, real estate sales, teaching, and independent consulting. One individual, who had already completed all the courses for a Ph.D. in engineering, surprised us by deciding he wanted to be a business manager rather than a technologist. He switched to business studies, left a high-paying technical job in industry, and became a very successful president of his own small nontechnical company.

Many dramatic changes in direction are not so far out as they initially seem. Often these changes involve active hobbies people have been studying and developing expertise in for years. For instance, one fellow, who opened a marina, had worked in a marina in his youth. He had maintained and developed his interest in boats over the years as a hobby. He knew boat construction. He understood marine engines. He had studied and then taught after-hours advanced powerboat courses. He made a big change when he quit a well-paying job in industry and jumped into this work full time, but it was not a leap into the unknown. He had done his homework first.

If you know nothing about boats and you decide to operate a marina, you need to ask knowledgeable people a lot of questions to find out what knowledge, experience, training, and skills are critical. Then you can make an informed decision if it is worth the effort. If it is, you spend a lot of time studying and developing yourself in the required dimensions before you quit your current job and take on the new task. If the data from the experts you talk to lead you to the conclusion it's not worth the effort or you're not interested, you cross off that door and move on to others until you find one that is worth the effort. That is how you end any impasse of daydreaming and making no decision because you have no data for a choice.

COUNSELORS CAN BE VERY FALLIBLE PREDICTORS

People usually narrow their hypothesis down to a practical range of options. However, it can be misleading to push practicality too far. No one can tell someone else with any certainty what they will or will not be able to do.

Many years ago one of our workshop participants was a young woman (we'll call her Maureen), who was a human resources trainee right out of college with a liberal arts degree. She focused very strongly on a hypothesis that she wanted to leave human resources and work toward becoming a manager of manufacturing in a highly technical division (staffed mostly with men who had technical graduate degrees) of a Fortune 500 company that had never had a woman manufacturing manager. It seemed like an impossible goal that could only lead to frustration and failure. For her own good, I was inclined to tell her this. Instead, some instinct prompted me to limit my comments. I simply pointed out the more obvious roadblocks and said that it might be difficult. I left the workshop worried that I should have been more straightforward.

After watching what later happened I concluded no amount of discouragement from me would have deterred Maureen at all. Several years later she had negotiated herself through a series of positions that led to her being appointed the company's first woman manufacturing manager. She later rose to become president of a major worldwide multimillion dollar technical business in the same company reporting directly to the CEO.

Maureen knew a lot more than I did about who she was and what she could do. Subsequently, in observing her progress, I discovered she had outstanding listening and interpersonal skills and enormous personal integrity. She generated trust in difficult situations where she could be counted on never to paper over any mistakes. She also did an extraordinary job of developing the specific core and leadership competency behaviors we will be describing later.

She collected a great deal of information about how others had achieved the positions she aspired to, and, with that information, she strategized how to do it her way despite huge obstacles.

Gathering data is how I move out of the "which door" impasse, make decisions, and get on with my life and career growth. This leads us to the next task in our *Taking Charge Process*, which involves conducting interviews to determine if the career paths that you've hypothesized really do match your personal criteria for success. We'll describe a well-tested technique for arranging these interviews and give you a format for conducting them.

CONDUCTING INVESTIGATIVE INTERVIEWS

W e need to find out whether the career paths we've identified as possibilities meet our criteria. Then we can make reality-based decisions that get us what we want. We can avoid wasting time by longing for—or even pursuing—career paths that look attractive on the surface but which, we may discover after expending great energy in pursuing them, really don't meet our criteria. Uninformed sampling of the smorgasbord is impractical busyness. Collecting and analyzing the facts are more productive and make better use of our time.

We suggest people collect the facts using a very tried and true process called the *Investigative Interview*. Over the years we've worked with many professional outplacement firms that help people find new positions after their old jobs have been eliminated by corporate downsizing or restructuring. Their clients include people at all career levels, including top executive positions. Based on their long experience, these firms pretty much universally recommend some version of the Investigative Interview as the most efficient and productive way to explore new career path possibilities. It's a well-proven process and people using it consistently find new, more rewarding jobs at or above their former salary levels.

INVESTIGATIVE INTERVIEWS

Many people are at a *which door* impasse, feeling guilty and depressed over their inability to choose a meaningful career path and making no effort to get the data required to make a choice. Many don't even perceive that lack of data is their problem. They'd never make a technical or business decision without collecting and analyzing data against specific criteria. However, somehow they think they can make career choices without this effort. Worse still, their managers or someone else in authority may be telling them what to do and sending them (unknown to both) down a career path totally at odds with their own personal criteria for success. As time passes they wonder why they're bored and not performing as well as they used to.

This is not a hypothetical possibility. I've worked with many people like this. Mark, for instance, was in a human resources staff position where he was very successful but had little enthusiasm for what he was doing. He used our techniques to develop his own personal criteria for success, did some Investigative Interviewing, and discovered he really wanted a career with a lot of customer contact in sales and marketing. His superiors felt he was an excellent human resources talent and did their best to discourage any job change. They said that he had no marketing credentials and the company would do nothing to help him switch career specialties. At some risk he persisted and finally convinced the people in marketing to give him a lower level job where he could learn. It was a step backward from his more advanced human resources position but he never regretted it. Over the years he moved up to levels of responsibility in marketing he felt he never would have achieved in human resources, primarily because he was more energized and excited by the work. As a human resources person myself, I hated to see my field lose a good talent. But I encouraged him to make the change because it was clear he was doing what was right for him.

How do you reach out and collect the data required to make autonomous (and practical) career decisions for you? You definitely don't wait for—or even expect—your manager or someone in human resources to collect the data for you. If your interests are in a type of work they haven't done themselves, they don't have the data and probably don't know how to get it. Also, they haven't been through the exercise of getting inside your head and figuring out what criteria are uniquely important to you. Instead, you ask successful people who are currently doing precisely the sort of things you think you would like to aim for, and you ask more than one.

If you ask three marketing experts what they do and how they got there, you'll get three somewhat different sets of answers and they will overlap. If five successful people in a given career field cite one particular skill or experience as important, you can consider that a core skill or experience. However, each will have unique insight. Each will have put a little different spin on his or her strategy for getting there. By comparing them, you can settle on the core requirements and be creative about what unique spin you can add to make yourself successful. That's what Maureen, who became her company's first woman manufacturing manager, did.

People you know (*e.g.*, managers, peers, friends, neighbors, mates, relatives, colleagues, or human resources people within your company) can help introduce you and set up interviews. You need to collect and analyze the facts yourself. This is the only way you can determine whether the potential career path(s) you hypothesized in Task 5 of the *Taking Charge Process* really do (or do not) meet the personal success criteria identified in Task 4. We suggest you conduct Investigative Interviews with people who currently hold positions that are at least five to ten years ahead of you on the career paths you've identified as possibilities.

These can be people within or outside your current work organization. The majority of people we've worked with have been in large companies they didn't want to leave. With a little diplomacy, almost all found they could obtain the necessary permissions for interviews inside their companies and negotiate more productive career paths that moved them

---

FIGURE 9 TAKING CHARGE PROCESS

Finding Your Calling

1. **Determining Your True Life Values**
2. **Tracking Your Life Stage Progression**
3. **Deciding What You Want to Do**
4. **Establishing Your Personal Criteria for Success**
5. **Identifying Potential Career Paths**
6. **Conducting Investigative Interviews**

in directions they wanted without changing companies. Others couldn't get permission for internal interviews, or couldn't find what they wanted even when they did interview within their companies. These usually used our process and moved successfully to new, more satisfying career paths outside their current companies. As shown in Figure 9, the Investigative Interviews make up Task 6 in the *Taking Charge Process*.

OBJECTIVES

The Investigative Interview is designed to help you identify and prepare for key future positions on your preferred career path. It serves several purposes. It can help you:

- Decide which future career paths do and do not meet your personal success criteria.
- Define what specific competencies are most critical for achieving your career aspirations.
- Look at various ways different successful people have met their competency development and experience needs.
- Identify which current strengths will make you most marketable on your preferred career path (important for communicating with future hiring managers).
- Determine your most important competency development needs vis-à-vis your preferred career path so you can focus development on those.
- Start building visibility and a network of contacts in your chosen field (important for future marketing).

All of the above are important steps in helping you turn your *career* into a more meaningful *vocation* or *calling* that energizes you and makes your time spent on the job more rewarding.

A POSITIVE EXPERIENCE

When we first introduce the concept of conducting these interviews to people, some initially resist the idea of asking people to spend an hour or more discussing career issues not directly related to immediate work pressures. They fear people will respond that they're too busy to talk. However, in our experience, if you position the interview appropriately, have a good interview protocol (sample in Appendix B of the *Career and Life Workbook*), and express a sincere interest in how they succeeded, most people willingly agree to the interview. Properly approached, they even feel it's a compliment to be asked.

INDIVIDUAL OR TEAM INTERVIEWS

The Investigative Interview can be conducted either as an individual or as a team interview. In some of our workshops people establish teams around similar interests. The team then conducts the interviews as a group whenever possible and assigns different interview questions to different team members.

A DIFFERENT KIND OF INTERVIEW

The Investigative Interviews are very different from the more standard job-seeking interviews. People conducting the more standard job-seeking interviews are typically either applying for an immediate job or exploring relatively near-term employment possibilities. Near-term employment is not the objective of an Investigative Interview, and that should be stated when making the interview request.

REQUESTING THE INTERVIEW

When requesting an Investigative Interview with someone, it is important to make it very clear you are thinking longer range and that you:

- Are not looking for an immediate job with their organizations but rather . . .
- Have completed some comprehensive long-range career planning
- Have concluded, after careful analysis, that the career path pursued by the individual you want to interview is one you would find highly rewarding

- Want to investigate how to prepare yourself for a similar career path in the long range
- Are asking this person for an hour because others (specific names if possible) have said he/she is a very successful and highly regarded expert in the career field you want to investigate

This type of introduction is important, even though you typically make the request through an intermediary who knows the person, because people frequently avoid talking with someone they think is looking for a job. Often they get too many immediate job applicant requests and don't have time for them all. Even more frequently, they don't like to be put in a position where they have to reject a job applicant.

On the other hand, successful people typically respond more positively to a request for an Investigative Interview because they:

- Like to be recognized as successful
- Like to talk about themselves if they don't have to worry about the person asking for a job
- Like people who want to be like them
- Like to share their wisdom with someone who looks up to them as having wisdom
- Are usually flattered that, after careful research, you have identified their career choices and successes as potential models for your own career

Suppose you had a friend call and say someone he knows well has been doing some career planning. After much soul searching this person has decided a career just like yours might be the most meaningful and self-fulfilling thing he or she could do. The person needs some information, however—such as what the work really consists of and how to prepare for it. Your friend has told this individual you are an expert who can give the best possible answers.

Would you talk to this person? No homework is required from you, and the individual is not looking for a job—just advice from an acknowledged expert.

What would you say? Our experience shows people up through very high levels say yes, and feedback shows they have fun in the interview.

One busy vice-president of a large insurance company rerouted himself on a cross-country trip so he could have an airport restaurant meeting with a small group of our workshop graduates who had requested an Investigative Interview with him but couldn't travel to his location.

ESTABLISHING THE CLIMATE

The following is a sample statement of purpose you can paraphrase at the beginning of each Investigative Interview to set the climate for an open dialogue and make it very clear why you are there:

Thank you for agreeing to talk with me. As you know, I'm not here looking for any specific employment opportunities. My purpose is longer range. I have been doing some fairly extensive career planning recently and . . .

- After a lot of analysis I've concluded a career path similar to yours would probably be very rewarding . . . especially for someone with my personal values and goals. *(Be prepared to be asked what your values and goals are. This can be a good way to establish rapport and show you've done some real homework. Keep your response brief, since you're there to learn about the interviewee.)*
- I'm looking at how I can best prepare myself for a similar career path.
- You've been recommended by *("specific name/names" if possible)* as someone who is highly regarded in this field . . . and who has a lot of expertise I could benefit from hearing.
- I appreciate your seeing me and I've done some homework on the questions to make the best use of your time. *(This prepares the individual for the fact that you will be using and taking notes.)*

WORKING THROUGH AN INTERMEDIARY

If you know someone who knows the person you want to interview, have that person act as your intermediary and ask the interviewee if he/she will speak with you. Prepare your intermediary with the above script, so the interviewee knows you're not asking for a job.

If you don't know an appropriate intermediary, use the same approach in contacting the interviewee yourself. Be prepared for some to refuse the interviews. Successful people say not being deterred by rejection is part of the success process. They get rejected more because they try more, but they also tend to have more successes because they learn from their failures and rejections.

I counseled one individual who worked in a small, remote New Mexico location of his company. Budgets were tight and he couldn't travel for interviews. He sent letters, using the approach described above, to a number of high-level managers in his company all across the country stating his purpose and suggesting a date and time for the call. A few ignored the request or sent negative responses so he had to tolerate some rejection. Some sent his letter to their human resources representative who tried to respond but didn't really know the details of their managers' jobs. Many, however, responded with enthusiasm. Some even had their secretaries call to suggest a different time because they weren't available at the time for which he had asked.

In talking to the people who did respond, he identified a critical experience gap that would eventually prevent him from qualifying for the general manager position he aspired to. In some tough give-and-take discussions with his current boss (who wanted him to stay right where he was), he negotiated himself into a position that filled the important experience gap and he eventually became a general manager. Later, he said he would never have achieved his goal without those phone calls.

Figure 10 shows a brief laundry list of some potential data sources. Use this list to stimulate your thinking on how to establish interviews with people on career paths of potential interest to you.

FIGURE 10 POTENTIAL DATA SOURCES

- Current incumbents in jobs identified
- Friends who know incumbents and can pave the way for you to interview them
- Past incumbents you or your friends may know
- Former associates now working in or near organizations, businesses, locations that interest you
- Human resources people in your own or other locations
- Your current manager and former managers
- People your manager can arrange an introduction/appointment with
- Library resources and periodicals describing different industries
- Other managers/friends (inside or outside your organization) who may be acquainted with areas/jobs that interest you, or who may know someone they can introduce you to

A FIVE-PHASE PROCESS

The Investigative Interview process is focused rather than hit or miss. It's also relaxed and nonthreatening. Properly conducted, it moves smoothly through five phases that are well-organized, concise, and designed to get the information you need. The interviewee sees that you are well prepared and that you respect his/her time. The five phases are:

Introduction
(Statement of Purpose, Establishing Rapport)

Job Content
(Results Expected, Relationships, Key Decisions, Communications Required, Future Growth Possibilities)

Important Qualifications
(Competencies, Experiences, Training)

Key Events
(Successes, Failures, High and Low Points, Values Met or Missed)

Closure

INTERVIEW FORMAT

Figure 11 shows a sample page from the recommended Investigative Interview form shown in Appendix B of the workbook. The left column under each interview phase contains suggested discussion topics and starter questions. The starter questions don't have to be used verbatim. You can rephrase them or add to them in your own words. Key words in the starter questions are **highlighted** in bold for quick scanning during the interview itself. Under *Personal Questions* the form gives you space to write your own questions. These should be tailored to collect additional information for helping you determine how well the interviewee's career path might meet your own individual values and personal criteria for success.

The right column provides space for you to take notes on responses to the questions. The backside of each page provides additional space for notes.

The questions are designed to collect specific data for comparison against your personal criteria for success. This form gives you an in-hand script, which helps show the interviewee you are well-prepared. Interviewees typically respond to this kind of preparation with thoughtful, candid, and enthusiastic answers.

COST-EFFECTIVE STRATEGIES

People we've worked with use organization directories, personal knowledge, any and all sources to identify successful people to interview in their identified fields of interest. If they work as a team they sometimes assign different interviews to different team members. If the person to be interviewed is within reasonable geographic proximity, several members of the team often go together and conduct a joint interview. If the interviewee is at some distant geographic location, they try to identify a team member whose normal business travel takes him or her to that area and this person does the interview.

We've found people are very inventive and autonomous at somehow finding ways to interview people all over the world. Many who saw our original program design expressed fears the whole thing would flounder

FIGURE 11 SAMPLE PAGE
INVESTIGATIVE INTERVIEW FORM

PHASE 3: IMPORTANT QUALIFICATIONS
(Competencies, Experiences, Training)

DISCUSSION TOPICS	NOTES (Complete during the interview)

DISCUSSION TOPICS

Competencies

What do you see as **the most important competencies** or skills required for success in **this job/career or path**?

- Technical?
- Functional?
- Leadership?
- Team-oriented?
- Others?

Experiences

Looking back over your career, are there any particular **experiences** or **challenges** that **stand out** as very **important in preparing you for success** in this work?

- On the job?
- Off the job?
- Hobbies, etc.?

Training

What type of **training** do you feel is **most important** in order to qualify for a career path like yours?

- **Degrees or formal certifications** required (and/or merely desired)?
- **Functional/Technical** training?
- **Leadership** Training?
- Etc.?

Personal Questions

on the cost of traveling to conduct the interviews. That didn't happen. Somehow people are motivated enough to find low-cost ways to do the job.

If a person-to-person interview is impossible, people do it by phone. A high percentage of those asked have agreed and these have displayed a surprisingly high level of candor in the interviews.

As we said, we recommend you have an intermediary, who knows both you and the interviewee, pave the way with a phone call. However, as our earlier example showed, many have done these phone interviews with nothing more than a brief advance letter stating their purpose to a stranger and saying when they will call.

We suggest our workshop participants start thinking as soon as possible about who they want to interview and when. Although you haven't completed the workbook exercises yet, you might benefit from taking a moment for the following reflection.

BRIEF REFLECTION

Is there any one individual, inside or outside your current organization, who comes to mind as someone you might want to conduct an Investigative Interview with to learn more about the requirements, challenges, and satisfactions of his or her career path? Who might that be?

BUILDING VISIBILITY IN THE NETWORK

Besides giving you data for making choices and plans, conducting Investigative Interviews also gives you significantly increased visibility and a broader circle of colleagues and acquaintances inside and outside your current organization. This can also contribute to your autonomy and ability to expand your options later.

The people you interview are usually impressed with the organization and obvious homework that went into your preparation for the interview. They find this unusual. They're surprised by the breadth and depth of the questions asked, and they tend to remember the person who interviewed them when later asked for candidate referrals on future job openings in their fields. Your network grows.

When you've completed your Investigative Interviews you move on to the task of choosing the right career path.

Choosing the
Right Career Path

When you've done the work up to this point in the *Taking Charge Process*, you've made significant progress in completing the essential ingredients we outlined for a successful career contract with yourself (see pages 54–56).

You've established your life value priorities. You've identified the preferred competencies or skills you'd like to exercise and grow in your future career endeavors. The *combination* of your *values* and *preferred competencies* has become your own unique set of *personal criteria for success.* You've identified a few potential future career paths that might best meet your criteria, and you've collected real-world data in the Investigative Interviews to see if these career paths really do meet your criteria.

Next you pull together the information you've gathered and make some data-based future career path choices. You do this by completing what we call a matching analysis.

Matching Analysis

In this process you look at the data collected in each of your interviews and analyze how well the job or career path of each person interviewed does or does not match your personal success criteria. You assess what important life values you would be most likely to achieve on each interviewee's career path and those that would most likely be jeopardized or not achieved. You also identify which of your preferred competencies you would or would not have the opportunity to use and develop. Then, on a scale of 1 to 10, you rate how interested you are in a similar career path.

| 1 | 2 | 3 | 4 | 5 | 6 | 7 | 8 | 9 | 10 |

Not Interested   **Very Interested**

Different people may interpret the numbers differently, but you will probably have a range of ratings with some career paths rated much higher than others. At this point you look at the different career paths you've rated and pick the one or two you've rated as having the very highest probability of meeting your criteria.

This is Task 7 in the *Taking Charge Process*. Here you cross off those doors (*i.e.*, career paths) that the interviews show don't meet your criteria. With those out of the way you can then focus much more efficiently on those that best meet your criteria and move on to Task 8 (see Figure 12).

FIGURE 12 TAKING CHARGE PROCESS

Finding Your Calling

1. **Determining Your True Life Values**
2. **Tracking Your Life Stage Progression**
3. **Deciding What You Want to Do**
4. **Establishing Your Personal Criteria for Success**
5. **Identifying Potential Career Paths**
6. **Conducting Investigative Interviews**
7. **Choosing the Right Career Path**
8. **Identifying Strengths and Weaknesses**

IDENTIFYING STRENGTHS AND WEAKNESSES

I n addition to helping you focus your career choices, the Investigative Interviews also help you identify:

- What strengths (*i.e.*, current competencies and work experience) you have that will make you most marketable on the career path you've chosen, and
- What critical weaknesses (*i.e.*, competency or experience gaps) you need to fill for success on that path.

A RESEARCH-BASED HEAD START

When you identify your own personal development needs, you don't have to rely solely on information gathered in your own interviews. As we said earlier, we have already conducted over 4,000 competency-focused Investigative Interviews across many career fields. To guide you in constructing your own interviews and to supplement your interview findings, in this chapter we will outline a set of *core* competencies our interviews have identified as important in just about any career specialty. We will also present a diagnostic tool you can use to assess yourself against these competencies. This can give you a significant head start in completing Task 8.

From the research we have specified 12 core competencies that are critical for successful performance in nearly all career specialties. When we introduce these to our workshop participants it gives them a solid base on which to build. This saves them a lot of time in collecting their own information. They use this data base as a starting point, and then build from there by conducting Investigative Interviews to identify what additional specialized competencies are important in their individually chosen career fields.

This process of observing and interviewing managers and nonmanagers in both large and small organizations has taught us a great deal about what successful career strategists do. It has also taught us about how they do it. Our interviews and focus groups have identified numerous things that successful and unsuccessful performers have in common—many behaviors both groups display regularly. But our analysis has focused on identifying a narrower, more practical set of distinguishing competencies and behaviors—things successful career strategists *do* that less successful people typically *do not* do.

If you know what these critical few are, you can focus your efforts on developing them—and eliminate much wasted time and energy spent on scattered and random personal development pursuits that have far less impact.

Our research shows the 12 core competencies can be very powerful assets in the pursuit of any career strategy. In presenting them, therefore, we want to emphasize that they should be exercised ethically and within the context of your broader spiritual as well as material life goals.

There are three groups of competencies you need to explore in career planning. Our research can provide you with significant information on two of these three groups before you even begin your Investigative Interviews.

THREE COMPETENCY GROUPS

The three groups of competencies our interviews have typically identified are:

Functional/Technical Competencies

These are function-specific technical competencies required on a given career path (*e.g.*, finance, engineering, or computer systems). Training is usually readily available in these competencies. They are typically taught in local universities and technical schools. Our undergraduate major or trade school gives us a basic foundation of competence in the specialty we choose. Because knowledge is moving ahead very rapidly in many of these specialties (*e.g.*, physics, psychology, or automotive mechanics) we usually have to keep ourselves up-to-date through ongoing reading, graduate studies, or periodic participation in specialized courses offered by local schools or professional societies. Often our work organizations offer a variety of in-house training to keep employees up-to-date in the specialized technical competencies required for their work.

Core Competencies

In our experience this is a frequently overlooked, underestimated, and ill-defined competency group, particularly among individuals who don't aspire to managerial positions. In current flatter and less hierarchical work environments anyone who wants to get his/her ideas heard and implemented will require a set of core competencies (*e.g.*, communication, influence, planning, organizing, and customer responsiveness) that in past, more hierarchical organizations have often been associated primarily with managerial positions. We call these core because they are not function-specific. Those who want or need others to listen to, fund, act on, or support their ideas will require these core competencies no matter what technical/functional career specialty they pursue—and whether or not they ever aspire to formal managerial positions.

Leadership Competencies

In addition to the core competencies, the research shows there are some further supplementary competencies required for success by those who aspire to positions involving leadership of other people. Like the core competencies these are generic across all career specialties. These leadership competencies are important in both formal managerial positions and in informal nonmanagerial leadership positions. For instance, in today's organizations people often serve as team or project leaders directing the technical work of others who do not administratively report to them. The people whose work they lead report administratively to other managers and move in and out

of their groups depending on when various projects need their
expertise. While the core competencies are required by everyone at
all organizational levels, the supplemental leadership competencies
evolve and change depending on the level of leadership involved.

FIGURE 13 EXAMPLES OF THE THREE COMPETENCY GROUPS

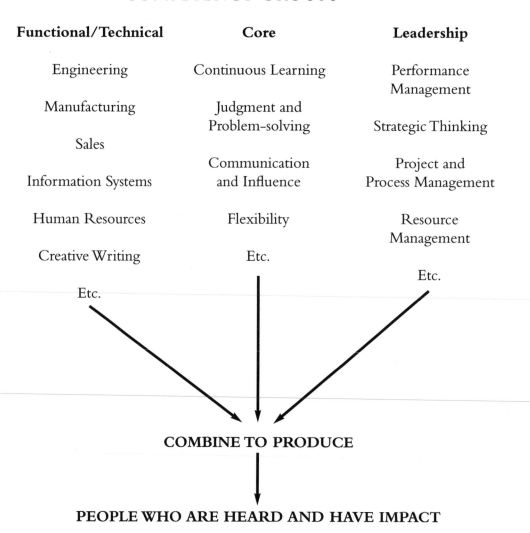

Functional/Technical	Core	Leadership
Engineering	Continuous Learning	Performance Management
Manufacturing	Judgment and Problem-solving	Strategic Thinking
Sales		
Information Systems	Communication and Influence	Project and Process Management
Human Resources	Flexibility	Resource Management
Creative Writing	Etc.	
Etc.		Etc.

COMBINE TO PRODUCE

PEOPLE WHO ARE HEARD AND HAVE IMPACT

Figure 13 shows some examples under each of these competency groups.

We focused our research on the identification of what specific competencies will be required for success in the current and predicted future career environments.

Functional/technical competencies varied, of course, depending on the specific business or technologies different organizations were pursuing. They were absolutely essential, but most organizations we interviewed thought they were at least competing on a level playing field in these areas. They could define what was required and usually had ready access to training resources equal to those their competitors were using.

THE CRITICAL DIFFERENCE

However, the core and leadership competency requirements presented a different story. Most felt these were harder to identify and define than the functional/technical competencies and that the universities and trade schools were doing very little to identify, define, or teach them. Because most organizations were having difficulty identifying and defining these competencies in any coherent and focused fashion, it was also difficult to learn much by tracking or benchmarking what other organizations did. Interestingly, most also felt these were the competencies most likely to give their organizations a competitive edge—or keep them alive if organization survival was an issue.

Core and leadership competencies were seen as critical catalysts. These provided the rare spark that was typically required to ignite innovation and new technology. These provided the energizing motivation that could steer innovation through the many roadblocks and tedious details required for successful implementation. Because the core and leadership competencies are often fuzzy and ill-defined, those organizations that can identify and focus on teaching them to their people will have a performance edge that can tilt otherwise level global playing fields in their favor.

But what makes the critical difference in the core and leadership areas? When we brainstorm in focus groups with top leaders in almost any specialty, we've found most can paper the walls with chart sheets listing competencies they feel are important in their fields. It is like choosing doors. The problem is not that we can't identify enough, but that we can speculate on too many. How do we focus?

In one half-day brainstorming session with top sales executives in a large company we identified over 200 competencies they felt were important for successful salespeople. Identifying over 200 is almost worse than not identifying any. It's total overload. With limited time and funding, where do you start? Which of those 200 are typically present in most salespeople—both successes and failures—and which few make the distinguishing difference? Which are present only in the successful performers? Which give them their performance excellence? What 20 percent of those 200 competencies should you focus on and develop to make yourself a more effective performer? You usually don't have the time or energy to focus on more than that at any given time.

To help answer these questions we moved beyond the brainstorming groups and conducted in-depth interviews with identified top performers—and some identified marginal performers—across a broad spectrum of organizations and functional specialties to identify the distinguishing differences. We focused on their specific observable behaviors on the job and looked for patterns the successful performers had in common. Based on that, we have identified a manageable number of core and leadership competencies we believe make the distinguishing difference in performance across different technical specialties and organizations.

THE MOST IMPORTANT FEW

Because the *functional/technical* competencies differed significantly depending on the type of organization and specific career specialties involved, the findings on those are too diverse to report here. Your own Investigative Interviews can identify those for the specific career field that interests you. Here we will focus instead on 12 *core* and a small number of supplemental *leadership competencies* that have emerged as most important for success across most career fields and organizations. Again, however, an obvious caution. While the competencies can dramatically improve job performance, they cannot in themselves guarantee career or life satisfaction. They will *contribute* to satisfaction only if they are exercised to support your broader life and *vocational* goals (*i.e.,* a *calling* that has meaning for you).

Twelve Core Competencies

Figure 14 shows the twelve core competencies identified in the research as important for everyone. The competencies are organized in three sections: *personal, team,* and *operational.*

FIGURE 14 CORE COMPETENCIES

Personal	1. Continuous Learning
	2. Initiative and Risk-taking
	3. Honesty and Integrity
	4. Flexibility
	5. Self-confidence
Team	6. Judgment and Problem-solving
	7. Teamwork
	8. Creativity/Innovation/Change
	9. Communication and Influence
Operational	10. Responsiveness to Internal/External Customer
	11. Planning and Organizing
	12. Quality Results-orientation

Of all the competencies identified in the interviews, these 12 are the core 20 percent that contributed most to the successful interviewees' effectiveness. When you have limited time, these 12 give you a highly leveraged starting point for identifying your own personal competency strengths and development needs.

REQUIRED BY ANYONE WHO WANTS TO
BE HEARD AND HAVE IMPACT

We find we have to continually stress that the core competencies are required, not only by managers and leaders, but by anyone who wants others to act on his/her ideas. When we reviewed our core competencies with the chief engineer in a multibillion dollar technical company, who was himself the winner of a presidential medal for outstanding personal technical contributions to aircraft technology, he said we were describing Thomas Edison. This surprised us. We had thought of Edison as an individual technical genius—essentially a loner who worked by himself and failed over 100 times before he got the right combination for the light bulb. The chief engineer agreed but said that, while Edison was technically brilliant, technology was not his distinguishing genius. Many people, he felt, had been as smart as Edison technically. Edison's real distinguishing genius, he insisted, was in his "perseverance despite failure and repeated rejection" and in his "influence skills"—in his ability to "get the financial community to fund multiple failures before he got it right." Edison, many feel, was really not much of a manager but everyone agrees he was heard and had impact.

The chief engineer used the Edison example to convince some of his top nonmanagerial technical talents they also needed some improved communications and interpersonal skills—especially when they felt the superiority of their technical solutions should be self-evident and stand by itself. He gave us an example of one near genius who said that if the marketing and financial people didn't understand his technical concepts that was "their ignorance." The chief engineer replied: "That may be so, but who isn't getting the funding?"

BEYOND THE LABELS

As shown in Figure 14, of course, these competencies are only labels. What do they mean? Labels alone are useless. You need to know how successful people act out these competencies in their behaviors. Here again the key is focus. You could take full semester courses on each of these individual competencies. You could learn a hundred different behaviors for each. However, with limited time it helps to know the distinguishing few. What are the 3 to 5 most important things the interviews showed successful people do to demonstrate each competency? Our research concentrated specifically on what these few most important distinguishing behaviors are. For example, Figure 15 shows the 5 most highly leveraged behaviors we found successful people demonstrate in performing the *Continuous Learning* competency.

FIGURE 15 CONTINUOUS LEARNING COMPETENCY

Critical Observable Behaviors

- Proactively defines and pursues personal development goals (*e.g.*, identifies and addresses development needs; negotiates growth assignments).
- Uses lessons learned from both positive and negative experiences to improve performance and effectiveness.
- Continuously looks for new and/or nontraditional ideas and approaches to improve personal and team effectiveness.
- Identifies appropriate role models, and adopts the effective behaviors and techniques they exhibit.
- Seeks and applies new information and concepts quickly.

We define these as *observable behaviors* because each describes a specific action or behavior you can perform—and you can readily observe whether you yourself and others are really performing them. These are not mysterious psychological traits. These are simple actions anyone can consciously choose to perform or not perform. If you rate yourself—or others rate you—as low on some of these behaviors, that doesn't mean you're defective. It simply means you are not remembering or choosing to do them. The simple solution is to start doing them. You always have that option if you want to improve things. Practice can bring significantly increased skill in exercising each of the behaviors.

On the surface, many of these behaviors may seem obvious. When they are spelled out this clearly, most people would agree these are things we should be doing. When I first read one of Steve's competency models my immediate reaction was "so what's new?" After years of working with competency models myself—and seeing the positive results others have gained from working with them—I now realize that what's new is having the most important competencies spelled out clearly and succinctly, and having a readily available checklist to remind me to do them. What's also new is knowing which few of the hundreds of good things I might do are most likely to have the highest impact.

When less successful people read through the key behaviors for the competencies they usually agree these behaviors are important, but typically they don't really do them and their excuse is they don't have time. Successful people acknowledge the importance of the behaviors and agree it's difficult to find time to do them. Typically, however, successful people tell us they force themselves to take the time because they've learned that doing these things saves much more time in the long run. It eliminates much wheel spinning and repetitive false starts that less successful people waste time on because they won't take time to rise above day-to-day fire-fighting and find a way to prevent the fires from starting.

LEARNING BY OBSERVATION

Successful people interviewed in the research said that they learned the critical competency behaviors by:

- Observing other successful people and copying what they did (*i.e.*, productive behaviors)
- Observing and learning from the mistakes (*i.e.*, critical behavior omissions and counterproductive behaviors) of unsuccessful people

GOOD AND BAD MENTORS

Successful people told us they didn't rely only on one or two mentors who might take them under their wings and consciously teach them critical behaviors. That was nice if it happened but it was not essential and they couldn't rely on that happening. Mentors can always get downsized and many successful mentors make cross-company or geographical moves their apprentices don't want to, or can't, follow. Instead, successful people identified many mentors—both successful and unsuccessful—who never knew they were mentors. Then they carefully observed what these mentors did (both good and bad). Interestingly, they felt they learned almost as much from poor mentors as from good mentors. Watching what behaviors—or behavior omissions—failed and learning to avoid them was extremely productive.

OBSERVATION CHECKLIST

Few of us are intuitive observers. We watch others' behavior but in the daily rush it isn't so easy to isolate what specific actions are making others successful—or unsuccessful—in their performance.

For instance, if I had the opportunity to observe a world-class surgeon perform a complicated operation, when it was over I'd have a hard time saying what he or she specifically did or did not do that made the operation successful. On the other hand, if a medical student with a written checklist of key surgical behaviors for that operation watched, he or she could continually compare the surgeon's actions with the checklist and learn a great deal about what the surgeon was and was not doing to succeed.

Most of us could benefit from a similar checklist of core competencies—something we can carry around in our day planners and glance at to diagnose what's happening when we see others performing successfully or unsuccessfully. The checklist can help us learn in real time what works and doesn't work. It can also be a valuable self-assessment tool. When we succeed or fail at a leadership or communications attempt, we can later sit quietly at our desk and pinpoint what we specifically did or failed to do that influenced the outcome.

CORE COMPETENCY SELF-ASSESSMENT FORM

Figure 16 illustrates the format we use for a competency assessment form designed to help you observe your own and others' behaviors. Here you see just one sample item from the three-page Core Competency Self-assessment Form we use in our workshops. The workbook has a complete

| FIGURE 16 | EXCERPT FROM CORE COMPETENCY SELF-ASSESSMENT FORM |

Key Competencies Enter the number indicating your current level of accomplishment on the line next to each behavior below.   *Rating Scale*   0   1 | | | | 5
                                                                                NA   Very Poor   Excellent

Average Score Sum of scores divided by number of behaviors actually displayed
Check Importance for Success
Comment on pertinent facts and critical incidents that show:
• Key Strengths (*i.e.*, behaviors often displayed)
• Important development needs (*i.e.*, behaviors seldom displayed)

PERSONAL

1. Continuous Learning Competency
• Proactively defines and pursues personal
  development goals (*e.g.*, identifies and
  addresses development needs;
  negotiates growth assignments).   _____
• Uses lessons learned from both positive
  and negative experiences to improve
  performance and effectiveness.   _____
• Continually looks for new and/or
  nontraditional ideas and approaches
  to improve personal and team
  effectiveness.   _____
• Identifies appropriate role models and
  adopts the effective behaviors and
  techniques they exhibit.   _____
• Seeks and applies new information
  and concepts quickly.   _____ Average _____   Importance _____

copy of the full form for your personal use later when you do the work-book exercises.

Our workshop participants use the full form to assess themselves against the core competencies. Then they focus even further and identify the top 3 observable behaviors they consider to be their greatest current weaknesses. These are those they most want to strengthen and develop further, either because they're weak (*i.e.*, got low scores) or because they believe they're especially critical for immediate growth on the career paths they've chosen. The following reflection can give you a quick idea what that's like.

BRIEF REFLECTION

Read through the 5 critical behaviors listed in Figure 16 under the *Continuous Learning* competency. Which one of these behaviors are you performing best today? Which 1 or 2 are you performing least well today? Can you benefit from improving your performance on these?

The *Career and Life Workbook* contains the complete self-assessment form you can use to complete your own self-assessment against all 12 core competencies when you do the workbook exercises later. In this profile, the word *customer* is used in its generic sense to indicate anyone, inside or outside your organization, who is the recipient of or relies on the work or product you produce. People sometimes think that only outside salespeople have customers. Actually we all have customers, often people inside our organizations who rely on the work we produce to do their jobs. And we are all customers of others whose output or product we rely on to get our work done.

Focus and Multiple Uses

Reading through the competencies in the profile can be informative in that it gives you a quick overview and probably some new insight. However, just reading through the competencies is unlikely to have much lasting impact on your personal growth. If you're like me, by the time you get to the last competency in just reading a list like this you may not remember much of what you've read.

The competencies only come alive when we assess ourselves against them. You can use the self-assessment profile to identify the few behaviors you want to focus on first. Then you can take action to improve your performance in those areas. We can't learn all the behaviors simultaneously.

Again, the key word—and the antidote to being completely overloaded with busyness—is focus. Also, as with Edison, persistence is important. We suggest you carry a copy of the profile in your day planner. You can use it on a day-to-day basis to help identify and maintain focus on precisely where you want to concentrate your personal improvement efforts. The profile has multiple uses that can help you maximize the limited time you have available for self-development by directing your energy to more highly leveraged areas with the greatest potential payoff. For example:

Observing Successful Performers
Like the medical student, you can use the profile to sharpen your real-time observations of various successful performers in action. In meetings, for instance, you can occasionally glance at the profile in your day planner to help pinpoint what these performers are doing—or avoiding doing—that is making them effective. As we said earlier, this type of observation is how people we interviewed told us they learned from many mentors who never knew they were their mentors. Having a tool can help those of us who are not always intuitive observers do the same thing.

Diagnosing Problems
When you observe unsuccessful performers failing, you can glance at the profile to diagnose what's causing the problems in real time—or you can go over it later to identify what happened.

Self-diagnosis
You can better analyze what went wrong in your own performance failures. After a specific incident where you have not been effective, you can sit quietly in your office or at home and use this tool to take a few minutes and identify what you can do better—or avoid doing—to be more effective next time.

Getting and Giving Focused Performance Feedback
The profile provides a tool to solicit feedback from others about your own performance, or to give more objective feedback to others who solicit it.

Identifying Personal Development Needs

With limited time and resources available for personal learning, you can use the profile to determine your most critical competency gaps and seek out and negotiate appropriate training and on-the-job development experiences to fill the gaps.

Organizations we have worked with often use a tool like this to focus their performance appraisal programs on more relevant and actionable feedback. They also use the profile to help people in their training programs pinpoint their most important improvement needs. Many do what has come to be known as a 360-degree feedback. Individuals give copies of the profile to a sampling of their managers, peers, customers, and subordinates (if they have any). These people rate them anonymously on the behaviors and E-mail or fax an answer sheet to our office. Then the individual being rated gets a confidential (*i.e.*, no one else in his/her organization sees it) computerized profile showing the averages of how various groups (*e.g.*, customers or peers) evaluated each behavior. The feedback report also highlights participants' top ten behavioral strengths and weaknesses, and identifies those areas where their own self-assessment differs most from the averages of how others rated them.

Most people say this is the most objective, relevant, and useful feedback they have ever received. They particularly like the profile's emphasis on specific behaviors they can choose to perform or not perform, as opposed to other more fuzzy or personality-trait-oriented feedback they've found to be less useful in the past.

LEADERSHIP ROLES

The research showed that individuals who aspired to and succeeded in positions requiring leadership of other people moved through a series of progressive leadership roles as they took on increasingly higher levels of leadership responsibility. There are four generic roles that leaders passed through as they moved from team member (*i.e.*, individual contributor) positions to increasingly more demanding levels of ad-hoc leadership and/or administrative managerial responsibilities. These are:

Team Member—(Individual Contributor)

Focuses on individual task completion and demonstration of personal competence. Typically a technical or functional contributor (*e.g.,* engineer, designer, financial specialist, creative artist, or salesperson).

Team Leader—(Coach)

Focuses on facilitating and coaching work done by others. Usually responsible for the completion of single team projects within limited time frames. Typical examples would be a front-line supervisor in manufacturing or perhaps a nonmanagerial ad-hoc special project leader.

Mid-level Manager—(Multiple Team Integrator)

Focuses on formal or informal leadership of multiple teams. Usually coordinates and allocates significant resources and is responsible for generating effective collaboration among diverse teams. Typical examples would be a plant manager or a multiproject facilitator (managerial or nonmanagerial).

Executive—(Strategist)

Focuses primarily on whole business or organization strategies. Must maintain perspective on markets and customers, and is future and long-term oriented. Usually a significant, large-scale managerial position. Typical examples would be a top functional leader (*e.g.,* engineering, manufacturing, or human resources) or a general manager of a business.

The workbook contains a *Role Determination Form.* When you do the workbook exercises later you can use this form to determine which role best fits your current responsibilities and which (if any) additional roles you might aspire to. If you aspire to one or more of the leadership roles, the workbook also contains a *Leadership Competency Self-assessment Form* that you can use to assess yourself against those few additional competencies required for each role.

On-the-Job Learning

Our research showed that people who moved successfully through the various leadership roles we've described did not follow any one clear career path, even when they were in the same career specialties. However, no matter what sequence of formal job titles they had, they did tend to move through some very similar on-the-job experiences or challenges that helped them develop the competencies needed for each successive leadership role. The list of these experiences is too lengthy to include here. However, if you aspire to higher level leadership roles and want to explore these experiences further, Appendix A in the workbook contains a complete self-assessment form. You can use this later, when you do the workbook exercises, to identify which experiences you already have had and which you might want to pursue next.

Not a Measure of Personal Success

It's important to emphasize here that movement through the hierarchy of leadership roles should not be considered a measure of personal success either in life or in a career. Leadership, especially administrative leadership, should be a matter of personal preference and never a measure of an individual's success to be pursued against one's personal inclinations. Trading off some of your most important personal values to achieve some position or title the culture or organization defines as success can, in reality, be failure for you no matter how much external recognition you receive. Some of the happiest and most successful people we interviewed have achieved enormous personal contribution and fulfillment in their areas of expertise—and even been very successful mentoring younger people in their fields and influencing the future directions of their organizations—without ever having held any formal administrative management positions. They would have found administrative management boring and unfulfilling.

Others, whose energies flow naturally into the type of competencies required for management, find administrative leadership very rewarding. Neither group is more or less successful than the other. In our value system both are successfully doing what is right for them.

SUCCESS IS MARCHING TO YOUR OWN PERSONAL DRUM

There is a danger that makes us almost reluctant to outline and define any hierarchy of leadership or management positions. In the materialistic and competitive culture most of us live in, hierarchy often implies a form of career progression where some move ahead and some are left behind. This fosters a subtle but harmful kind of win-lose competition that destroys trust, distorts communications, inhibits community-building, and makes personal, spiritual growth on the job more difficult.

We have no solution for eliminating the insidious one-upmanship that excessive competition for hierarchical progression brings to many organizations. The best we can do is suggest that you stay aware of it but don't let yourself get unrealistically caught up in it. Leadership, even top level leadership, can be a very valid, reasonable, and ethical goal. But don't let it dictate, distort, or destroy your personal values—your internal awareness of who you are and who you want to become. Occasionally doing the following reflection may help you keep things in perspective.

BRIEF REFLECTION

Think about the culture in your own organization or work group. Are there any formal or informal status norms in your organization that pressure people to compete excessively or against their will for movement up the leadership and managerial hierarchies? If you are competing for leadership jobs, is that what you really want or are you reacting to outside pressures? If higher level leadership is what you really want, are you monitoring yourself to make certain you're pursuing it ethically and with appropriate consideration for others?

Stay centered in what's important to you. Use the tools and techniques in this book to identify and follow the course you set for yourself. That will be success for you. That's also where you'll probably make the greatest contribution to others.

ELEMENTS OF STABILITY IN THE CHAOS

In today's work environment new technology, global competition, and new computerized information techniques are continually redesigning our workplace. Job requirements are evolving so rapidly that job descriptions seem to go out of date almost as soon as they're written. The core and supplemental leadership competencies can provide an anchor in an otherwise chaotic career world. Developing these competencies can give you a set of consistently reliable core skills you can use not only to survive, but to grow and prevail in facing whatever challenges unpredictability and chaos might bring.

CONTINUOUS DUAL FOCUS

In using the various career planning tools presented in this section of the book, it's important to keep in mind the broader concepts we discussed in earlier sections. We can't overemphasize the need for continually maintaining a higher, longer-range focus as you develop and implement your career strategies.

The competencies we're presenting have a specific and limited purpose. They describe behaviors that make individuals successful in careers that are usually in or related to communal, organizational settings. However, career success must be kept in perspective as a limited goal, meaningful only if it supports and does not conflict with a personally and spiritually satisfying total life journey that, to quote our preface, "transcends career success and keeps it in perspective as merely one, and never *the* ultimate criterion for success in life."

Pursued with the right mindset the competencies can be used very effectively to keep our life journeys focused on the right targets. They can be powerful aids in defining and negotiating careers that help us meet important life values and fill the void many currently feel around their emotional, spiritual, and communal life at work.

Pursued with the wrong mindset, however, they can lead us in the wrong direction—toward accomplishment of materialistic, organizational, or self-centered success goals that violate our true values, and prevent a meaningful life journey without our even noticing this is happening.

Stay alert. Don't unconsciously replace your internal spiritual compass with conflicting cultural or organizational norms. You don't have to. Our experience shows that maintaining your spiritual compass can keep you focused, less driven, and more, not less, productive for the organization.

Keep tuned in to your compass by periodically asking yourself questions such as:

- Do your career plans or competency improvement targets conflict in any way with your broader life values and goals (*e.g.*, service to and building community with others and pursuit of a broader purpose beyond just work)?
- Have you looked at potential conflicts and synergies between your career goals and the more spiritually satisfying personal growth goals you want to accomplish (*e.g.*, effective progress through each life stage)?

At this point we've walked you through each task of Step 3, *Finding Your Calling*, in our 5-step career planning approach. Once you've found the calling you want to pursue in life, the next step is to take the necessary actions and *make it happen*.

1. BREAKING OLD MINDSETS

2. CONTRACTING FOR RENEWAL

3. FINDING YOUR CALLING

4. MAKING IT HAPPEN

5. STAYING THE COURSE

STEP 4

MAKING IT HAPPEN

In **Step 4** we continue to converge—to narrow our focus even more by showing what you can do to achieve the goals you defined in Step 3. Here it's important not to lose momentum. Your objective is to really live the important life values you've defined. You don't want that to become a fuzzy, unattainable dream. You want to **make it happen**.

To make it happen you usually have to get down to earth and practical. You have to fill critical competency gaps. You also have to look at reality—at how the world and people around you really operate (*e.g.*, in filling positions you aspire to) as opposed to how you might want them to operate—and at barriers that typically arise to block your progress. Then you have to address these realities. The successful people we interviewed didn't wait for their environments to improve. They looked at the realities, helpful and not helpful. Then they identified and took some ethical and practical actions to deal with what they saw.

In Step 4 we share more lessons learned in our own and others' research. We describe effective coping techniques people have used and show you how to use them.

First, we'll summarize what the tasks we've described so far in the *Taking Charge Process* do for you and introduce the remaining tasks.

Second, we'll give you a format for identifying and negotiating desired and needed new job enrichment experiences into your current position.

Third, we'll outline a strategy for identifying and marketing yourself for new positions when and if your goals require that.

Fourth, we'll describe a technique many have found useful for anticipating and overcoming inevitable barriers to progress.

Fifth, we'll describe what for many will be a new communications mindset for hearing and being heard in the two-way negotiations that are essential for obtaining the support of others in accomplishing your goals.

TAKING CHARGE PROCESS CONTINUED

At this point we've described each task of Step 3, *Finding Your Calling*, in our 5-step career planning approach. Everything you've learned in the *Taking Charge Process* up to this point will later be summarized when you do the *Career and Life Workbook* exercises designed to help you accomplish each task. As you complete the workbook exercises you will develop brief, focused, and synthesized definitions of:

- the **top life values** you want to achieve today—and those you'll want to find you've achieved at the time you retire
- your most personally satisfying **peak accomplishments** to date
- the types of **preferred competencies** you want to develop and grow in future jobs

The combination of your top life values and preferred competencies will then become your unique **personal criteria for success**. The workbook exercises will also help you:

- identify what **future career paths** might meet your personal criteria and record a consolidated list of the top 3 to 5 paths
- identify a list of people you want to explore these career paths with in individual and/or team **Investigative Interviews**

In the workbook you can also take advantage of the extensive interviews we've already completed in our research to identify and record:

- the most important **core and leadership** (if any) **competencies** you want to develop and grow next
- the most important **developmental experience gaps** (if any) you want to fill next in your current and future jobs

Completing these tasks will give you a set of clear career goals (*i.e.*, the career path or *calling* you want to pursue and the critical competency gaps you need to fill for success in your pursuit).

Next we'll describe the final four tasks in the *Taking Charge Process*. These involve the critical activities required for *Making It Happen* (see Figure 17). In the first *Making It Happen* task you look at ways to better meet your career and personal growth needs right within your current job.

FIGURE 17 TAKING CHARGE PROCESS

Finding Your Calling

1. **Determining Your True Life Values**
2. **Tracking Your Life Stage Progression**
3. **Deciding What You Want to Do**
4. **Establishing Your Personal Criteria for Success**
5. **Identifying Potential Career Paths**
6. **Conducting Investigative Interviews**
7. **Choosing the Right Career Path**
8. **Identifying Strengths and Weaknesses**

Making It Happen

9. **Enriching Your Current Job**
10. **Marketing Yourself for Future Jobs**
11. **Overcoming Predictable Barriers**
12. **Communicating with a New Awareness**

Enriching Your Current Job

A Place to Start Now

When we interviewed people who had successfully identified and pursued personally satisfying careers or vocations we found they were very action-oriented. They didn't rely on fate or wait for their management to provide the on-the-job learning and experience they'd identified as essential to meet their goals. They developed some very proactive strategies to get what they wanted. Often this involved negotiating new and enriching learning challenges into their current jobs.

Three Kinds of Competencies

First, let's briefly review what kinds of competencies you might want to develop. Then we'll look at how they define the overall goal you want to achieve in terms of job enrichment. So far we've looked at several kinds of competencies. They are:

Functional/Technical
These are specialized technical, function-specific competencies (computer programming, creative writing, etc.). They vary significantly depending on the special expertise you want to pursue. Because of this they are too numerous to describe here. You can identify them by conducting Investigative Interviews with people five to ten years ahead of you on the career path you choose (see pages 128–130).

151

Core and Leadership

Our research interviews have identified these. They are the more generic competencies required for basic performance effectiveness and/or (if desired) leadership growth in just about any career specialty or organization (see pages 128–130).

Preferred

These are the competencies you enjoy exercising and want to develop further. You identify them in the *Taking Charge Process* through analysis of your past peak accomplishments. They usually include a combination of the above functional/technical, core and (if desired) leadership competencies (see pages 95–101).

MAXIMIZING THE OVERLAP

Your career goal is to negotiate maximum possible overlap between your preferred competencies and the competencies required on the career path you choose. In other words, the more the various functional/technical, core and leadership competency requirements of your job match the

FIGURE 18 SMALL OVERLAP

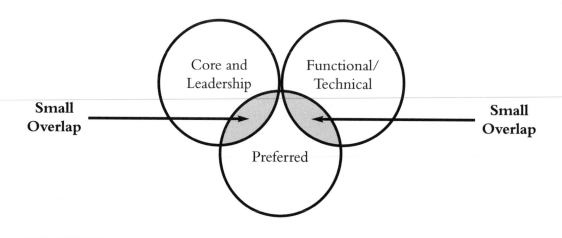

FIGURE 19 INCREASED OVERLAP

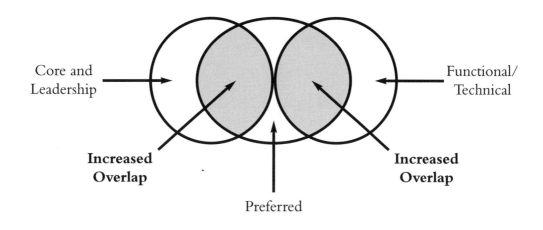

There are two ways you can bring the requirements of your job

preferred competencies you want to exercise and grow, the more likely you are to find satisfaction and meaning in your work. You'll have more fun and be more energized, and you will be moving in directions you want to go.

Chances are you will never attain an absolutely perfect match. No matter how much we love our work most of us will always have some parts of the job we find boring or tedious. However, instead of the relatively small overlap shown in Figure 18 most of us can, over time, increase the overlap and raise it to something more like that shown in Figure 19.

TWO STRATEGIES

There are two ways you can bring the requirements of your job more in line with the preferred competencies you want to exercise and develop. Current job enrichment is one way. Today's flatter, more boundary-less organizations tend to offer more opportunity to do this than the more rigid and hierarchical structures of the past. They often allow more leeway for negotiating to structure (or restructure) your present job duties.

The other way to bring your job requirements more in line with what you want to do is to change jobs or organizations. We'll talk about that later. Most people prefer to work on enriching their current jobs first.

IMMEDIATE POSSIBILITIES

Too often people developing career strategies focus only on career growth opportunities that might be available in future positions. However, successful people interviewed in our research did not focus solely on future jobs. At any given time most recognized that their current jobs provided the best, and certainly the most immediate, growth opportunities. Once they had identified their key competency and experience gaps, many were very creative in finding ways to fill them through enriching their current positions.

In our current jobs we can begin our growth right now and it would be unwise to overlook that. Our workshop participants use a format provided in our *Career and Life Workbook* to think through how they can build needed experience and competency growth into their current jobs. You can do the same thing when you complete the workbook. Next, they work in small groups and learn from each other's ideas. We'd recommend you also brainstorm ideas with a few other people when you do this task. Most find the dialogue with others enlightening. It gives them new ideas that had never occurred to them before.

Figure 20 shows a very brief list of ideas we give people to get them started. However, most don't need our list. They usually brainstorm far more creative ideas than we could ever suggest. There are too many possibilities for us to include them all on our list.

The last bullet is one that usually needs special attention. In most people's overloaded schedules something has to go before they can take on significant new challenges. However, many find that when they really think it through there are things they do that don't really need doing or can be done more simply. Many discover they can delegate a lot more than they thought they could even when they have no managerial or supervisory authority.

We should regularly look at what we do to decide what is and is not

FIGURE 20 POTENTIAL JOB ENRICHMENT ACTIONS

(A Starter List)

- Proposing a special project
- Requesting assignment to existing or upcoming special projects
- Negotiating special task force assignments
- Arranging to attend meetings you normally don't attend
- Proposing improved processes/approaches
- Obtaining and reading reports you don't normally receive
- Setting up informal lunches with peers to share ideas on how to work together more creatively and productively
- Attending professional society conferences and bringing back new ideas for improved work procedures
- Eliminating unneeded tasks or delegating tasks to provide time for enriching your work

essential. This often helps us pare down the nonessentials. Then we can take action to restructure and enrich our work content in ways that let us accomplish more for ourselves and our organizations/clients in less, not more, time. For instance, one individual we know initiated a series of meetings with peers to develop ways of eliminating overlap and unnecessary activities in the work they did together. The time they saved by instituting more efficient processes allowed them to create a new advanced computer program that enhanced all their skills, gave them new challenges, and eliminated even more unnecessary work.

BRIEF REFLECTION

Think about one new skill or work experience you would like to build into your current job. Are there ways you can make it happen? What less important or unnecessary tasks could you eliminate to gain the needed time?

When and if you have exhausted the enrichment opportunities in your current job, it may be time to move on to the next task. Here you develop a strategy to market yourself for new positions that can better provide the skills development and additional experience you need to pursue the career goals you've chosen.

MARKETING YOURSELF FOR FUTURE JOBS

PROVEN MARKET STRATEGIES

At some point you may decide to identify and pursue a completely new position, one which offers needed growth opportunities that can't be built into your current job. In this task we'll present some proven strategies for finding the type of future jobs you're looking for. These strategies are based on research about how managers hire and what criteria they use.

A TACTICAL DECISION

To decide when and if it is time to seek new job opportunities, you look at your current job and decide if it's still leading you toward where you want to be five or ten years from now. Are you:

- Well-placed on a steep learning curve that is still teaching you things you need to know to move in the directions you've chosen?
- On the right path but in a flattening out or declining learning curve that can be revitalized by negotiating some appropriate current job enrichment?
- In a position where you have exhausted the job enrichment possibilities and it's time to move on to a new job or assignment?
- On the wrong path altogether and it's time for a change?

Whichever it is, you next make a tactical decision. You decide whether you need to look for a new position. If the answer is yes, you decide when (now or later) and what kind of new job that change should involve.

The *Taking Charge Process* helps you identify what strengths you already have to help sell yourself. It also identifies what key competency and experience gaps you need to fill if you want to qualify for your longer-range career goals. Your next job should be chosen as carefully as possible to fill in those gaps. You'll have to sell yourself for a job that will do this. You'll develop a much better personal sales strategy if you first understand the realities of how managers hire.

STANDARD HIRING CRITERIA

When we ask people what they think managers look for when they hire to fill key jobs, the typical criteria they list include education, experience, self-confidence, communication skills, etc. You'd probably give us a similar list, and for good reason. These are all real criteria that most managers use. However, important as they are, these are only the visible, surface criteria. There is another criterion that is less visible but even more important.

ONE OVERRIDING MEGACRITERION

In any hiring decision it's usually the hiring manager (*i.e.*, the person the job candidate will actually report to) who makes the ultimate decision on who will be chosen to fill the job. The human resources function may offer advice and counsel, but it's the hiring manager who makes the final decision. And hiring managers seldom rely solely on human resources to find candidates for their openings. They do a lot of searching on their own.

In our observations, and in studies others have done to determine what criteria hiring managers typically use in searching for and selecting candidates for key positions, a clear and not surprising pattern emerges. As much as possible, managers want the candidates to be fail-safe (*i.e.*, risk-free). Each of the other standard criteria (education, experience, etc.) become merely pieces of data the managers use to assess whether or not a candidate meets this fail-safe standard.

Hiring managers are human. Like everyone else, they don't like to fail. They know the success or failure of a candidate they hire will have significant effects on their own reputations and careers. If a key subordinate they hire fails to perform, they will share that failure.

AVOIDING THE UNKNOWN

Selecting the right candidate to fill an important position becomes a process of risk reduction, and most managers reduce the risk by avoiding the unknown. They search for candidates whose performance they have already observed. Personal knowledge of an applicant's past performance has significant influence on a manager's hiring decision.

BOTH WHO AND WHAT YOU KNOW

Of course, this is the same old game of politics. It isn't what you know but who you know. Right?

No, not right at all. In fact, very wrong. What you know is very important. Who you know is irrelevant unless those people have reason to believe you are competent. Performance is critical.

Remember, the basic standard is to reduce the risk of failure. A manager doesn't reduce risk by hiring a crony he knows is incompetent. He reduces it by hiring known competence.

A PREDICTABLE SEQUENCE

Combining known research with our own personal observations over many years working with hiring managers at all levels, we have concluded managers follow a fairly predictable sequence in seeking fail-safe candidates.

1. First, they look for someone they already know and whose performance they have observed (*e.g.*, former employees, peers, or people they have worked closely enough with to observe their performance).
2. Next, they ask close friends, colleagues, and other people whose judgments they trust to recommend candidates.

3. Then, if the first two approaches don't pay off—or if their human resources system requires it—they look at résumés of strangers submitted from outside the company or from their organization's internal human resources inventory systems.

Often managers already have candidates identified before they communicate their openings to their human resources departments. If human resources forces them to post the job, managers frequently ask people they have already identified through personal contacts to apply.

ORGANIZATIONAL INVENTORY SYSTEMS

When managers go to their organizations' recruiting or internal inventory systems for paperwork on unknowns it's often only because:

- They can't identify enough known candidates on their own.
- Organization policies require them to look at inventory candidates in addition to candidates they've personally identified.
- They have some personal candidates identified but want to check the marketplace on the off-chance they can do better.

This is not cynicism or negative politics. It's merely the basic human tendency to feel more comfortable and less at risk with the known than with the unknown. This doesn't make their behavior ideal, or even the most productive, but it does make it understandable.

PEOPLE WHO KNOW PEOPLE

When receiving résumés on candidates they haven't personally identified, managers will narrow them down to a reasonable number for in-depth research. Then they will immediately start checking out personal friends and associates who might know the identified candidates well enough to give a good "reading" on them. Reference information from previous managers or associates tends to provide the information most trusted by hiring managers. More often than not the reference sources contacted are known personally or at least by reputation to the hiring managers.

Strategy Options

Faced with the above realities, you have a choice to make:

- You can denounce the system as negative politics and spend your time in *Ain't It Awful* discussions with other *Ain't It Awful* prone people who would rather denounce than cope . . . or
- You can avoid *Ain't It Awful* and devote the energy and time thus liberated to productive coping.

It's more productive simply to recognize the normal human dimensions of the selection process, analyze them dispassionately, and use your awareness of these realities ethically to improve your marketing strategy.

Understanding that visible candidates have the edge, you can deliberately and systematically work at becoming visible to people who have influence in the selection process. In this way, you are more likely to be selected for work that will lead toward your personal career goals.

I once asked an influential human resources consultant—who earned his living developing candidate slates for high-level positions in his company—if he didn't find it discouraging that managers typically rely more on personal contact than on professionals like himself to identify candidates. He said, "No." He knew the realities and simply incorporated them into his process. He devoted much of his energy to helping high-potential candidates become visible in parts of the company where they wanted to grow.

Sometimes he did this by having them interviewed in situations where he knew they would not get the job simply so they could be met and remembered by the people who interviewed them. He said that if these individuals were sent back into the same environment six months later, they would have significant advantages over candidates the interviewers had never met. Because they were slightly more known, the risk of hiring them would be slightly reduced.

Visibility, Good and Bad

Visibility in the organizations and career fields that interest you provides significant marketing advantage. However, visibility is an asset only when it reveals competence. Visible incompetence scares potential employers off, particularly your best friends if they think you might ask them for a job.

Apparent contradictions to this don't tend to hold up when we look beneath the surface at what's really happening. All of us can cite examples of people we've seen in high-paying jobs who were not competent. Almost always they got there through someone's mistake. Someone who erroneously believed they were competent put them there. Managers are not always the world's best evaluators.

If such an individual and his or her manager have become friends, the manager often finds it difficult to face the situation when incompetence surfaces, as it must. At the same time, he or she usually finds it very risky to leave an incompetent with any real power or decision-making authority. The manager may compromise by letting the individual maintain status, income, even an impressive title—but the real decisions subtly shift elsewhere. If times are good, incompetents can hang in (usually unhappily) for a while to no one's real advantage, least of all their own. Raises slow down or stop. The boss becomes uncommunicative and difficult to reach. The job becomes boring. The situation is uncertain and scary.

While I've seen managers maintain incompetents on the payroll because they found it too unpleasant to face the situation, I've never seen a manager voluntarily take recognized incompetents along when he or she was promoted. When a manager moves on or up, the organization breathes a sigh of relief and expects all the cronies to move along too. Not so. Only a few competent cronies move on. It is the departing manager who breathes the sigh of relief, grateful to be unburdened of any cronies who were not performing. They get left behind for the next manager to handle, and any safety the nonperformers had in their powerful friendships deteriorates rapidly.

IT IS LESS FATIGUING TO BE COMPETENT

Incompetents don't always get fired, but neither do they get much challenge, growth, fun, or even any internal feelings of security on the job. It is easier, safer, and far less fatiguing to be competent. Depending on friends is risky. They might leave the organization, lose their influence inside the organization, or simply decide you are inappropriately taking advantage of their friendship. The only real security lies in being competent and in making sure people, many people, particularly people who can influence your career, know you're competent.

Who and what you know are both essential. Too often the *Ain't It Awful* people see only the who-you-know side in the two-dimensional who-and-what formula for success.

To come out a winner in the selection process you must perform successfully and be visible. The more visible you are—the more people who know your talents and can honestly recommend you—the greater your chances of getting the work and career progress you want in a fail-safe oriented marketplace.

Résumés Are Still Important

None of the preceding discounts in any way the importance of developing a good, marketing-oriented résumé for inclusion in your organization's *internal* human resources inventory system, and for use in periodically sampling the market *outside* your organization.

We have never seen anyone hired strictly on his or her paperwork, but we have seen hundreds rejected on poorly prepared paperwork, often at very high levels in the organization. Busy executives don't have time for personally interviewing large numbers of candidates. Given 15 résumés of strangers, they will quickly eliminate ten and narrow down their consideration to the four or five who look best on paper. Then they will get into their personal network to check these few out.

A Self-defeating Circle

Not maintaining a well-written résumé in your organization's internal human resources system can lead to a self-defeating circle of events. Many don't get included on internal candidate slates for promotions or growth enhancing moves because their paperwork is shoddy. Because they never get contacted or interviewed for internal openings they assume the system is worthless—so the next year they again submit hastily prepared,

low-quality paperwork. Where does it end? By remaining passively igno-
rant they assure themselves of never finding out. Another corner of their
own making. Obviously, shoddy résumés don't get them very far in
searches for jobs outside their companies either.

WHICH ICEBERG?

If the iceberg pictured in Figure 21 represents all available jobs in
your chosen career field, you can pretty safely assume that only about 20
percent will be filled from a slate of candidates all of whom are unknowns
to the hiring manager. The other 80 percent will be filled from slates containing some candidates who are known to some degree and are therefore
of lower risk. We have no statistical proof of this 80–20 ratio, but we've
talked with many recruiting experts and this figure generally represents
their experience, particularly concerning openings requiring a college
degree or equivalent.

The above, of course, is no surprise if we consider how managers
hire. Managers really don't want much paperwork on complete unknowns. Even executive search firms that recruit full time bypass much of
the unsolicited paperwork they are besieged with, and use the phone and
personal contacts to find candidates.

How do you become a visible, low-risk candidate on the iceberg of
your choosing? How do you make certain your name leaps forward in the
minds of people most likely to influence the selection of candidates when
a job you want opens up there?

The first step is to choose your iceberg carefully. The ocean of career
opportunities is crowded with many icebergs (*e.g.*, different businesses,
organizations, and career specialties)—far too many for one individual to
explore them all (see Figure 22).

Here again, as in our earlier "which door" dilemma, you need to
focus. If you scatter your attention and energies across too many icebergs,
you will become known in none well. Leaving all doors open is a non-
choice. You'll get swept through one by chance and find yourself riding
the wrong iceberg, drifting in directions you don't want to go.

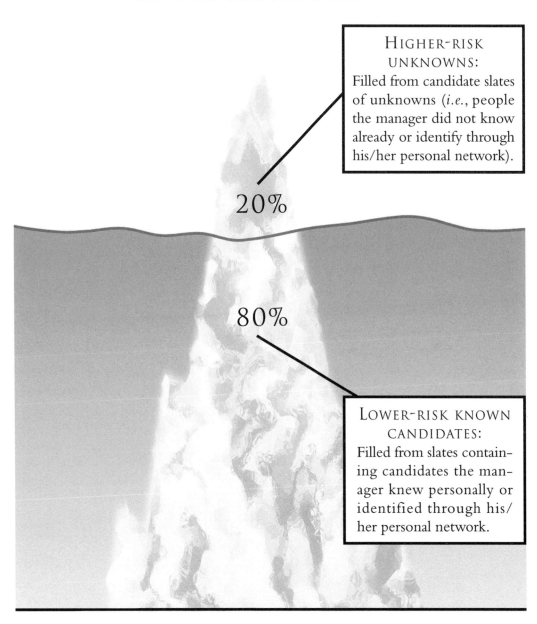

FIGURE 21 ICEBERG OF AVAILABLE JOBS IN YOUR CHOSEN FIELD

HIGHER-RISK UNKNOWNS: Filled from candidate slates of unknowns (*i.e.*, people the manager did not know already or identify through his/her personal network).

20%

80%

LOWER-RISK KNOWN CANDIDATES: Filled from slates containing candidates the manager knew personally or identified through his/her personal network.

FIGURE 22 MULTIPLE ICEBERGS

(Focus Using the Taking Charge Process)

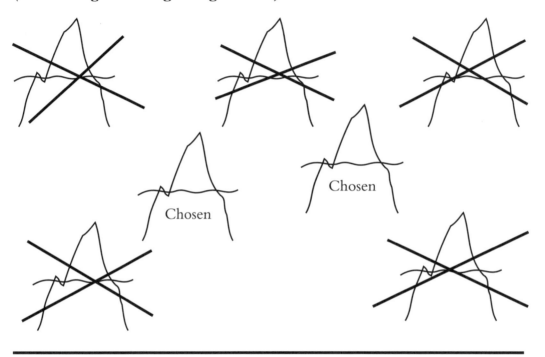

Conserve your energy. Avoid confusion. Use the *Taking Charge Process* to define your personal success criteria and focus attention on the one or two icebergs most likely to meet them (see Figure 22).

TURNING YOUR RÉSUMÉ INTO A MARKETING PROPOSAL

Assuming you now have your sights focused on the right iceberg, how do you climb aboard? How do you tap into that 80 percent below the surface? If you've done your research, you know what the most likely requirements are for success on your iceberg. You also know which of the required competencies you already have, and what new competencies and job experiences you need to round out your credentials further. Knowing all this you can now strategize a multiple visibility assault on the iceberg of your choice.

You begin by drafting a résumé that's carefully worded to market your strengths. Using the specific vocabulary most likely to be understood and accepted by the people doing the hiring, you highlight those specific aspects of your background most likely to be marketable in your target organizations. This would include brief descriptions of specific, relevant *accomplishments* in your work to date. Most hiring managers want to know more than what your *responsibilities* were in past jobs. They want to know what you *achieved* (*i.e.*, the practical results of your efforts) and they'd like to see accomplishments that are relevant (*i.e.*, predictive of success in the jobs they're recruiting to fill).

Preparing a good, marketing-oriented résumé requires homework. Through reading, personal contacts, and Investigative Interviews you learn about the target organization, its objectives, needs, the challenges it faces, and its business vocabulary. You use this information to tailor your résumé accordingly, and make relevant responses in any personal or interview contacts.

Most of us don't bother to do this homework. Most of us write one quick résumé that is supposed to attract all possible buyers. Because it makes sense to us, we expect it to appeal to everyone. We fill it with buzzwords, abbreviations, and acronyms understandable only to someone who has worked in the same organizations or on the same projects we have. We then sit back with the arrogance of the expert and assume it is the readers' problem if they don't understand our shorthand.

The arrogant expert who won't take the time to communicate in understandable English has a loser's perspective. Some simple questions help put things back into correct perspective. Whose problem is it when hiring managers discard résumés that don't communicate? Who has the most to lose? Who loses the opportunity for a job he or she wants? Who is left rejected and not knowing why? Who caused the rejection?

MULTIPLE REWRITES

We've seen winners rewriting their résumés 10 to 15 times, preparing several versions designed (truthfully) to highlight those different aspects of their experience that their homework shows will most appeal to different potential organizations. They ask for feedback from peers, friends, professional society colleagues, and anyone else who will read their résumé and aid in multiple rewrites.

NETWORKING TO BUILD VISIBILITY

One clever tactic many winners use is to build a visibility network by seeking out friends, former associates, and friends of friends in their specific target organizations. They ask these people to critique a résumé and make suggestions for rewrites that will make it more marketable in their organizations. This serves several objectives. It increases visibility because the critic becomes aware of them and their important qualifications. It develops support and more mutual ownership of their career objectives because people are more likely to recommend and sell someone whose career move they have helped strategize. It also helps them write a better marketing proposal (*i.e.*, résumé).

It helps if we think of our résumés as formal marketing proposals for our most valuable commodity—ourselves. Everyone knows you have to put this kind of effort into a marketing proposal for a product. Few of us realize the same sort of effort must go into marketing our personal résumés. It's useful, and motivating, to notice that some of the other candidates for positions you aspire to are putting this level of effort into their paperwork.

When you're asking people to critique your résumé, make it clear that you're seeking expert advice and not asking for a job. They usually respond positively because people like to be asked for advice. It's flattering in a positive sense. Also, people like to see their advice pay off. They're likely to keep the advice seekers in mind and remember them if they become aware of potential openings.

BECOMING FAIL-SAFE

Assuming you now have a well-written, understandable, and persuasive résumé, it's still a cold piece of paper to anyone who doesn't know you. How do you warm it up? How do you become more visible and less of a risk as a candidate in your target organizations? You make a multiple assault. Get your carefully tailored résumé into the hands of as many residents on that iceberg as possible. Find ways to phone, meet, and talk to as many people there as possible. Use all avenues of access you can find to establish your visibility in key places, and persist inventively and tirelessly, sometimes in the face of indifference and repeated rejection.

One assault seldom achieves the goal. We've seen determined candidates focus on a target organization and persist in their campaign a year or more before scoring a hit. Six months is a fairly standard minimum. One individual we knew campaigned for two years before he succeeded in negotiating a move from a government-oriented division of his company to a consumer-oriented division. Even after two years it was a lateral move, not a promotion. The consumer-oriented work filled a critical experience gap, however. Filling that gap made it possible for him to take on successively higher level consumer-oriented jobs and to eventually become chief executive officer of a different company.

Another individual wanted to leave her job in a large company and become an outside consultant. In a long campaign she collected advice and information from everyone she knew in consulting work. Then she developed a marketing strategy and sold herself for a job in a consulting firm where she could learn the business.

In the more lengthy efforts we've observed, the individuals had clear, well-articulated goals at stake or they never would have persisted.

Different avenues of access to targeted organizations would include such things as:

- Contacting former managers or peers, who work there and asking them to critique your résumé and get the final version into the hands of the right people, talk about you, make personal inputs on your skills, and stay alert for opportunities
- Contacting friends or former school associates who work there and asking the same of them
- Asking friends who don't work there to recommend you to any friends they have who do work in the target organization
- Doing after hours' freelance or volunteer work in activities where you can make contacts with people who work in or know about your target organizations

- Having your current managers contact people they know there (assuming your managers have agreed to your search and are willing to recommend you)
- Having your human resources representative(s) refer you to the target organization's human resources people with an appropriate endorsement of your capabilities (assuming your human resources people have agreed to your search)

Asking your manager(s) and human resources representative(s) to help you (last two bullets) usually assumes you are looking for new opportunities within your current organization (*e.g.*, in a different sub-unit, business, or geographical location of the same company) and that you've negotiated your current manager's permission to seek new opportunities. Most companies we've worked with allow and often encourage this type of internal search if the individual has been in his/her current position a reasonable amount of time. Policies on what constitutes a reasonable amount of time tend to range from two to four years on the current job.

We've listed only a few examples of the more obvious ways to gain access and build visibility in your target organizations. You can be creative and come up with many other ways not on our list. This type of multiple access can be the key to making your competence visible in that critical 80 percent of the iceberg below the surface where most of the real action takes place (see Figure 23).

The more points of contact you have in the target organizations, the higher the probability you'll score a hit when the type of job you want opens up. The more people you have recommending your competence, the more likely you will be chosen over lesser-known applicants.

Waiting passively for the formal system to advance your career by placing you in one of the jobs that surfaces on the top of the iceberg is like playing Russian roulette. You may never score a hit. Or even worse, by relying on chance you may score a hit on the wrong iceberg and drift away from your real needs and values for years without knowing what's wrong.

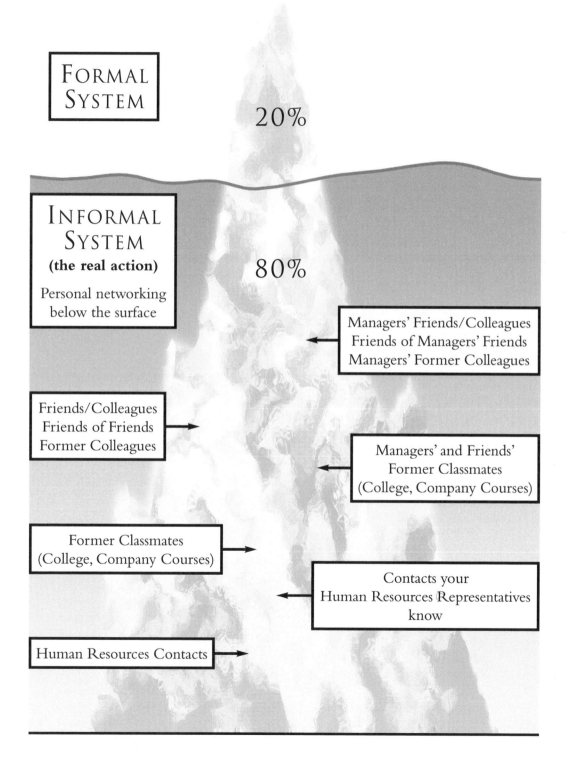

FIGURE 23 MULTIPLE ACCESS TO BUILD VISIBILITY

FORMAL SYSTEM

20%

INFORMAL SYSTEM
(the real action)
Personal networking below the surface

80%

Managers' Friends/Colleagues
Friends of Managers' Friends
Managers' Former Colleagues

Friends/Colleagues
Friends of Friends
Former Colleagues

Managers' and Friends'
Former Classmates
(College, Company Courses)

Former Classmates
(College, Company Courses)

Contacts your
Human Resources Representatives
know

Human Resources Contacts

USING BOTH THE *FORMAL* AND THE *INFORMAL* SYSTEMS

If your current organization has a formal internal human resources personnel inventory system don't neglect it. Meet all its requirements with quality paperwork. It's always possible some good jobs that meet your criteria will come along if you just wait for the formal system to call on you. It's also possible that the more formal approach of simply answering want ads or mailing your résumé cold to organizations you're interested in might pay off. However, because much of the real action happens in informal networking activities, it's wise to supplement the formal system by engaging in proactive networking.

The many possibilities for multiple access on the iceberg you choose (whether inside or outside your current organization) multiply rapidly once you consciously and systematically begin to identify them. The proper sequential timing of your contacts, a personalized approach to the specific contacts, tact, finesse, good salesmanship, and so forth are important if you are to avoid the overkill of a mass mail-out. You want to communicate that you are competent, interested, and potentially available, not desperate. You can usually trust your instincts to strategize that and learn profitably from any mistakes made.

If your organization has been downsized and your job has been eliminated you may well have a desperate need for a new job. Even in those situations, however, it's better to plan ahead and figure out ways you can stay calm and articulate other very valid reasons you want a job change (seeking new challenges, looking for something more in line with your longer-range career goals, etc.)

SPECIAL COVER LETTER PARAGRAPHS

When you ask people in your network to refer you or your résumé to others, it helps if you give them a few brief statements that summarize the most important assets you can bring to the organization(s) you are targeting—a few brief marketing statements they can have on the tip of their tongues. These statements should be carefully worded to make someone want to read your résumé. With this in mind we suggest you prepare two or three short, focused paragraphs that can be incorporated into a cover letter when you or others distribute your résumé. These paragraphs should highlight:

- Your strengths and accomplishments that are most marketable in the targeted organization(s)
- How these strengths meet the targeted organizations' specific needs

If you're targeting more than one organization you may vary these paragraphs since you might have different strengths that meet different organizations' specific needs. These paragraphs should make it clear you're asking letter recipients to keep you in mind not only for near in, immediate job openings but also for longer-range future opportunities.

PERSONAL RÉSUMÉ DISTRIBUTIONS

When you self-distribute your résumé to people you know personally in your target organization(s) your cover letter should include:

- Thank you comments to those who helped you in your résumé editing or spent time with you in an Investigative Interview
- Your special marketing paragraphs
- A request that they keep you in mind and refer you for any openings they become aware of now or later

Be sure to send your résumé and cover letter to everyone you spoke to in your Investigative Interviews. They can become particularly strong allies in your future job searches since they have spent personal time with you. Hopefully, they've also been impressed with the professionalism of your career planning and the intelligence of the questions you asked them in the more relaxed Investigative Interviews where you weren't asking for a job.

Résumé Distribution by Others

When you ask others to distribute your résumé to people they know in your targeted organizations, suggest they send it with a cover letter from them including:

- Comments that you are a high potential talent who has special interest in a career with their organization(s)
- Your special marketing paragraphs (or paraphrases in their own words)
- A request that they keep you in mind and refer you for any suitable openings they become aware of now or later

Other Marketing and Visibility-building Mechanisms

There are, of course, many other ways of marketing yourself and building needed personal visibility. All of us can find our own personal ways matched to the circumstances of our specific situations. Examples would be things such as:

- Special project assignments requiring interface with your targeted organizations
- Negotiating assignments on special task forces that also have members from your targeted organizations
- Participation in professional organizations that have membership from multiple companies
- Participation in extracurricular activities such as church groups, social clubs, athletic teams, or social service organizations

Networking is a skill you build with practice. And the more networking you do the more likely you are to meet others who share your interests and values. This not only helps you find jobs in organizations compatible with your interests and values, it also builds your sense of being in community with others whose company you enjoy.

A Safety Net

Networking has also provided a valuable safety net for many by giving them an immediate pipeline for locating new opportunities when downsizing, restructuring, or the sale of their current organizations left them without a job. It's wise to maintain an ongoing network of people who can help you find another job if you get in trouble where you are. Paradoxically, this safety net often makes us more willing to risk innovations that ultimately make us more valuable and even more secure in our current organizations.

Persistence

People who get what they want and need are usually very persistent in their marketing campaigns. Effective campaigns usually take time and involve some rejections. Successful people tend to experience more rejections because they attempt more. Rejections don't destroy their self-esteem. Instead, rejections teach them lessons that ultimately make it possible for them to succeed.

A Case History

One persistent and inventive individual I knew (we'll call her Martha) did financial analysis work in a large automobile manufacturing company. Martha decided she wanted to develop her already good computer skills and make a career move into the company's information systems organization. She took the following approach when her manager repeatedly refused to let her interview for information systems openings inside her company. Because she felt it was important to start expanding her computer background immediately she:

- identified organizations outside her current company that offered the type of work she wanted
- ranked these organizations according to their desirability as places to work

- began by testing her résumé and interview skills with the lowest ranked, least desirable outside organizations and probed for feedback when she was rejected
- used the feedback to improve her résumé and interviewing skills
- used her perfected résumé and interview skills to approach the higher ranked outside organizations that most appealed to her and received a job offer

The confidence she was able to build from this approach—and the viable safety net she had generated with the outside offer—put her in a position where she could overcome the opposition of her current manager and generate a very attractive information systems offer in her own company. Without the safety of the outside offer, Martha felt she couldn't risk taking a stronger stand for a move inside her own company.

Sometimes, despite all the well-meaning human resources policies to the contrary, we have to generate good visibility and viable options elsewhere before we can take on the economic risk of addressing an obstacle or breaking out of an impasse in our own organizations. Sometimes we have to go all the way. Large organizations are full of top-level people who broke through an impasse and got what they wanted by leaving, establishing a visible reputation elsewhere, and then returning at a higher level to do what they wanted to do and couldn't before.

A good friend of mine, for instance, left his job as an engineering manager in a well-known Fortune 500 company because, after repeated rejections for higher level jobs, it became obvious they weren't going to give him any more promotions. He built such a record of accomplishment in a different, smaller company that his original company came looking for him six years later. They hired him back as president of a major division reporting directly to the chief executive officer. That was well beyond anything he could have achieved if he hadn't left. We've encountered many such cases.

REALITY TESTING AS A KEY MARKET STRATEGY

One of the best door openers for establishing contacts and visibility in new places is, of course, the Investigative Interview process we've described for collecting data to help develop your career goals. The very same strangers who met you, got to know you, counseled you, and helped you strategize your selection of an iceberg now live on that iceberg, probably in key positions influencing which people are brought aboard.

The Investigative Interview is an excellent multipurpose tool for collecting facts, selecting doors, and establishing your visibility with people who can help you. In this more comfortable, mutual exchange of information discussion they will probably get to know you even better than they would in the more tense job interview situation where they face the decision of accepting or rejecting you as a candidate. As a process, the Investigative Interviews are practical, effective, energy conserving, straightforward, honest, informative, and fun. They not only help you choose doors; they also help you open doors.

THINKING AHEAD

Many of the people we work with conclude they can grow in their current jobs for the immediate future. However, even when you're not planning any short-term changes, it's always a good idea to think ahead—to at least ask yourself a few questions about where and how you are networking to build visibility for future opportunities.

BRIEF REFLECTION

What are your current thoughts about changing jobs? Might you someday want to move into a different job than the one you hold now? If so, when might that be? What type of job do you think you'll be looking for?

Even if you're not currently planning any moves, what are you doing to grow a network and build market visibility for your longer-range future career aspirations?

Is there anything else you can or should be doing?

OVERCOMING ROADBLOCKS

As you move into actual implementation of your career plans and marketing strategy you will usually have to persist, in Churchill-like fashion, by pursuing our next task. You'll have to continually anticipate and overcome multiple roadblocks. You will, inevitably, encounter some very predictable and some not so predictable barriers to progress. There is a technique many have found extremely useful for anticipating as many of these barriers as possible, and for calmly developing strategies to overcome them.

Overcoming
Predictable Barriers

In the *Taking Charge Process*, you identify your career and personal growth goals and summarize them in your *Career and Life Workbook*. In Figure 24, the line from the lower left to the upper right corner of the graph illustrates an ideal straight progression as you move from your current situation toward achieving the longer-range goals you've recorded.

This is the ideal. Inevitably the progression will not be that straight. You will continually encounter barriers as indicated by the downward arrows in Figure 24. Many of these barriers are highly predictable. Earlier we discussed several generic barriers including myths, lack of focus, etc., and there are always others that are specific to each individual's situation (*e.g.*, family responsibilities that prevent a geographical transfer to your ideal job location).

It's foolish and unnecessarily energy-depleting to be surprised by predictable barriers when they occur. It's much more useful to identify and list as many of these barriers as possible in advance. Then you can make contingency plans to avoid or overcome them. The engineering manager we cited earlier would never have achieved his long-range career aspirations if he hadn't recognized the barriers to promotion where he was and left his company to build the necessary credentials elsewhere.

Avoiding an Imbalance

Barriers, however, are only one of the elements we need to consider in implementing career plans. It's equally useful to identify all the potential aids in our environment (as indicated by the upward arrows on the

179

FIGURE 24 BARRIERS AND AIDS

(Actions to Overcome the Barriers and Enhance the Aids)

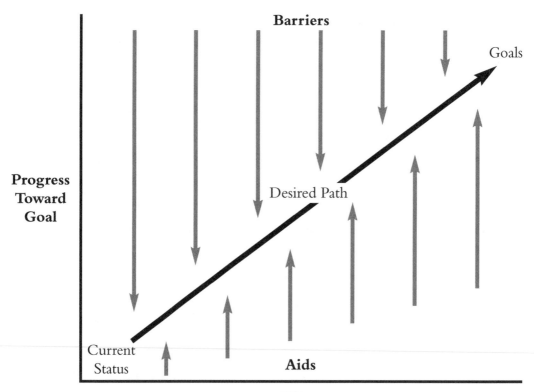

graph) that might help us achieve our goals. Then we can make plans to increase and enhance these aids as much as possible.

Too often we see only the barriers and fail to notice the aids. Years ago psychologist Kurt Lewin wrote about how we can improve our success rate in overcoming barriers that inhibit our progress. He said that it's important to avoid a narrow-minded "barriers only" focus. We can overcome this narrow focus and expand our action options by continually identifying various balancing aids in our environment as well. When people see only the barriers and fail to notice the aids they tend to become discouraged, often to the point where they remain passive and do little that is proactive.

On the other hand, people with a more positive outlook—people who end up achieving what they want—tend to:

- accept the barriers more calmly as a normal part of any planning process, and strategize proactively to avoid or overcome as many of them as possible.
- search out and identify as many counteracting aids as they can and plan proactively to enhance them.
- learn a great deal from the effort.

Figure 24 and the process of anticipating barriers and aids by incorporating both into your plans were derived from a very practical future action planning technique developed by Lewin. He called it *Force Field Analysis.*

The more you can plan actions to minimize or overcome the barriers and enhance (*i.e.,* take maximum advantage of) the aids, the more you can keep your line of progress on track toward your goals.

Brainstorming Both Sides

When we ask people to brainstorm potential barriers to achieving their career goals they typically include things that are specific to each individual's work situation such as:

- Managers don't have time for counseling and can't predict future needs (even for their own careers)
- Family (*e.g.,* my spouse has a career in this location and I can't move)
- Human resources systems in my organization are not helpful
- Budget limitations (*e.g.,* no training funds)
- Restructuring (*e.g.,* flatter organizations and fewer promotional opportunities)

They also consider various generic barriers, applicable to almost everybody, which we've described earlier. These include:

- Myths and self-defeating old mindsets
- Undefined or conflicting values priorities
- Loss of Spirit in the workplace
- No systematic process for taking charge, developing more focused goals, and marketing themselves

Typical aids they identify in many of their work situations include:

- Increasingly more open and de-layered organizations that allow more flexibility and opportunity for current job enrichment
- Rising business and government organization awareness that training is an essential investment in the future
- Ongoing business meetings, seminars, and conferences that provide opportunities for informal networking, Investigative Interviewing, and developing visibility
- Possibilities for negotiating special assignments to build essential competencies

In addition, the various career planning tools presented in this book were designed as enhancers to help everyone bypass or overcome many predictable barriers (*e.g.*, value prioritization, *Taking Charge Process*, competency assessment tools, and marketing techniques).

ACTION PLANS

After you identify potential barriers and aids, you can use the format in the *Career and Life Workbook* to develop a list of the most important *getting started* actions you can take to overcome the barriers, enhance the aids, and begin implementing your personal career action plans over the next 30, 60, and 90 days.

COOPERATIVE BRAINSTORMING

Workshop participants meet in groups of four to share their aids and barriers lists, and describe the actions they've identified to deal with them.

Hearing others' ideas gives people new perspectives on their own lists and helps each expand his/her own inventory of effective action options. When you later do the barriers and aids exercise in the workbook, we recommend you also share the results with someone who can help by giving you new ideas.

A Concise and Action-oriented Take-away

The barriers/aids analysis and action planning exercises complete the entries in the *Career and Life Workbook*. In the workbook you can summarize insight gained from each task in the *Taking Charge Process* and develop concrete next-step action plans. Workshop participants tell us the slim, focused goals and plans summaries they document provide important, often life-changing, new insight. These and a much more empowered personal mindset are frequently cited as the most important workshop take-aways. Participants also say the workbook provides a much needed discipline, with concrete tools they can use the rest of their lives for periodic career and life planning updates as they move through progressive life stages.

BRIEF REFLECTION

Looking at your own situation, what is the number one barrier you think might cause difficulty in the pursuit of your career and life goals? Are there any aids in your environment that might help you work around or overcome this barrier?

Communications Barriers

In our experience, by far the biggest barrier to successful career planning is a lack of the communication skills that are crucial for obtaining others' support. As we've observed people in multiple career specialties over many years, a clear pattern has emerged. Those who have trouble with communication are usually approaching it with the wrong mindset. Our next task involves developing a new, more productive mindset.

Communicating
with a New Awareness

Most of us know that communication is important. It's obvious. Earlier we showed how lack of communication skills kept the smartest individual in a talent assessment program from getting his solutions heard in group problem-solving. Effective communication is especially important if you want to nurture your spiritual as well as material growth and work in more rewarding community with others. To accomplish your career and life planning goals, you need to build understanding and negotiate the backing of others who are in a position to support your pursuits.

To improve our communication skills we usually take courses and read books on how to organize our presentations—how to present our thoughts in clearer, more rational, and irrefutable arguments. This is good. The courses help us. We don't want to ramble incoherently, but clarity and logic are not enough. The gentleman who was told "being right was irrelevant" was very organized, logical, articulate, and precise. It wasn't enough.

Receiving Before Transmitting

Many of us need a new communications mindset—a new paradigm for hearing and being heard—in both our personal and career-oriented interactions. As we work on improving our communication skills, we typically concentrate primarily on transmission. How clearly are we transmitting the facts of our positions to others? How well we transmit information is very important, but focusing on transmission first may be putting the cart before the horse. As we have watched effective communicators over the years we've noticed most focus first on their own perceptions—on how well they are receiving information. How objectively and accurately are they hearing and assessing their own internal voices? How well are they filtering out their biases, and hearing the legitimate, unfiltered realities of others' feelings, opinions, needs, and assessments of the issues?

More than Logic and Presentation

Early in my career, I worked on several projects with the head of human resources in a large research company. We'll call him Jim. At first glance, he was not very impressive. I wondered how he ever got where he was. He was small and unimposing. Surrounded by peers with Ph.D. credentials from nationally known technical universities, he had a non-technical bachelor's degree from a small, relatively unknown college. In noisy meetings with highly educated, sophisticated, and articulate contemporaries competing for air time, he was soft-spoken. In fact, he didn't seem to talk much at all. Nonetheless, he was highly respected. Everyone knew he was the single most influential person in the company below the president.

I asked a staff psychologist who worked with him regularly how anyone so quiet could be so influential. The psychologist had an interesting answer I never forgot. He said: "Jim doesn't talk much, but watch him in meetings. He almost always talks last and when he talks everyone listens. When the meeting is over the decisions usually go in the directions he orchestrates or recommends." I later decided the key verb was "orchestrates." Orchestra leaders make few sounds of their own during the performance. They bring out the best in others.

Emptiness

I didn't know what to call it then but I learned years later that Jim's credibility came from his ability to communicate from what spiritual writers have referred to for centuries as *emptiness*. Emptiness is an ancient spiritual concept that M. Scott Peck's writings have reintroduced with powerful new relevance into modern organizational psychology.

Jim had the ego strength to listen while others competed for recognition. He listened until he really understood where others in the room were coming from. He was able to set aside or *bracket* any preconceived notions or solutions with which he entered the room. He knew how to assess his early conclusions against the data being generated in the discussion before he spoke. He questioned and drew on others' expertise before he offered his own. He modified his thinking when others gave him new insight, often openly admitting errors in his thinking, and then developed new, more accurate conclusions. He apparently also had the humility not to care if he got personal recognition for any of the ideas incorporated in the ultimate solutions. He waited until he was "moved to speak" (another centuries-old spiritual concept contemporary social scientists have given new pragmatic significance to in the world of work). When Jim did speak, he usually made suggestions that synthesized and openly recognized the best thinking from each person in the room. People listened because his comments, even the vocabulary he used, showed he had listened to them while everyone else had been too busy jockeying for position to hear even themselves. The others also knew, from long experience, that Jim would never take personal credit for the solutions, but would instead recognize them for what they rightfully were, the best cooperative efforts of a community of peers. The other people had never heard of emptiness as a communication concept, but they knew Jim behaved differently. That difference gave him credibility. Emptiness is a concept that needs some definition. What is it?

> Emptiness is a word relating to space. It means "nothing in space."
> However, emptiness is also a metaphor suggesting making room or
> space for others (or the spirit) by removing one's self from that space.
> If we are very full of ourselves—with whatever makes up our self-
> identifications (credentials, opinions, the personal images we want to
> project, etc.)—it is often difficult to be accepting and understanding
> of others. Our ego gets in the way. We tend to block out our percep-
> tions of other people's individual value—of the information or ideas
> they might have that can help us improve our own ideas and treas-
> ured assumptions. Emptiness, or the process of emptying oneself,
> means making space for others and for new information. When we

make space for others, they begin in some way to make space for us, even when they may not be making much space for each other. Community can begin to happen.[23]

By letting other people and information in, we find out important things about ourselves—things we may have been blocking from our consciousness. Often this is critical data that can form the foundation for a new growth spurt and pinpoint new directions for the next stage in our journey. Emptiness demonstrates the wise paradox pointed out by mystics for centuries. By letting go of our egos we can more easily find and dramatically expand our *true* selves. We can tune in and hear the internal voice of the *Spirit* that is trying to break through and give us needed guidance.

By emptying and listening, we also bring upon ourselves the profound risk of having to change. Somehow, even when we know it's progress, admitting we have changed our minds or opinions is painful. Aware people usually accept this temporary pain as far preferable to the long-term pain of stagnation that comes from freezing their designs.

Effective career planning often involves change. Avoiding change can keep us stuck in an unrewarding career rut we really need to rethink. Practicing emptiness can help us get in touch with and clear away the biases and fears that prevent important needed change in our own thinking and perceptions. It can also help us hear, acknowledge, address, and overcome various fears or concerns of others (*e.g.*, our bosses or clients) that may be preventing them from giving us the support needed to pursue career goals.

I don't know why it's easier for some people to develop Jim's skill at communicating from emptiness. Steve, my collaborator in this book, comes by it easily. Like Jim, he seems to have been born with it while I've struggled with it all my life. I usually reach a clear early idea of what needs to be done and I want to convince everyone as quickly as possible. But I've learned, frequently and painfully, that I don't succeed when I behave like that. For me, emptiness is a learned skill, one I have to continually force myself to practice and use. Now that I know the term, emptiness, it's easier but not easy. When I'm failing to communicate, when I see people's eyes glaze over or their counterarguments build in precise proportion to the irrefutable logic of my presentation, I know I'm doing it again. When I'm lucky, the word *emptiness* flashes like a red warning light in my head and I tell myself to shut up and listen before I present or recommend another thing.

When Steve and I introduced new training programs in Europe and Asia, we had a firm rule that we would make no recommendations on the first trip. We would listen to their needs. We had an agreement that if either of us noticed the other drifting into recommendations we would gently but firmly silence him. It worked. Several months later I had to make the second trip to all the same places myself. Steve had coached and prepared me with a new script that said: "Did we hear you correctly? If we heard you correctly, here are some of the things we can recommend. If we didn't hear correctly, let's talk about how we can modify things to better meet your culture's needs." The programs we had developed in the United States spread within two years to 14 countries. Most of these countries would never have accepted any programs designed by two Americans if we hadn't first asked for their local experts' opinions and tailored the content to their unique cultures' needs.

WE DON'T HAVE TO WAIT FOR OTHERS

Practicing emptiness can help us achieve two needs we hear people express in the work world. First, emptiness can help clear our heads of the din of false assumptions, myths, and preconceived notions. It can give us some much needed space and internal silence so we can better listen to and comprehend our own inner voices when they speak about our careers. Second, emptiness can help us experience working in greater, more meaningful community with others.

It would be ideal if everyone practiced communicating from emptiness. It would be nice if everyone, as Jim did, focused on sorting out his/her own internal biases and bringing out the best in others. We can all work and hope for that. However, our observations across many career fields show you don't have to wait for others to start first. In reality, it can be very naive and self-defeating to postpone our own practice of emptiness until others begin practicing it. Jim didn't wait. And his rewards for not waiting were enormous. He simply went ahead on his own, using emptiness to stay calm, to sort out his thoughts and biases, and to hear others and empathize with them even when their needs prevented them from cooperating with each other. In the end, Jim usually developed a sense of community with them and they felt community with him, even when they weren't hearing each other.

We've said most people yearn for more meaning in their work lives. "They have a sense that in order to find meaning, they have to find authenticity, reality, and connection and relationship. . . . What they are yearning for is more authentic and meaningful communication."[24] When he intuitively practiced emptiness, Jim was authentic. He came across as real. People sensed this. With him, they somehow felt more comfortable connecting and being authentic themselves. Their own communications with him tended to become more genuine and effective.

I learned from Jim that I don't have to wait for others to change before I can have influence. Just who I am and what I do personally can and does make a difference. My state of being and the way I behave as an individual can have enormous positive impact.

I've since met quite a few people like Jim. Somehow they seem connected even in the midst of disconnected, tense, and anxious contemporaries. People gravitate to them without knowing precisely why. People tend to trust them and return their trust, even when these same people don't trust others. As I look back, I realize my mother, like Jim, practiced emptiness intuitively and unconsciously. As a widow struggling to earn a living in a cold and cutthroat New York media environment, she trusted, empathized, and refused to compete negatively or judge others. Somehow, incredibly I thought, her trust was usually returned. In my skeptical youth and early adulthood, I thought her refusal to compete negatively wasn't really very smart or cool. I decided her success must have come from sheer luck or naiveté. I was well into my thirties before I realized she was operating from real wisdom.

SPEAKING WHEN MOVED

Emptiness is only one of the important interpersonal communications concepts I've learned from the Foundation for Community Encouragement (FCE), a nonprofit educational foundation whose mission is to teach the principles of community—or healthy communication with and between groups. The FCE was founded by author M. Scott Peck, his wife Lilly, and nine other community-oriented professionals dedicated to achieving Peck's visions. The FCE has also taught me the importance and enormous contemporary effectiveness of another ancient spiritual concept, *speaking only when moved*.

While emptiness is not an easy thing to practice, it is relatively easy to understand. There are specific behaviors, which we will describe shortly, that constitute acting from emptiness. You can use them as a personal diagnostic to keep you on track. Most of these behaviors are very concrete.

Speaking only when moved is a more elusive but equally important concept. It requires more openness to mystery and to the less concrete. The FCE encourages us to speak only when moved by the internal voice of "that spirit that imparts a wisdom greater than our own." This refreshingly recognizes the reality of a higher power—a power that virtually all great religions of the East and West tell us must be acknowledged, listened to, and heeded before anyone can find lasting meaning, peace, or satisfaction. Specifically, the FCE tells us that the person who wants to act effectively from emptiness must continually:

> remain open to and listen for the inner voice of that *spirit* which imparts a wisdom greater than his/her own . . . and . . . discern when he/she is or is not moved by the *spirit* to speak or act—and respond appropriately.[25]

How do I know when I am or am not moved by the Spirit? The FCE doesn't give us a checklist for that. Instead it tells us that this discernment requires some tolerance for mystery. And it assures us that if we use emptiness to silence the din of too many external voices and erroneous assumptions—if we listen internally and purposefully—we will know when we are moved.

When I first heard this as a pragmatic, business-oriented consultant I was very skeptical. It sounded much too soft and elusive. What did it really mean? How could waiting to be "moved" ever work in concrete, rational, and time-pressured business situations? I remained skeptical and wasn't convinced for a long time.

Over a year or more, however, after participating in several FCE workshops and watching the practice of "speaking only when moved" work very effectively for others, I began to experience it working in myself. I will never be a natural expert like Jim. However, the more I work on it, the more I begin to experience what I imagine Jim and my mother felt naturally—a sense of tuning in to where people are coming from, of somehow being closer to them and appreciating them more. I begin to sense that when I feel moved to speak in this mode, somehow the words that come are better heard and understood.

ONE-MINUTE REVIEWS

I often finish a workshop or book feeling exhilarated and highly motivated to practice new behaviors and improve my actions based on new insight gained. Then I enter the real world where few know or practice what I have learned. My memory is short. The concepts get hazy. I lose them and don't have time to go back and reread the workshop materials or book. I need a handy tool I can carry in my day planner and occasionally look at for one minute to help me remind myself. As we've worked together developing numerous competency models, Steve has taught me the most useful tool for developing and practicing a new skill is a behavioral checklist—a brief summary of specific behaviors that will contribute most to my developing the skill. They have to be behaviors (*i.e.*, things I can do or not do) and they have to be observable so that I can notice when I am or am not doing them and correct course (*i.e.*, remind myself and start doing them).

My real need for a concrete crutch led me to work with the FCE on the development of a Communications Self-observation Checklist (see Figure 25) to help me discern when I am and am not practicing emptiness effectively. I refer to this checklist when I notice people tuning out—when I begin to wonder what I'm doing wrong that's preventing me from feeling connected or being heard.

As these behaviors indicate, listening to others is critical, but emptiness requires much more. Emptiness requires listening to, assessing, and

FIGURE 25 COMMUNICATIONS SELF-OBSERVATION CHECKLIST[26]

Authentic, effective communication is one of the most important elements required for negotiating and achieving both career and day-to-day work goals. Below are some behaviors that can help you accomplish this. Use the scale below to rate yourself on how well you follow each behavior. Then circle your rating on the three behaviors you most need to work on to improve your effectiveness.

5	4	3	2	1	Rating
Always	Usually	Sometimes	Seldom	Never	1–5

- **Use "I" statements when you speak** (*i.e.*, speak personally and specifically and not generally and abstractly). _____
- **Take responsibility for your own feelings and actions.** (Don't blame or project them on others.) _____
- **Focus on critical issues.** Clearly identify the most important issues and bracket (*i.e.*, put aside) other potentially distracting issues that might interfere with personal or group progress. _____
- **Respect confidentiality.** _____
- **Listen from understanding** (*i.e.*, as a friend, not an adversary, even if you disagree). _____
- **Be inclusive and avoid all forms of exclusivity** (*e.g.*, don't exclude anyone or discount their opinions based on race, nationality, sex, creed, etc.). _____
- **Remain open to and listen for the inner voice of that Spirit which imparts a wisdom greater than your own.** Discern when you are or are not moved by the Spirit to speak or act—and respond appropriately. _____
- **Listen carefully and with respect to what another person is telling you.** Do not formulate your response while someone is speaking but wait until the other has completely finished. _____
- **Be aware of your own barriers such as prejudices, expectations, ideologies, judgments, preformed opinions, or a need to control.** _____
- **Commit to "hang in there" even when it is difficult.** _____
- **Pay attention to your own and others' nonverbal as well as verbal behaviors** (realizing that nonverbal participation/interaction can be as important as verbal interaction). _____
- **Operate on the philosophy that each person (including you) is responsible for the success of the group.** _____
- **Use or suggest brief periods of silence** (where appropriate) to help you and the group return to effective focus. Be comfortable with silence, your own and others. _____

managing our distracting thoughts, feelings, assumptions, biases, expectations, and judgments. And emptiness demands that we notice when it's
appropriate to let go and give up our natural desire to control the dialogue or the outcomes.

I Can Only Start with Me

This is a short list but it asks a lot of us. I find the list easy to understand, but not easy to remember and not easy to act out in a distracting
and fragmented environment filled with people who are not practicing, or
even aware of, emptiness. I'm tempted to wait for someone else to start.
But I find I don't feel very good about myself when I wait. I feel better
about me and even about others when I doggedly remind myself to follow these behaviors. I have to continually remind myself to get out my
checklist when people are responding negatively and, instead of blaming
them or waiting for them to change, look at what I can do better. It isn't
very productive to lecture other people or try to teach them emptiness.
It's simpler just to model it. Eventually they will probably notice and start
behaving more openly and civilly at least toward me. I've seen it work.
I've seen people have enormous influence by, paradoxically, ignoring the
common assumption that we must all strive, continually competing with
each other, for visible, measurable recognition and reward.

Real Humility Is Not Weak

Practicing the behaviors in Figure 25 requires real humility. It takes
humility to acknowledge and bring out the strengths of others, rather
than bolstering our weak self-esteem by denying our errors or making a
show of speaking out when we don't really have much to say.

Humility is a frequently misunderstood, even maligned, word in
many work cultures. Humility is confused with excessive meekness, lack
of self-esteem, or a reluctance to speak up and be heard. That is not real
humility. It takes not low, but high self-esteem to practice emptiness, to
admit mistakes and uncertainties, to search out biases.

Real humility is a paradox. Real humility, the type Jim had, is not a
weakness but a strength. It results not in lack of impact but often in enor-

mous influence. Real humility, again paradoxically, is noticed. Others may not understand it, but they notice it. Intuitively, they respect it. Ultimately, because they feel less need to compete with the humble person, they hear that person better and pay more attention to what he or she says.

Jesus Christ is a powerful role model for real humility, but he was never weak. His influence has been enormous and lasting.

PERCEPTION, NOT NAIVETÉ

Emptiness and real humility are not naive. Instead they help us become, in a positive sense, much more shrewdly perceptive. We don't fail to notice weakness, or even deceptive tendencies in ourselves and others. If we can silence some of our internal distractions and become even a little less externally driven, we become much more objectively aware. Our previously dulled perceptions sharpen. We notice more and cope better. We start to perceive not only our own, but others' feelings, biases, and preconceived notions. We can anticipate potential emotional blocks and other barriers to ideas we want to present, and carefully tailor our communications to deal with these. If our communications fail the first time we can persist. We can listen carefully to find out why and, armed with these facts, redesign our approach to try again later. We can persist, not through stubborn repetitiveness, but rather flexibly, quietly strengthening our presentations based on an increased intuitive awareness of what is really going on with all parties involved.

I worked for years with the first woman vice-president of a large international company. She was a genius at anticipating barriers and overcoming them before she made key presentations. She did this by identifying and correcting mistakes that might trigger resistance in advance. She practiced the presentations with people who knew the individuals in her intended audience. She'd ask them to raise every possible objection anyone might have—rational or emotional, objective or biased. Then, humbly, she would admit and correct mistakes uncovered on her part, and plan a strategy to avoid triggering other specific objections. Or she would have suitable answers on the tip of her tongue if questions were raised. Her goal was to have no surprise objections in the final presentation. She usually succeeded.

Her goal was also to practice and hone her skills at hearing what people were saying so that in the final presentation she could listen, learn, and build ownership in her audience by integrating new insight gained from their comments.

She knew that feelings, emotions, and biases (both rational and irrational—her own and others') are facts that can't be ignored in any work setting. They are, whether we acknowledge them or not, just as real as any numbers that come off a computer.

Naiveté is pretending that everyone should be objective and rational, or feeling guilty or angry when we/they are not. It's more practical to calmly notice, accept, and deal with both the rational and the irrational. I copied and practiced her techniques. It greatly improved my communications success ratio.

Practically speaking, practicing emptiness expands our perception and significantly improves the accuracy, volume, and breadth of information we receive. The increased awareness this brings then improves the accuracy, objectivity, and credibility of the information we transmit. Tuning in to the complexity of others' sensitivities and needs before we transmit too much also helps us design and tailor our transmissions so they are most likely to be received. It helps us put them into a form and vocabulary that can be accepted and seen as meeting everyone's needs rather than just our own. Accurate perception, especially of our own internal voices and needs, is a critical prerequisite for communicating with others whose support we require in defining and pursuing our life and career goals.

MERE MEANS TO A MUCH MORE IMPORTANT END

This completes our discussion of various tasks in the *Taking Charge Process* we recommend for ongoing career and life planning. We've presented some very practical "to do" techniques and given you some time-tested and proven tools for better charting and navigating your own evolving life course.

The next challenge is to stay the course, to notice when course correction is needed, and to remember that no career is an end in itself. Careers are merely means—and not at all the most important means—to achieve a much more important end we all share. Whatever career or series of career options you might pursue in this life, they have significance only if they help you keep your eyes on the true and lasting values, and on the only ultimate destination that can give real meaning to anyone's life.

1. BREAKING OLD MINDSETS

2. CONTRACTING FOR RENEWAL

3. FINDING YOUR CALLING

4. MAKING IT HAPPEN

5. STAYING THE COURSE

STEP 5

STAYING THE COURSE

Step 5 deals with the important process of **Staying the Course**—the process of keeping your eye on the only truly satisfying ultimate goal, and not allowing yourself to get derailed into temporarily enticing but counterproductive way stations.

We've stressed the importance of defining clear life values with focused goals and career plans to support them. But career success, however recognized in this world, is not enough. It can never be a satisfying final end in itself.

In recent years our most advanced psychological and medical research has begun to discover anew what great spiritual leaders have told us for millennia. To have an ultimately fulfilling life we all need a larger purpose—a mission beyond pure self and mere career success.

Running the Race to the Finish

We've talked a great deal about research and technique. As we conclude, it's probably a good idea to look again at the bigger picture—at overarching meaning and purpose. Why are we doing this? Why even bother with career and life planning? What's the bottom line? Where is it all leading?

The Ultimate Purpose and Reward

Shortly before his death, when St. Paul knew he was about to be beheaded, he wrote from his Roman prison:

> The time has come for me to depart. I have fought the good fight to the end, I have run the race to the finish, I have kept the faith.[27]

Why and where had he been running? By all worldly standards, Paul faced death as a failure. In the eyes of imperial Rome, and even in the opinions of his rabbinical peers in Jerusalem, Paul's career had led nowhere. He was penniless and reviled by both the Roman and Jewish authorities. He had no standing, recognition, or authority in the society of his day. His accomplishments were questionable. Through untiring effort, personal sacrifice, and suffering, he had managed to convert small groups of people, usually at lower social levels, in a number of scattered cities like Corinth and Ephesus. But even they tended to waffle and backslide so much he had to write endless letters in a frustrating and often seemingly fruitless campaign to keep them in the faith. He had no guarantee at all that they would pay any lasting attention to what he had taught them, or that anything enduring would result from his years of toil and anguish. In society's view he had no tangible, measurable output or accomplishments to show for his life.

By contrast, he was dying surrounded by people who had achieved enormous worldly wealth, success, recognition, and power—people such as the emperor Nero, Vespasian, the illustrious general who later became emperor, and the powerful men and women who made up their entourages. Rome ruled supreme. The emperor and Roman authorities who were executing Paul had visible, measurable, and undeniable results to show in their lives. They were revered and feared. People knew who they were, and most envied the lavish lifestyle that came with their fame, power, and possessions.

Where are those Romans today? How often have you had the things Nero and Vespasian said quoted or read to you recently? What have been the long-term results of their labors? What has been their final and eternal reward?

By comparison, ask yourself the same questions about Paul. Whose life had the most real meaning—Nero's, Vespasian's, or Paul's?

THE ULTIMATE VICTORY

Who won the ultimate prize? And what is the ultimate prize? The Romans, like us, were very busy. Conquering the world was not a casual pastime. War, presumably, was not relaxation. What drove them to pursue it? What inner need could not be filled even by their immense material comfort and grandeur? What was the missing ingredient that motivated their restless territorial expansion but could not be found in all their busyness and conquests?

Paul knew. Paul, who had been a dedicated and driven persecutor of everything Christian, had a revelation on the road to Damascus. Paul listened to the revelation, developed a dramatically different mindset, and changed. He tuned in to a new, more accurate view of what values are and are not worth pursuing in life—which have lasting payoff, and which are transitory, ultimately leading nowhere. Are we tuning in? Or are we too busy, too dazzled, and confused by the more immediate short-term pay-offs of the modern Romes we inhabit?

The new Paul's overwhelming desire was to pursue God's will, whether or not it brought any personal recognition. He knew it would be absurd (vanity of vanities) to take any personal credit for whatever good his efforts might produce. And he could never be certain how much he really had accomplished. The epistles he wrote were not very widely recognized or accepted in his time. Relatively few even knew about them. He could hope, but he couldn't be sure people would even keep them around. They might just be thrown away as most letters are.

Paul was a smart man. His intelligence, coupled with his coveted Roman citizenship, gave him unique and powerful credentials for worldly success, if he had chosen to use them that way. But popularity and recognition from his Roman peers would have required compromising his newly discovered values. His writings would have had to become less honest and more in vogue with the contemporary mores of the society around him. He resisted that temptation because he knew those mores were transitory and wrong. Instead he held on to his principles, never giving up and never visibly prevailing over his contemporary critics.

Paul died trusting, but not knowing, that there would even be any lasting results from all his efforts. That was undoubtedly frustrating but he had grown to the point where it was also OK. He had learned to listen as much as he possibly could to the Spirit. He had worked very hard and continuously to monitor and clear away his own self-serving internal biases and insecure pride. He practiced emptiness to make space for God—so he could better hear what God wanted him to do.

Paul believed his task was to make the effort—to stay true to his real values and beliefs—regardless of the outcome. The outcome, the results, were up to God. And he had learned to accept whatever happened as long as he had done his best, even when what happened was frustrating and not what he intended. He trusted a wisdom greater than his own, and he persisted in that trust even as he faced seeming failure, dishonor, and execution.

Paul's journey was focused and efficient. He had one simple goal ahead. He sought only to do God's will as best he could determine it. He died believing he had succeeded at least in that. He could truthfully say he had done his "best in the race." And he died believing he had achieved the only *personal* accomplishment—and won the only *personal* victory—he really and ultimately cared about. In his own words:

> From now on the crown of righteousness awaits me, which the Lord, the just judge, will award to me on that day, and not only to me, but to all who have longed for his appearance.[28]

Undoubtedly, if Paul's pagan Roman contemporaries had read the above, they'd have thought it unsophisticated, naive, impractical, fuzzy, unscientific, and unprovable. In their more pragmatic, worldly wisdom they would have pointed out their own more concrete achievements and rewards in life, certain they were right as they watched Paul lower his head on the executioner's block.

What do you think? Who was right? What victories and rewards will you seek for the rest of your life? Wealth, recognition, power, and influence—the immediate concrete payoffs that others can see, revere, and envy—are just as popular today as they were in ancient Rome, maybe even more so. Pursued (or envied) out of balance, these can become false gods every bit as distracting and harmful as any pagan gods Rome ever had.

THE MOST CONSEQUENTIAL DECISION WE WILL EVER MAKE

We all stand at a fork in the road. Which way will we choose? Paul took what M. Scott Peck calls "The Road Less Traveled." Which road will you take—immediate payoff now or more lasting rewards later?

This should be an easy and obvious choice but unfortunately most of us don't find it so. In the frantic, harried, and distracting pace of today's *instant-satisfaction* and *must-have-everything* society, choosing which road more often becomes a tough decision. We try not to think about it. We procrastinate and try to avoid it. But it can't be avoided. If we listen to centuries of spiritual and philosophical wisdom, this is unquestionably the most important and seriously consequential decision we will ever make. Avoiding it is too risky because we have no idea how long we have left to make it. It may be years, but it may also be that tomorrow will be too late.

Even if we still have years, avoiding the decision will only make the passing of those years far less productive, meaningful, and satisfying.

KEEPING THE FAITH

"Keeping the faith" was important to Paul. Knowing he had kept it was a critical ingredient in his final satisfaction and reconciliation with both his life and his death.

What is "keeping the faith"? Again, Steve and I are not theologians. However, after over two decades of career counseling with professionals and managers at all levels of the hierarchy in a wide spectrum of different career fields, we've formed some definite opinions. We can point out what our observations lead us to believe are at least a few of the more essential requirements for keeping the faith if you want to keep it *on* as well as *off* the job—if you want to fill the painful void many feel today because they have split their spiritual longings off from their careers, leaving their souls at home when they go to work and then returning home with no energy left for their souls.

First of all, to keep the faith you must have a faith. You have to know and decide what you believe in. Are you a *Naturalist*, as defined in our earlier chapters, who believes the best you can hope for is a flawed and incomplete heaven on earth in an equally flawed, incomplete, material, and too often amoral world? Or are you a *Supernaturalist* who aims for something higher and more enduring—who believes you can lift your gaze from the mud and hope for more than a comfortable and undemanding final decade in the sun? Have you been seduced, consciously or unconsciously, by the distracting and discredited promises of various materialistic "isms"? Or have you discovered a higher reality? Have you looked beyond, like Hubble, Einstein, and the other scientists Jastrow describes, who pulled themselves over the peaks of ignorance and were "greeted by a band of theologians who have been sitting there for centuries"?[29]

Chances are you're a Supernaturalist. Most people consider themselves believers. But simply believing isn't enough. Keeping the faith means really living up to your beliefs—every day—especially some of the more obvious basics like the ecumenically, almost universally accepted (if often ignored) Sermon on the Mount. Believing but not living is almost the same as not believing.

Even Paul knew that living his principles and beliefs was not easy. He writes about his own struggles to keep on the right path despite personal weakness, distractions, temptations, and frequent setbacks. For Paul the road less traveled was never a straight and simple path. Like the spaceship heading for the moon, it was a zigzag path maintained only through noticing mistakes and constantly correcting course.

Keeping the faith also involves really living your life values. To do this you have to keep your values conscious, clear, and straight. Knowing your value priorities is essential. If your values are fuzzy—if you're avoiding and letting yourself be distracted from making important value decisions and trade-offs, you won't be living the life you want to lead. You won't be happy, fulfilled, or satisfied. Your life will lack meaning, and you will definitely not be keeping the faith.

FIGHTING THE GOOD FIGHT TO THE END

Paul did more than keep the faith. He acted it out day-by-day, year-by-year, even when he was tired, distracted, and overwhelmed. He was proactive. He didn't wait for people to ask for and reward his message. He spoke it, he lived it, he modeled it in his behavior despite frequent rejection and disbelief on the part of his contemporaries. He persisted despite obstacles. He was tenacious and flexible in finding ways to overcome setbacks.

Few of us will face the level of opposition Paul faced and few of us are asked to make the heroic sacrifices he made. But few of us will travel a smooth road. If we're truly going to live and act out our values and beliefs, it would be nice to have some help. It would be helpful to hear how others have succeeded in fighting the good fight, to be able to anticipate and plan in advance how to avoid or overcome the predictable barriers they faced. It would be useful to have some proven tools or techniques, some weapons that can give us an edge in fighting the good fight. Hopefully, this book and its appendices will give you much of the help you need, at least in the areas of identifying and negotiating a career path that is consistent with your faith and spiritual longings.

Another key part of keeping the faith, of course, is your religious life. We can't claim any special expertise in the specifics of your life of faith but we hope you have one—and we hope you take it seriously enough to allocate real time for it. When people don't, our observations are that the secular side of life can get really out of balance. Busyness escalates and becomes less and less satisfying or productive.

As I drove to my office to work on this chapter, the newscast on my car radio reported that a significant new research study has developed strong statistical proof that people who are "religious and go to church religiously" tend to live much longer than those who don't. There have been numerous recent studies that support this conclusion about the physical health as well as spiritual benefits of having and *practicing* a strong faith.

Religion, like work, is a community activity. No matter how pure our intentions, it's difficult, prideful, and ultimately naive to think we can go it alone. We need each other's support in the community endeavors that religion sponsors (regular services, seminars, and retreats, etc.). We need the wisdom and humility to learn by paying attention to what centuries of recognized spiritual giants have been telling us about how to bring meaning to our lives.

And we need to do our part to encourage others in the faith we share with them. You may not personally feel that you gain much from a particular religious activity—but your just being there may be a very real help to others. The growth we experience from a particular religious activity comes not merely from what we get from it but—perhaps even more importantly—from what we give to it.

Tools Can Only *Support* Intent

The tools and techniques we've presented can help you accomplish what you decide you want to do with them. But they can only support, never supply or guarantee your intent. Only you can determine your motivation, positive or negative. We hope you will periodically critique and evaluate your own intent because, like any tools and techniques, those in this book can be misused.

It's important to remember that movement up a hierarchy of leadership roles should never be considered a measure of personal success either in life or a career. Buying into the myth (strongly promulgated by many if not most hierarchical organizations) that upward movement in the pecking order or size of financial reward defines success can be disastrous. This myth may have caused more unhappiness, lack of meaning, lost values, and failure to "keep the faith" than any other misguided organizational banality we've encountered.

There's nothing wrong with hierarchical leadership or financial success if they're kept in balance, if they don't become false gods, and if they support rather than distract from your unique personal values and success criteria. People like Paul, Mother Teresa, Shakespeare, Einstein, Francis of Assisi, Martin Luther King, and Gandhi (to name just a few) had nonhierarchical personal success criteria. They had intensely unique personal visions of their missions in life. Fortunately, for them and us, they kept their focus and didn't let the world distract them.

It's interesting to note, however, that each of the above probably had great intuitive expertise in many of the core and leadership competencies we've described. Their life histories seem to indicate they used these competencies very successfully for pursuits other than hierarchical ambition.

MEGAMISSION

We've talked about the often elusive task of finding our missions in life, the special vocations or callings that can give each of us our real reasons to be. We long for a career that will include some sense of spiritual fulfillment and still provide a decent living. We should hold on to that longing. It's our ally, not our foe. It may be the most important mechanism we have for keeping us on track.

If we're to find real meaning and purpose, elements that often seem missing in the day-to-day specifics of almost any occupation (sales, accounting, law, business, writing, acting, teaching, etc.), we will need some sense of mission beyond the specifics of our work, beyond even our accomplishments no matter how much they're recognized. Even when we speak with highly renowned people in what appear to be very exciting careers, such as TV and movie-making, they complain about spending much of their time on tedious, boring detail. For instance, movie actors and actresses often spend hour after hour waiting for scene setups. And they frequently shoot the same two-to-three-minute scenes over and over again until they get them right.

Great accomplishment and acclaim can never substitute for a sense of mission. And people who lack a sense of mission, no matter how successful, usually end up feeling a boredom or ennui that is not new to our generation. It's nagged the human race for most of recorded history. One spiritual writer described this condition as "an oppressive sorrow that so weighs upon a man's mind that he wants to do nothing." This description was written over 700 years ago by Thomas Aquinas. However, as Peter Kreeft points out, it is "a pretty exact, clinical description of what we call depression."[30]

How do we overcome this all too common restlessness and depression? How do we find an energizing sense of mission that can give some meaning even to the overload and tedium in our lives?

People who seem to find inner peace and satisfaction keep their eyes on a higher purpose. They don't frantically try to escape and deny their boredom through self-important busyness. Beyond their work they know they are pursuing a more important, overriding megamission that encompasses, but is not limited to, the specific accomplishments of their chosen occupations.

These people somehow intuit and march to a higher drum. They're very much *in* the world, including their occupations, but, as the Bible says, they're not completely *of* the world. They have a certain sense of what spiritual writers describe as detachment from the pressures of fleeing contemporary mores. Not being completely *of* the world includes the ability to practice emptiness and, paradoxically, it makes them even more intensely present and tuned in to their environments, their work surroundings, and their peers. People hear them even if they disagree with them.

What is this megamission? In its broader definition it's absurdly simple. But in the details it's more subtle and complex. The great spiritual writers seem to agree what it is, but it isn't easy to describe. They've used a variety of parables and analogies to communicate it. In recent decades various leading-edge psychologists and psychiatrists have focused their research on this megamission. Their findings and theories have correlated very closely with what both modern and traditional theologians have been telling us.

In its broader definition Kreeft has given us a simple and direct description of our megamission. He says:

> Our primary business in life is not business, or construction work, or sales, or teaching, or even motherhood, but becoming a human being.[31]

Obvious, right? But what does that mean and how do we do it? How does that play out in the details?

Looking at the best contemporary research, we've found a pretty good consensus that our megamission is actually progression through key life stages, independent of what career fields we pursue. That's how we become complete human beings. That's where we find overarching meaning and lasting satisfaction. Completing this progression by acknowledging and resolving the issues of each stage (*e.g.*, those described on pages 85–192), and by helping others move through the stages, provides the ultimately rewarding mission that supersedes and can't be replaced even by outstanding success from any *in-this-world* career ambitions. This is a mission we can pursue with enthusiasm right to the very end, always anticipating a higher and more lasting payoff, as Paul did, despite any and all setbacks and failures in the lower-tier and temporarily satisfying ambitions of our worldly careers. The goal is to keep growing and to behave in ways that will help others grow. Often we make our greatest progress in pursuing this goal by learning from failures to achieve our more material career or other worldly goals.

The six stages of adult development we presented in Step 3 were synthesized from the work of many who have studied the human and spiritual growth processes. Other experts word their descriptions of the stages a bit differently and some categorize their findings into a different number of stages. However, there tends to be good general agreement on the themes and the direction movement takes through various stages as we grow. There is also agreement that this growth is our most profound purpose in life.

MISSING THE MEGAMISSION

Stalling out in our progression by refusing to acknowledge and work through the issues of a given stage can leave us stuck and self-frustrated in lower stages we need to move beyond. Levinson, for instance, talks about people who deny and are unwilling to resolve the polarities of the mid-life transition (see pages 87–88). Many have had great worldly success. They want to focus only on that, not on themselves and their need to complete themselves and grow. They can't acknowledge the inevitable dark side of the behaviors that brought them their successes (*e.g.*, their sometimes less-than-constructive activities on the way up). And they don't find their successes very satisfying. They look back at their worldly accomplishments and somehow feel cheated. "Is this all there is?" To avoid facing the next growth step they want to go back to their twenties and start all over again. They want to avoid the pain of growth and again feel the more comfortable, self-deceiving, naive, and uninformed energy of a more callow youth.

Often these people have trouble when they reach retirement. They can't bury their real issues and needs in busyness. The fleeting sense of self-importance that comes from having the phone ring to distract them with more mundane, and more easily acknowledged work needs is gone. Frequently these people don't have much fun relaxing in the sun. Work distractions were all they had. They have failed to grasp the great mega-mission altogether.

When we get stuck, or stall out in our progression, the answer is usually to raise our eyes from the mud so we can feel the pain, and the glory, of a higher vision—so we can quit trying to *be* God and learn instead to humbly trust and *serve* God who knows we aren't perfect, and who still stands by offering unending love and support through the pain of growth—if only we will accept the offer.

LOVE SUPPLIES THE ENERGY

Another thing most spiritual writers of all faiths agree on is that love supplies the needed energy. Love is the fuel and the essential reality that sustains and supports us in our megamission growth. But they're not talking about just any love. Even love, it turns out, has a series of progressive stages.[32]

The lower level is *romantic infatuation.* This love is typical of teenagers or young adults. It is a form of early fascination with the newly discovered love object. The good thing about romantic infatuation is that it usually feels wonderful. Even the pain that sometimes accompanies it somehow feels good. The dark side of infatuation is that it is often possessive and self-centered, not other-centered. Ultimately, its interest is not so much in the other person as a separate being but rather as someone who can complete your own being—meet your own needs and magically fill in for all your inadequacies without distracting you with needs of his or her own. This kind of love typically loses much of its steam (often in 18 to 24 months). Then you start to notice the other is not really an extension of you but a separate being with needs and sometimes even conflicting demands of his or her own. That can become very frustrating. If infatuation doesn't move on to at least the next stage, the relationship often ends. One tells the other "I just don't *feel* that way about you anymore." Many of today's disrupted relationships involve people who move from one short-lived romantic infatuation to another rather than face the next growth step.

The next stage is *reciprocal* love. Here the relationship becomes more tolerant and two-way. There are trade-offs. Instead of having things flow one way, you sense, accept, and meet each other's separate needs. You negotiate and reach resolution on conflicting needs. Relationships and friendships in this stage can last for years, even lifetimes, to the great mutual benefit of the involved parties.

The highest stage is one of the principal goals in our journeys through life. Its Latin name is *caritas,* and it is what Christians call *charity.* Charity becomes one way again but this time in a different direction. Charity is not self-centered, but other-centered. If you have charity you love, even serve, not only your friends but also your enemies. It's nice if charity is reciprocated. That's the best case of all. However, if you have real charity you love, even serve, others, when there is no reciprocation. As an example of charity, Augustine cites the elderly couple where one serves and is totally dedicated to the needs of the other, despite the fact that the other is senile and doesn't even know who is helping. Charity moves much closer to God's love. Charity is difficult to achieve—and even when we reach it we typically have many setbacks—but charity is what we are striving for—our ultimate experience of love—and it brings the highest ultimate rewards.

We know a number of people who work tirelessly and very productively with the poor and downtrodden all over the world. They warn new, aspiring social service people never to enter this type of work if they expect gratitude. Gratitude is nice if it comes but they can't rely on it. And they have to carry on with or without it. Those who need to be rewarded with gratitude often become disillusioned to the point where they burn out and eventually quit—or they grow and learn to operate from a charity that demands no gratitude or personal worldly rewards.

In recent years, my work has brought me into contact with quite a few people who seem to operate from this level of selfless charity. Paradoxically, they are some of the most serene, joyful, and genuinely self-fulfilled people I've ever met. For me, just being in their presence is very humbling.

The following poem, paraphrasing Archbishop Alban Goodier, describes the terrors and the rewards of love at its highest stage.

> When love has passed you by
> Asked for the last drop of your blood
> And told you it isn't enough
> Ignored you and passed coldly by
> As you lay in the ditch.
>
> If you persevere then
> Then you shall know
> What eye has not seen
> And ear has not heard
> And it has not entered into
> The hearts of humankind to think.[33]

A tough prescription—a very challenging goal. Many of us will achieve this level of love occasionally, but it may be that few achieve it permanently, with no regression, in this life. Nevertheless, it's a goal that can keep us challenged and energized—and a goal we can't help but gain from pursuing. Paul pursued it, admittedly with great difficulty and frequent setbacks. And he grew tremendously in the race.

We've used Paul as our prime example in this chapter. However, as we said, Paul's conclusions about what is and is not ultimately valuable in life are reflected in some fashion by the writings of most great Christian *and* non-Christian spiritual leaders from both the Eastern and Western traditions.

MULTIPLE SECOND-TIER MISSIONS

Below our megamission there are multiple second-tier missions that help support it. These include things such as your important family goals and activities, your community and social service projects and, of course, your career endeavors.

Your career is a critically important second-tier goal because it dominates so much of your time. If you don't define, negotiate, and pursue career goals that ultimately support your deepest values and beliefs, and enhance your upward progression through the life stages, you will probably find yourself harried, frustrated, and unable to focus on tracking and achieving your megamission.

However, there is a danger in believing that your career *is* your megamission. We hope you now agree that it is not. Your career is one very important second-tier goal that supports your megamission. That's why we've devoted so much time to the "how to's" of career planning in this book.

There is a danger too in the frequent, but erroneous, belief that career planning is a once-in-a-lifetime endeavor—that you decide sometime in your twenties or early thirties what you want to be in life and believe you've failed if you later deviate from that. We hope you agree that is nonsense. Career planning is an ongoing activity. Many of us will change career fields several times over the years as circumstances change, or as we achieve some values and want to focus more on others. Any work you do to support your growth toward becoming a more complete human being can advance you in your megamission. Our belief is that if you do work you find intrinsically satisfying and interesting you will find it easier to grow. We hope you'll use the tools in this book, not only to focus on and pursue that type of work, but also to notice when it's time for a change and plan/negotiate the needed course corrections.

Despite your best planning you still must always be prepared to make the best of—and find the growth opportunities in—unanticipated events beyond your control. There are countless examples of people who have done this. Psychiatrist Victor Frankl, for instance, used the unwanted experience of being incarcerated in a World War II concentration camp as the inspiration to write *Man's Search for Meaning*, one of the most inspiring and life-changing books of the twentieth century. Another example is Bill Wilson, the founder of Alcoholics Anonymous. His unwanted struggle with and ultimate victory over alcoholism led him unexpectedly into an incredibly productive career as a writer and counselor. His twelve-step program for overcoming addiction has become the worldwide standard for helping millions recover their belief in a higher being and conquer addictions of all sorts (alcohol, gambling, drugs, food, etc.). If you can get clear about where you're going in your megamission, as he did, you'll be much better prepared to handle unexpected setbacks and turn them into real growth opportunities.

DOING GOOD

So far we've talked about the megamission primarily in terms of personal growth. We hope it is obvious, but it's worth mentioning, that we're not talking about staying *only* self-focused and egotistically centered on *our own* growth. Obviously that would defeat our purpose. Paradoxically, as virtually all spiritual experts agree, the more we overcome a self-centered focus—the more we become other, as opposed to self, focused—the more we accelerate our progress in growing the self. To achieve our personal and internal growth objectives we have to focus outward. We need to do our best to do good and help others. This becomes clear in the Sermon on the Mount and in Matthew 25 where we read:

> Come, you that are blessed by my Father. Come and possess the king-
> dom which has been prepared for you ever since the creation of the

world. I was hungry and you fed me, thirsty and you gave me a drink, I was a stranger and you received me in your homes, naked and you clothed me, I was sick and you took care of me, in prison and you visited me. (TEV)[34]

Doing good is a more elusive, less definable and measurable goal than self-growth. Somehow, intuitively, we know when we are and are not growing ourselves. If we're honest with ourselves—and this is a big if—we can track our progress through both the stages of life and of love. We can sense when we're making progress and when we're stalling out or regressing. It's often very difficult to know when we really are and are not helping others, no matter how hard we're trying. We can track only our own intentions and actions. The results—the output—we usually have to leave up to God.

When we find this frustrating it helps to remember what John Henry Newman concluded despite the many setbacks and great personal difficulties in his own life endeavors:

God has created me to do some definite service, God has committed some work to me which He has not committed to another. I have my mission. I may never know it in this life but I shall be told it in the next.[35]

Newman, who has worldwide respect today, faced tremendous opposition and criticism when he was alive. But he took comfort in his faith and in his firm belief that all anyone, including himself, could do was his or her very best. Not only is that all we are asked to do. Even more importantly, that's all we have been given the power to do.

When it comes to doing good for others—to improving the world somehow—we probably do have a specific mission but, more often than not, we never know precisely what it is. This is true not only for saints and philosophers but even for ordinary people like ourselves. Ultimately in the vast and subtle interconnections of the human race what each of us does, no matter how small and unimpressive at the time, will probably have a level of impact on other people we could never dream of. This means that while we can never control the outcome we should certainly monitor our intent. If we intend good then good will probably be the ultimate and unknowable-to-us result, no matter how discouraging the immediately visible results might be. As the rest of our quotation from Newman shows, he was optimistic about ultimate outcomes.

> I am a link in a chain,
> a bond of communication between persons.
> God has not created me for naught.
> I shall do His work. I shall do good.[36]

Trusting God, however, is not passive. It doesn't mean we just sit back and wait for events to unfold. Trusting God requires that we work hard and continually at discerning God's will, at listening to the Spirit and tracking what we think God's will is.

TOOLS TO HELP

We've presented five steps and a series of tools and techniques we believe can help you navigate a successful life journey. Of course, tools and techniques are merely helpers, not end goals. The real objective is not completing the exercises in the workbook, but using the tools and exercises to move your life in directions you want to go. The tools were developed to help you make the career planning process simple and concrete enough to try different things. They give you a method for exploring directions you might not consider otherwise. Tools, however, provide only one of two critical ingredients we believe are essential for successful career and life planning.

AN EMPOWERED MINDSET

The most important single ingredient in life and career planning is your mindset—your view of reality and belief in what can be done. This includes the accuracy and breadth of your awareness, and the personal vision with which you view the world and decide what is and is not important for you. Successful life strategists continually expand their awareness. They see mistakes and disappointments, however temporarily distressing, not as disasters or proof of worthlessness—but as critical learning experiences. Lessons learned from failures help them progress ever more effectively toward goals that energize and have intrinsic meaning for them.

PRAYER AND MEDITATION

As we've continually stressed, to find enduring meaning in life, our pursuit of success must include spiritual growth. We need to balance our worldly pursuits with a great deal of prayer and meditation. Christ, for instance, tells us to pray so that we don't collapse along the way. Since the beginning of recorded history spiritual leaders of all persuasions, throughout the East and West, have constantly reminded us to do this and agreed it's essential. In prayer we lift up our minds and wills to God seeking his grace and asking that he continually be with us and guide us. In meditation we prayerfully compare our lives and goals with what we accept as God's guidance and instruction.

HARD BUT EXHILARATING WORK

Career and life planning are tough. Facing the hard reality that it's I—not some organizational villain or Santa Claus—who bears the responsibility for defining and achieving my life's goals is real work. But it doesn't have to be boring or discouraging work. Addressed with the right mindset, it can be exhilarating, energy-generating work.

We have talked about responsibility. This is a word we like to hyphenate. Hyphenated *response-ability* is an asset, not a burden. Response-ability is our capacity to respond effectively to life's challenges with freedom, autonomy, and a clear awareness of the world's true realities. That has been the essence of this book.

Undoubtedly, there will be anxieties. We've pointed out that anxiety doesn't need to be suppressed as something bad. Anxiety can be your most important road signal for needed course correction. Anxiety can trigger awareness. Awareness makes you periodically stop and notice where you are. Awareness gives you important data to compute new, more exciting courses.

A Larger Purpose

As you work through the various exercises and competency tools we've presented, we urge you to remember this book's and your life's real purpose—an enhanced personal and spiritual journey focused on ultimate goals and lasting meaning. Keep your career goals and achievements in clear, pragmatic perspective as mere influencing factors that can enhance your progress or derail you, depending on how well you take charge and manage them. Don't let them manage you.

In each step of the process we outlined, check your mindset. Ask yourself:

- Will the career goals and competencies I am deciding to work on meet my long-term as well as my organization's short-term needs (or will they at least not conflict with my values or prevent me from meeting my deeper needs)?
- Will the actions I am deciding to take enrich not only my own life, but the lives of others in my immediate network and broader community (or at least not harm myself or others)? Will they put me in more or less meaningful community with others and do they link with a broader purpose beyond myself?

Like Paul, we all need a larger purpose beyond ourselves. Pursuing this larger purpose has a leveraging effect. It enhances our impact and gives increased meaning to everything we do. Regularly, we see articles in the research journals and press citing beneficial effects of career and life strategies that link our actions to a broader community interest and purpose. This linkage enhances not only our spiritual growth but also our health, longevity, and everyday satisfaction in this world.

Theologian Reinhold Niebuhr often spoke about the importance of having a larger purpose. Niebuhr once wrote about attending the birthday party of an octogenarian friend who said with gusto and joy, "I'm still working on my larger purpose. God is not finished with me yet." Commenting on his friend's remark, Niebuhr added, "Remember, throughout life, we are engaged in an ongoing pursuit of unearthing our larger purpose for being on this earth—what we are meant to do . . . what we are meant to be."[37]

Everything Steve and I have learned in years of observing and inter-viewing people has led us to agree with people like Niebuhr and New-man that real satisfaction and life fulfillment usually do not come from any specific career goal or accomplishment. Instead they come from keep-ing the faith and staying the course, from continually reminding ourselves that no matter where we are in the life stages, as long as we draw breath, "God is not finished with us yet." We can still grow and joyfully "run the race" toward our never completed megamission of becoming better human beings—of preparing ourselves for another life beyond anything we can imagine. We believe in this megamission. We think it is absolutely the most important thing in life. And we hope our book can make your very personal race to complete your megamission a bit more understand-able, productive, and fun.

NOTES

[1]Robert Jastrow, *God and the Astronomers* (New York: W. W. Norton, 1978), p. 28.

[2]*Ibid.*, p. 116.

[3]C. S. Lewis, *The Abolition of Man* (New York: Macmillan, 1955), p. 87–88 (*Italics added*).

[4]Peter Kreeft, *Back to Virtue* (San Francisco: Ignatius Press, 1992), p. 22.

[5]*Ibid.*

[6]St. Paul, 1 Corinthians 2:9.

[7]Blaise Pascal, *Pensees*, trans. Krailsheimer (Baltimore: Penguin, 1966), pp. 157–159.

[8]Kreeft, pp. 74–76.

[9]Erik H. Erikson, *Childhood and Society* (New York: W.W. Norton, 1963).

[10]Daniel J. Levinson *et al.*, *The Seasons of a Man's Life* (New York: Alfred A. Knopf, 1978).

[11]Daniel J. Levinson in collaboration with Judy D. Levinson, *The Seasons of a Woman's Life* (New York: Alfred A. Knopf, 1996).

[12]V. A. Punzo, *After Kohlberg: Virtue, Ethics and the Recovery of the Moral Self* (*Philosophical Psychology*, Volume 9, Number 1, 1996). p. 7.

[13]Selma Kramer, Salman Akhtar, Alan, Sugerman, *Mahler and Kohut: Perspectives on Development, Psychotherapy, and Technique* (*Journal of the American Psychoanalytic Association*, Volume 44, Number 1, 1996), p. 334.

[14]James W. Fowler, *Stages of Faith: The Psychology of Human Development and the Quest for Meaning* (New York: Harper & Row, 1981).

[15]Fr. Benedict J. Groeschel, C.F.R., *Spiritual Passages* (New York: The Crossroad Publishing Co., 1992).

[16]We would highly recommend both Fowler's book, *Stages of Faith*, and Fr. Benedict Groeschel's book, *Spiritual Passages*, to anyone interested in paying more attention to his/her own spiritual development.

[17]Robert Graves, "In Broken Images," from *Collected Poems* (Garden City: Doubleday & Co. Inc., 1961), p. 104.

[18]Figure 3 is a modified and expanded version of a values list used in Mr. Weiler's earlier book, *Reality and Career Planning*, and in the workshops derived from that book.

[19]Kreeft, pp. 28–29.

[20]*Ibid.*, p. 79.

[21]The concept of these three polarities was originally developed by Dr. Daniel J. Levinson, coauthor of both *The Seasons of a Man's Life* and *The Seasons of a Woman's Life*. While our descriptions of these polarities are not direct quotes from Levinson, we based our writing of them on insight gained in personal conversations with Levinson over a period of years.

[22]John Henry Newman, *Meditations and Devotions* (Westhampstead, Hertfordshire: Anthony Clarke Books), pp. 6–7.

[23]The description of "emptiness" and most of the words elaborating on the "emptiness" concept in this paragraph are paraphrases of a similar description in the workbook for the Foundation for Community Encouragement's "Leadership Education Program." Copyright © 1995, The Foundation for Community Encouragement. Used by permission.

[24]Excerpted from the Foundation for Community Encouragement's "Leadership Education Program" workbook, Spokane, Wash, 1995. Copyright © 1995, The Foundation for Community Encouragement, Box 17210, Seattle, Wash. 98107–0910.

[25]Excerpt from "Emptiness" competency behavioral descriptions developed in consultation with M. Scott Peck, M.D., and Mary Ann Schmidt, president of the Foundation for Community Encouragement, in 1995.

[26]Developed in consultation with Mary Ann Schmidt, president of the Foundation for Community Encouragement, in 1995.

[27]St. Paul, 2 Timothy 4:6–7, *New Jerusalem Bible* (New York: Doubleday, 1985), p. 1968.

[28]St. Paul, 2 Timothy 4:8, *New American Bible* (Iowa Falls, Ia: World Bible Publishers, Inc.), p. 1316.

[29]Jastrow, p. 28.

[30]Kreeft, p. 156.

[31]*Ibid.*, p. 15.

[32]The different types and stages of love have been a recurring theme in philosophical and theological writing since Plato. As with the life stages, some cite more categories and use different adjectives to name them, but there tends to be good agreement on general themes and the direction growth takes as we progress. For simplicity's sake, we give very brief descriptions of only three love stages here.

[33]Benedict J. Groeschel, C.F.R., paraphrasing comments written by Archbishop Alban Goodier in *The School of Love* (St. Meinrad, Ind: Grail Publications, 1947), pp. 12–13.

[34]Matthew 25:34–37, *Good News New Testament* (New York: American Bible Society, 1992), p. 51.

[35]Newman, pp. 6–7.

[36]*Ibid.*

[37]Reinhold Niebuhr commentary, *Christianity and Society Journal*, Volume 76, p. 4.

SELECT BIBLIOGRAPHY

Listing every book that contributed to our thinking would produce a bibliography too lengthy for most readers to find useful. Instead, we are presenting a relatively short selected bibliography. We hope this will provide a practical starting point for further exploration of the subjects we have covered.

Some of the authors mentioned below have written numerous other excellent books in addition to those listed here. For the contemporary reader, we would particularly recommend further reading of various other books by authors Erikson, Groeschel, Lewis, Levinson, and Peck.

Erikson, Erik H., *Childhood and Society*, New York: W.W. Norton, 1963.

Fowler, James W., *Stages of Faith: The Psychology of Human Development and the Quest for Meaning*, New York: Harper & Row, 1981.

Frankl, Viktor E., *Man's Search for Meaning*, New York: Pocket Books, a division of Simon & Schuster, 1984.

Groeschel, Benedict J., C.F.R., *Spiritual Passages*, New York: The Crossroad Publishing Co., 1992.

Jastrow, Robert, *God and the Astronomers*, New York: W.W. Norton, 1978.

Kreeft, Peter, *Back to Virtue*, San Francisco: Ignatius Press, 1992.

Lecomte du Nouy, *Human Destiny*, New York: Mentor Books, 1958.

Levinson, Daniel J., et al, *The Seasons of a Man's Life*, New York: Alfred A. Knopf, 1978.

Levinson, Daniel J., with Levinson, Judy D., *The Seasons of a Woman's Life*, New York: Alfred A. Knopf, 1996.

Lewis, C.S., *The Four Loves*, San Diego: Harcourt Brace Jovanovich, 1960.

Lewis, C.S., *Mere Christianity*, New York: MacMillan Publishing Co., 1960.

Newman, John Henry, *The Heart of Newman, a Synthesis*, arranged by Erich Pryzwara, S.J., San Francisco: Ignatius Press, 1997.

Pascal, Blaise, *Pensees*, trans. Krailsheimer, Baltimore: Penguin, 1966.

Peck, M. Scott, M.D., *The Different Drum*, New York: Simon and Schuster, 1987.

Peck, M. Scott, M.D., *The Road Less Traveled*, New York: Simon and Schuster, 1978.

Index

YOUR SOUL AT WORK

Five Steps to a More Fulfilling Career and Life

CAREER AND LIFE WORKBOOK

By
Nicholas W. Weiler
In collaboration with
Stephen C. Schoonover, M.D.

When you have finished reading *Your Soul at Work*, we suggest you use this workbook to develop your own individual career and life plan. This is what people do in our workshops.

The workbook is designed to help you personalize lessons learned from the research and techniques presented throughout the text. It contains a series of exercises and self-assessment forms you can use to establish your own personal criteria for success, identify what career path will best meet your criteria, and create a practical action strategy to achieve the goals you define along that path.

As time passes, we suggest you review your workbook entries periodically to track your progress and assess how your values and goals may be evolving as you progress through each life stage.

The workbook leads you step-by-step through the completion of each task in the *Taking Charge Process* shown on the next page.

In addition, the workbook contains two appendices. **Appendix A** contains a self-assessment form and exercise you can use to determine what developmental experiences you might need for various leadership roles (if any) you want to pursue. **Appendix B** contains the complete Investigative Interview form and instructions.

TAKING CHARGE PROCESS

Finding Your Calling

1. Determining Your True Life Values
2. Tracking Your Life Stage Progression
3. Deciding What You Want to Do
4. Establishing Your Personal Criteria for Success
5. Identifying Potential Career Paths
6. Conducting Investigative Interviews
7. Choosing the Right Career Path
8. Identifying Strengths and Weaknesses

Making It Happen

9. Enriching Your Current Job
10. Marketing Yourself for Future Jobs
11. Overcoming Predictable Barriers
12. Communicating with a New Awareness

DETERMINING YOUR TRUE LIFE VALUES

Before you do this exercise sit quietly and get in touch with your thought processes. Monitor any voices in your head from other people (*e.g.*, society, the media, peers, teachers, your organization) telling you what to value. Tune them out. Then listen to your own inner voice. Doing this exercise may force you to make trade-offs you've been avoiding. That may be temporarily uncomfortable but it can also bring enormous progress.

Start with the list of sample life values on the next two pages. If you have some important personal values you don't find on the list add them in. For this exercise, forget the practicalities of earning a living. Get in touch with what you *really* want, whether or not it seems immediately practical. As we become more aware of our inner selves, we often develop new insight. That helps us develop creative options we didn't see before. Our possibilities expand.

You may find it helpful to get someone else (a partner or friend) to do this exercise with you. Discussing our choices with someone else sometimes helps to clarify our thinking. In our workshops, we have participants share in groups of four, comparing notes and discussing their reasons after each card drop. However, we stress that they should make no attempts to influence each other's preferences. Instead, we tell them to empty themselves of any group or organizational norms and concentrate on their individual preferences.

- **Friendship**   To work with people I respect and to be respected by them.

- **Location**   To be able to live where I want to live.

- **Enjoyment**   To enjoy my work. To have fun doing it.

- **Loyalty**   To be committed to the goals of a group of people who share my beliefs, values, and ethical principles.

- **Family**   To have time with my family.

- **Leadership**   To motivate and energize other people. To feel responsible for identifying and accomplishing needed group tasks.

- **Personal Development**   To learn and to do challenging work that will help me grow, that will allow me to utilize my best talents and mature as a human being.

- **Security**   To have a steady income that fully meets my family's basic needs.

- **Wisdom**   To grow in understanding of myself, my personal calling, and life's real purpose. To grow in knowledge and practice my religious beliefs. To discern and do the will of God and find lasting meaning in what I do.

- **Community**   To be deeply involved with a group that has a larger purpose beyond one's self. To perform in effective and caring teamwork.

- **Wealth**   To earn a great deal of money (*i.e.*, well beyond my family's basic needs). To be financially independent.

- **Expertness**   To become a known and respected authority in what I do.

- **Service**   To contribute to the well-being and satisfaction of others. To help people who need help and improve society.

- **Personal Accomplishment**   To achieve significant goals. To be involved in undertakings I believe personally are significant—whether or not they bring me recognition from others.

- **Prestige**   To be seen by others as successful. To become well-known. To obtain recognition and status in my chosen field.

- **Power**   To have the authority to approve or disapprove proposed courses of action. To make assignments and control allocation of people and resources.

- **Independence**   To have freedom of thought and action. To be able to act in terms of my own time schedules and priorities.

- **Integrity**   To live and work in compliance with my personal moral standards. To be honest and acknowledge/stand up for my personal beliefs.

- **Health**   To be physically and mentally fit.

- **Creativity**   To be innovative. To create new and better ways of doing things.

-

-

-

LIFE VALUES

Get some blank 3 by 5-inch cards or small pieces of paper. Write each of the 20 values listed on the previous two pages on a separate card. If there are other important values you added, make cards for them too. However, to start with we suggest no more than 25.

Step 1
Lay the cards out in front of you and look at them. Assume your situation is such that you have to give up 5 of these values. Which would they be? Drop them out.

Step 2
Look at the 5 cards you dropped. Who really dropped them? Was it your inner voice or were they dropped by someone else (*e.g.*, your parents, boss, peers, or organization)? If necessary, change what you dropped to make certain they reflect only you. Then rank order them (*i.e.*, lowest ranked is the one you'd be most willing to give up).

Step 3
Drop 2 more cards (or more if you added values). Get down to 13.

Step 4
Drop 2 more cards. Get down to 11. If you're doing this with other people tell them your reasons. Hear their reasons for what cards they dropped but remember it's OK if you are dropping different cards. You may be at very different points in your life stage progression.

Step 5

Drop 2 more cards. Get down to 9. By now it should be getting more difficult to choose. Discuss what you dropped or, if you are doing this alone, think about the reasons.

Step 6

Drop 2 more cards to get down to 7. At this point you probably don't want to give up a single other value.

Step 7

Drop 2 more cards. Stop at 5. Then look at your final 5 cards. Rank order them. Think about why you kept these particular values. What do they mean to you? Change cards if this gives you new insight.

Step 8

Capture this snapshot in time. Record your values in the space provided on the next page. List them in rank order according to how you dropped them (*i.e.*, number 1 becomes the value you dropped *last* and would be least willing to give up and number 20 becomes the value you'd be *most* willing to give up). Then look at your list. Any surprises? Think about your final ranking for a while.

Step 9

Consider your behavior today versus the ideal values you have just ranked the highest. Are you achieving your most important values? If not, why not? This is data you need to be aware of if you want to develop more productive career strategies.

LIFE VALUES RANKING

From #1 *(least willing to give up)* **to #20** *(most willing to give up)*

Top 5 Life Values

1. _____
2. _____
3. _____
4. _____
5. _____

Other Life Values

6. _____
7. _____
8. _____
9. _____
10. _____
11. _____
12. _____
13. _____
14. _____
15. _____
16. _____
17. _____
18. _____
19. _____
20. _____

If you added other values, also list them wherever you put them in the above rank ordering.

TRACKING YOUR LIFE STAGE PROGRESSION

As you prioritize your life values it's a good idea to consider where you are today in your progression through the life stages. What stages have you passed through and which do you face next? How does this influence your thinking and feelings about your work and life today—and about your choice of life values to focus on at this point in time? The exercise below will help you make this assessment.

Before you do this exercise, you might want to do a brief review of the narrative life stage descriptions beginning on page 85 of the *Your Soul at Work* text. Also, remember that the ages shown for each stage are only rough estimates. An individual may pass through the stages several years earlier or later than the estimates shown.

LIFE STAGES

Read down each column under the categories listed across the top of the ***Adult Life Stages*** chart on the following two pages (Key Issues, Self-image, Relationships, etc). Using an erasable pencil, put a check mark (✔) in the box under each column that best defines where you think you are today. It may not be a perfect fit, but pick the one that comes closest. Then look at the boxes above the one you checked and put a question mark (?) in any you feel may still need some attention.

Look at what you've done. What does this tell you? What impact might it have on the life values you've ranked as most important to you right now? How might your priorities be changing if you are currently in a transition between stages? Come back and look at this again after you complete the other exercises in this workbook.

ADULT LIFE STAGES

Stage	Key Issues	Self-image
Autonomy and Tentative Choices **(18–26)**	Autonomy vs. Dependence, Tentative vs. Lasting Choices	Developing sense of personhood as separate from parents and child-hood peer groups
Young Adult Transition **(27–31)**	Turmoil vs. Certainty, Settling Down vs. Keeping Things Open	Questioning sense of self and who/what we want to become
Making Commitments **(32–40)**	Master vs. Apprentice, Permanent vs. Tentative Choices	Firming up/establishing a more permanent sense of self and who/what we want to become
Mid-Life Transition **(41–48)**	Resolving Key Polarities—Immortality vs. Mortality, Constructive vs. Destructive, Nurturing vs. Aggressive	Reexamining realities of projected ego and image vs. true self and struggling to define/accept true self
Leaving a Legacy **(49–65)**	Contribution vs. Personal Benefit, Other vs. Self-Centered, Social vs. Independent Accomplishments	Letting go of earlier inaccurate ego images and accepting oneself as a worthwhile being with weaknesses as well as strengths
Spiritual Denouement **(66 and Beyond)**	Hope vs. Despair, Survival of Spirit vs. Mortality, Surrender vs. Control	Accepting self as dependent on a wisdom greater than one's own, recognizing that wisdom as benev-olent, and submitting one's self and life to that wisdom's will

Goal Focus	Relationships	Community
Defining self as an individual and establishing an initial lifestyle	Testing out new relationships (*e.g.*, love interests, peer groups, and friends)	Realigning focus from family of origin to new peers and groups
Reassessing initial lifestyle and making more permanent choices/ commitments	Sorting out and deciding which relationships will become more permanent	Rethinking and evaluating commitments and connections
Deciding a life direction and defining/ aggressively pursuing a dream of what we want to accomplish in life	Making more permanent commitments to love relationships, friends, and peers	Establishing more permanent connections and community ties/ responsibilities
Questioning the dream whether or not it was achieved and developing a more mature sense of what is really important	Recognizing/ acknowledging one's own negative, as well as positive, impact on relationships and correcting course for deeper, more authentic connections	Disengaging from group and cultural pressures/norms to reevaluate and restructure priorities
Making the best of the time one has left to help others and leave a positive legacy	Settling into more realistic and rewarding relationships based on recognizing/forgiving each other's imperfections as human and helping each other grow	Re-engagement on a deeper, more objective, less driven, and more productive level with family, friends, and society
Tying things up and completing the development of the person/spiritual being we want to become	Accepting others and recognizing/respecting humankind's diversity as part of a greater wisdom's plan	Recognizing that life is only part of a larger, more enduring spiritual community and helping others understand that

You recorded your *current* life value priorities on page 10. Now look at these same values from the perspective of a different point in time by doing the following exercise.

LONGER-TERM LIFE VALUES

Considering the Adult Life Stages chart you just reviewed (and the more detailed life stage descriptions beginning on page 85 in the *Your Soul at Work* text), look ahead to your retirement.

From that vantage point, what *top 5 values* do you think you will want to look back on and feel you have achieved in your life? Record these in the space below.

Top 5 Values
(Looking back from retirement)

1. _____

2. _____

3. _____

4. _____

5. _____

These may or may not be the same as your top 5 current values. If they are different, that may just be a question of where you are now on the life stage growth curve. When you really do retire, your growth through the life stages between now and then will probably have given you new insight you don't have now.

DECIDING WHAT YOU WANT TO DO

To decide what you want to do in the future (*i.e.*, what type of skills or competencies you want to exercise and grow on the job), it helps to look at what activities have been most satisfying for you in the past.

PEAK ACCOMPLISHMENTS

You can start to determine this by looking at your past peak accomplishments that are defined in the *Your Soul at Work* text as follows:

> A *peak accomplishment* is something you personally enjoyed doing and found highly satisfying whether or not others (*e.g.*, bosses, peers, mentors, teachers) recognized and rewarded the accomplishment as significant. It energized you, made you feel good, and had real meaning for you.

Your peak accomplishments may or may not have anything to do with your current field of work. They may have been in school, in athletic or artistic endeavors, in social activities, in community or local volunteer government work, in crafts or in other part-time hobbies.

Complete the following exercise to identify your own top peak accomplishments.

PEAK ACCOMPLISHMENTS

Think about and identify your own top 5 peak accomplishments to date. Again, as you do this be sure your list represents you. Identify any intruding voices (organizations, mentors, media, peers, or others). For now factor them out.

Then record the details of your 5 peak accomplishments in the space provided on the ***left*** side of the following form. At this point don't write anything on the right side of the form. You'll complete the right side in a later exercise.

PEAK ACCOMPLISHMENTS...
...AND PREFERRED COMPETENCIES

YOUR PEAK ACCOMPLISHMENTS (Describe in some detail. What happened? Who was involved? What did you do?)	YOUR PREFERRED COMPETENCIES (List skills used in each accomplishment. It doesn't matter if you repeat some of the same skills on more than one accomplishment.)
1.	
2.	

PEAK ACCOMPLISHMENTS...
...AND PREFERRED COMPETENCIES *(continued)*

YOUR PEAK ACCOMPLISHMENTS	YOUR PREFERRED COMPETENCIES
3.	
4.	
5.	

PREFERRED COMPETENCIES

Determining what you did to achieve *each* of your top 5 peak accomplishments can help you identify the type of competencies or skills you most enjoy exercising and want to grow in the future. These are your preferred competencies, which are defined as follows in the *Soul* text:

A *preferred competency* is a set of behaviors or skills you enjoy exercising and want to develop or grow further in the future. It can also be something you want to learn in the future.

It's important to identify which competencies you used *in each of* your top peak accomplishments. This way you are less likely to overlook some important ones you used in only one accomplishment and not the others.

Complete the following exercise to identify what types of competencies you prefer to exercise and grow in the future.

PREFERRED COMPETENCIES

EXERCISE

Review the 5 peak accomplishments you listed on the *left* side of the form on pages 16 and 17.

Think about the types of competencies you exercised on *each*. Make a complete list of these on the ***right side*** of each accomplishment. If this gets repetitive (*i.e.*, you find yourself listing similar competencies for more than one of the accomplishments), that's OK. This is the pattern you are looking for.

There may be some important competencies you want to develop in the future that aren't related to your list of peak accomplishments. These might include competencies you've already mastered and new competencies you want to learn. Add these to the bottom of the form.

ESTABLISHING YOUR PERSONAL CRITERIA FOR SUCCESS

The *combination* of the top *life values* you want to achieve plus your most important *preferred competencies* becomes your own unique set of **personal criteria for future success**. Complete the following exercise to record these criteria for use in identifying possible future career paths that might meet them.

PERSONAL CRITERIA FOR SUCCESS

Top 5 Life Values
(As listed on page 10)

1. _____

2. _____

3. _____   → **Personal Criteria for Success**

4. _____

5. _____

Preferred Competencies
(Consolidated from pages 16 and 17)

• _____   • _____

• _____   • _____

• _____   • _____

• _____   • _____

• _____   • _____

IDENTIFYING POTENTIAL CAREER PATHS

REDUCING THE SMORGASBORD TO A PRACTICAL SIZE

With clearly defined success criteria you can now narrow down the smorgasbord of career possibilities to a manageable few. In the following exercise, you make some focused best guesses (*i.e.*, hypotheses) about which career paths might best allow you to achieve as many as possible of the personal criteria for success you listed on the previous page.

FUTURE JOB HYPOTHESES BRAINSTORMING

Brainstorm future positions 5 to 10 years from now, which you think might best meet the personal criteria for success you recorded on page 20. List them in the space provided below. At this point be creative, open to many possibilities. List as many options as you can. Don't feel you have to restrict your ideas to any one profession, organization, or career path. At this point, you might also want to ask selected other people some very focused questions about what career paths they think might meet your criteria.

Be as specific as you can. What do you feel might be the job title, type of organization (*if any*), and geographical location for each possibility listed?

FUTURE JOB HYPOTHESES *(Brainstorming List)*

* _____
* _____
* _____
* _____
* _____

* _____
* _____
* _____
* _____
* _____

CONSOLIDATION

Just as you did with your preferred competencies, now use the following exercise to look for duplications or overlaps and consolidate.

FUTURE JOB HYPOTHESES CONSOLIDATION

Look at the future positions you have hypothesized. Are they each unique and separate, or are there overlaps? Do some naturally fall together into allied constellations of jobs that are similar or have much in common?

Purify your list. Eliminate any obvious duplications (*i.e.*, different titles but the same or very similar jobs).

Now organize your list. Look for patterns (*i.e.*, groupings of similar jobs). See if any of the possibilities you listed can be combined. Also think in terms of which possibilities are most appealing to you (*i.e.*, most likely to meet your success criteria).

List **your 3 to 5 top options** (*i.e.*, your best guess on which possibilities have the highest probability of meeting your criteria) in the space provided below. These may be creative combinations of 2 or more related possibilities from your brainstorming list.

FUTURE JOB HYPOTHESES *(Consolidated List)*

• _____

• _____

• _____

• _____

• _____

CONDUCTING INVESTIGATIVE INTERVIEWS

The next task is to conduct Investigative Interviews. You collect information to determine if the career path(s) you've hypothesized really do meet your success criteria. Even if you're not contemplating any near-term career changes we suggest you think about the longer-range future and complete the following exercise.

INVESTIGATIVE INTERVIEWS PLANNING

In the space below, list the 3 people you might like to contact first for Investigative Interviews to start networking and researching the longer-range future career path(s) you now think might be most interesting to you. Also write down anyone you'd like to join you in any team interviews.

Just enter types of positions/functions if you don't know specific names of people in the jobs you want to investigate. This entry is just to make you start thinking.

INVESTIGATIVE INTERVIEW POSSIBILITIES

- _____
  (Date to initiate contact _____)

- _____
  (Date to initiate contact _____)

- _____
  (Date to initiate contact _____)

List the names of any colleagues or friends you think might like to join you in conducting team interviews with any of the above individuals.

- _____

- _____

- _____

CHOOSING THE RIGHT CAREER PATH

This is another important task. However, ***do not complete this task at this point in this workbook***. You complete this task only *after* you have completed the rest of this workbook and *after* you have finished your Investigative Interviews. We've placed this task here in the workbook just to remind you how it fits into the *Taking Charge Process*.

On this task you look at the information you've collected in Investigative Interviews and do a matching analysis. You decide how well the careers of the people you interviewed do or do not match your personal criteria for success. You rate each career path you considered on a scale of 1 to 10 based on how many of your high priority life values it will allow you to achieve and how much it will allow you to exercise/grow your preferred competencies.

Code each career path you investigated with a letter (*e.g.*, A, B, C). Then write each letter on the scale below at the point where you rate the career path it represents.

1	2	3	4	5	6	7	8	9	10

Not Interested   **Very Interested**

Different people may interpret the numbers differently but you will probably have a range of ratings with some career paths rated much higher than others. You look at the different career paths you've rated and pick those you've decided have the very highest probability of meeting your criteria. Hopefully, only 1 or 2 will stand out above the rest. Then you list these below.

Career Paths Most Likely to Meet Your Personal Criteria for Success

• _____

• _____

• _____

Remember, go on to the next task and complete the rest of this workbook, *before* you use the form in Appendix B to conduct any Investigative Interviews or attempt any matching analysis on your own.

IDENTIFYING STRENGTHS AND WEAKNESSES

You don't have to rely solely on information gathered in your own Investigative Interviews to identify your most important personal competency growth needs. To supplement your own interview findings, our research has identified 12 *core* competencies that are critical for successful performance in nearly all career specialties.

Use the following exercise to self-assess your current strengths and growth needs on these 12 core competencies and on the observable behaviors that demonstrate each competency.

CORE COMPETENCY SELF-ASSESSMENT

Complete the following *Core Competency Self-assessment Form*. Do a relatively quick run through. Trust your intuition and don't agonize over the details.

Next look for patterns and check (✔) your top 3 to 5 overall *competency* improvement needs based on two criteria—your *rating scores* and your perception of *importance* or immediate need in your present job or preferred career path.

Then go to the next level of specificity. Look at the *observable behaviors* listed under each competency. Check (✔) your top 3 to 5 *observable behavior* improvement needs based on your *rating scores* and perception of *importance* or immediate need. These may or may not be behaviors associated with your top competency improvement needs. It's OK if they fall under different competencies.

In the right-hand column write a few examples or evidence of why you need to improve these specific behaviors.

Then record your results in the space provided on page 33.

CORE COMPETENCY SELF-ASSESSMENT FORM

Key Competencies Enter the number indicating your current level of accomplishment on the line next to each behavior below. *Rating Scale*   0   1 | | | | 5
NA   Very Poor   Excellent

Average Score Sum of scores divided by number of behaviors actually displayed

Check Importance for Success

Comment on pertinent facts and critical incidents that show:
- Key Strengths (*i.e.*, behaviors often displayed)
- Important development needs (*i.e.*, behaviors seldom displayed)

PERSONAL

1. Continuous Learning Competency
- Proactively defines and pursues personal development goals (*e.g.*, identifies and addresses development needs; negotiates growth assignments). _____
- Uses lessons learned from both positive and negative experiences to improve performance and effectiveness. _____
- Continually looks for new and/or nontraditional ideas and approaches to improve personal and team effectiveness. _____
- Identifies appropriate role models and adopts the effective behaviors and techniques they exhibit. _____
- Seeks and applies new information and concepts quickly. _____

Average _____   Importance _____

2. Initiative and Risk-taking Competency
- Proactively anticipates events well in advance of action to ensure a successful outcome. _____
- Actively explores with others the advantages and disadvantages of a course of action. _____
- Takes calculated business and technical risks when appropriate. _____
- Seeks responsibilities that add value beyond the normal scope of the job. _____
- Formulates and follows through on goals and work plans that support organizational objectives. _____
- Makes effective decisions based on limited information when appropriate. _____

Average _____   Importance _____

3. Honesty and Integrity Competency
• Acts with integrity in business transactions.____
• Builds trust with co-workers across organizational and functional boundaries. ____
• Ensures that individual and team actions build the organization reputation for excellent business practices or missions (*i.e.*, appropriately subordinates individual goals to those of the larger organization). ____

Average ____ Importance ____

4. Flexibility Competency
• Works cooperatively and capably with a wide variety of people.   ____
• Shifts focus smoothly and quickly among activities.   ____

Average ____ Importance ____

5. Self-confidence Competency
• Demonstrates a strong, but realistic belief in own capabilities.   ____
• Displays authority and self-assurance when dealing with people at all organizational levels.   ____
• Demonstrates a sense of urgency and a positive *can do* attitude.   ____
• Takes personal responsibility for mistakes or omissions.   ____
• Personally models desired values, behaviors, and work practices for workers.   ____
• Seeks constructive feedback and responds to it as a challenge and opportunity to improve.   ____

Average ____ Importance ____

TEAM

6. Judgment and Problem-solving Competency

• Selects the right activities or issues to work on from a range of competing alternatives. _____

• Approaches situations and issues in an informed and structured manner (*e.g.*, reduces problems into manageable parts). _____

• Utilizes key sources of expertise and information within and outside the organization (*i.e.*, knows when and how to seek help). _____

• Manages multiple tasks in an efficient and effective manner. _____   Average _____   Importance _____

7. Teamwork Competency

• Contributes to a team environment that balances individual initiative and team accomplishments. _____

• Collaboratively develops and tracks team mission, goals, and plans with team members. _____

• Actively promotes teamwork and information sharing across organizational boundaries to improve team performance. _____

• Shares success with team members. _____

• Supports decision-making and accountability at all levels of the organization. _____

• Supports experimentation and prudent risk-taking in self and others. _____   Average _____   Importance _____

Key Competencies Enter the number indicating your current level of accomplishment on the line next to each behavior below. *Rating Scale*

	0	1 _|_|_|_|_ 5
	NA	Very Poor Excellent

Average Score Sum of scores divided by number of behaviors actually displayed
Check Importance for Success
Comment on pertinent facts and critical incidents that show:
- Key Strengths (*i.e.*, behaviors often displayed)
- Important development needs (*i.e.*, behaviors seldom displayed)

---

8. Creativity/Innovation/Change Competency
- Introduces new ways of thinking and behaving; encourages innovation and exploration of nontraditional ideas from team members. ____
- Quickly applies new ideas and technologies to adapt to changing work demands. ____
- Continuously seeks out and shares best practices. ____

Average ____   Importance ____

9. Communication and Influence Competency
- Actively solicits inputs from others to clarify key issues and potential actions before acting. ____
- Takes action to help ensure that key strategies, goals, and plans are understood by all team members. ____
- Provides important information quickly and accurately to internal and external customers. ____
- Acknowledges and addresses problems and issues in an honest, up-front, nonjudgmental manner. ____
- Understands and responds appropriately to the underlying (often unexpressed) motivations, values, and concerns of others. ____

Average ____   Importance ____

OPERATIONAL

10. Responsiveness to Internal/External Customer Competency
- Clarifies customer requirements and develops approaches to address them. ____
- Continuously clarifies customers' evolving goals, strategies, and concerns to maintain responsiveness. ____
- Looks for ways to add value for the customer by improving his/her processes. ____
- Generates customer confidence that their needs are given the highest priority. ____

Average ____   Importance ____

Key Competencies Enter the number indicating your current level of accomplishment on the line next to each behavior below. *Rating Scale*   0   1 | | | | 5
                                                                NA   Very Poor   Excellent

Average Score Sum of scores divided by number of behaviors actually displayed
Check Importance for Success
Comment on pertinent facts and critical incidents that show:
- Key Strengths (*i.e.*, behaviors often displayed)
- Important development needs (*i.e.*, behaviors seldom displayed)

11. Planning and Organizing Competency
- Develops and applies criteria for prioritizing changing tasks. _____
- Accurately assesses scope of effort and time required for completion of tasks. _____
- Develops well-thought-out plans that include work breakdown structure and timeline. _____
- Tracks and revises project plans and milestones as required to achieve goals. _____   Average _____   Importance _____

12. Quality Results-orientation Competency
- Relentlessly identifies and eliminates unnecessary work and all nonvalue-added activities. _____
- Seeks out cause/effect relationships of key work processes and addresses root problems wherever they exist. _____
- Analyzes costs and benefits of various work alternatives and recommends/ selects best alternative. _____
- Meets commitments with minimal supervision while being responsive to organizational needs and time frames. _____
- Performs all tasks and achieves results in an accurate and timely manner. _____
- Continuously develops and improves key work processes; develops better, faster, more efficient ways of doing things. _____   Average _____   Importance _____

CORE COMPETENCIES
(Rank ordered in terms of your current proficiency scores)

When you've finished assessing your core competency strengths and weaknesses, rank order the competencies in terms of your current proficiency scores. Your greatest competency strength will be #1 and your weakest (*i.e.*, greatest current competency improvement need) will be #12. Record your rank ordering in the space below. Then check (✓) your ***top 3 to 5*** current competency ***improvement needs*** (based on both your scores and your immediate need in your present job).

CURRENT PROFICIENCY RANKING

Top 3

1. _____

2. _____

3. _____

Middle

4. _____

5. _____

6. _____

7. _____

8. _____

9. _____

Bottom 3

10. _____

11. _____

12. _____

TOP OBSERVABLE BEHAVIOR
IMPROVEMENT NEEDS

Look at the observable behaviors listed under each competency on the Core Competency Self-assessment Form. These are the behaviors that demonstrate each competency. Select the 3 observable behaviors that you consider to be your greatest current weaknesses (*i.e.*, those you most want to strengthen and improve further), either because you *rated them low* or because you believe they are *critical* for success in your current job or preferred future career path.

Record these 3 behaviors below:

• _____

• _____

• _____

LEADERSHIP ROLES
AND COMPETENCIES

The next few pages provide additional detail on the leadership roles mentioned in the *Soul* text. These pages can help you decide what, **if any**, type of leadership role you may aspire to. The accompanying self-assessment forms can help you identify your current competency strengths and future growth needs for whatever role you might choose.

LEADERSHIP ROLES

The research showed there are four generic roles that leaders passed through as they moved from team member (*i.e.*, individual contributor) positions to increasingly more demanding levels of ad-hoc leadership and/or administrative managerial responsibilities. As summarized in the *Your Soul at Work* text, these are:

Team Member—(Individual Contributor)

Focuses on individual task completion and demonstration of personal competence. Typically a technical or functional contributor (*e.g.*, engineering designer, financial specialist, creative artist, or salesperson).

Team Leader—(Coach)

Focuses on facilitating and coaching work done by others. Usually responsible for the completion of single team projects within limited time frames. Typical examples would be a front-line supervisor in manufacturing or perhaps a nonmanagerial ad-hoc special project leader.

Mid-level Manager—(Multiple Team Integrator)

Focuses on formal or informal leadership of multiple teams. Usually coordinates and allocates significant resources and is responsible for generating effective collaboration among diverse teams. Typical examples would be a plant manager or a multiproject facilitator (managerial or nonmanagerial).

Executive—(Strategist)

Focuses primarily on whole business organization strategies. Must maintain perspective on markets and customers; and is future and long-term oriented. Usually a significant, large-scale managerial position. Typical examples would be a top functional leader (*e.g.*, engineering, manufacturing, or human resources) or a general manager of a business.

In addition to the *core* competencies, the leadership roles require some shifts in emphasis and some supplemental *leadership* competencies that are different for each progressive role.

Many decide, very appropriately, that they don't want to be distracted from the individual technical or creative work they love most. Taking on additional leadership responsibilities would not constitute success for them (*i.e.*, would fail to meet their personal criteria for success). In today's flatter organizations, many remain in team member roles not only because flatter hierarchies offer fewer opportunities, but also because they feel the addition of administrative managerial responsibilities would detract from other values they consider more important. The brief descriptions and exercises in the next few pages may help you decide what's right for you.

The following are the additional competencies our research showed are required for each different leadership role. Details of the observable behaviors required to demonstrate these competencies are presented later in the self-assessment form.

ALL LEADERSHIP LEVELS

There are two competencies required across all leadership *roles beyond team member.* These are:

- **Performance Management**

- **Strategic Thinking**

TEAM LEADER—(Coach)

Some competencies required for success as a team member have to be modified or given less emphasis to avoid failure in a team leader role. For example, one of the critical shifts in becoming a team leader is to focus less on personal task completion and shift more attention to managing and motivating others to complete tasks. If you aspire to this role, the following two additional competencies are required.

- **Project and Process Management**

- **Team Leadership and Development**

MID-LEVEL MANAGER—(Multiple Team Integrator)

People who want to move into the next mid-level manager role have to modify or suppress some competencies required for team leadership and master other new competencies. For example, as they take on responsibility for integrating activities across multiple teams, they have to suppress some of their previous *hands-on* management techniques. They have to add a range of new skills including coordination of multiple projects, and resource acquisition/management. They also have to develop significantly greater capabilities around network building and influencing constituencies across organizational boundaries. The following new competencies must be developed for success in this role.

- **Resource Management**

- **Cross-team Integration**

EXECUTIVE—(Strategist)

The much smaller group of individuals who have the desire and values priorities that drive them to top leadership jobs in organizations must again change the way they allocate their time. They typically have to suppress their former strong emphasis on detailed day-to-day leadership. Instead, they have to focus on more future-oriented, less easily defined issues such as defining, articulating, and relentlessly pursuing a longer-range vision and strategy. They have to work on motivating the entire work force in a continuously changing environment and on driving the organization through major transformation and change initiatives (often unpopular and difficult to communicate). Two new competencies are of particular importance here.

- **Visioning and Alignment**

- **Strategic Planning**

The next exercise will help you determine what role you are currently performing and which (if any) you aspire to next.

ROLE DETERMINATION EXERCISE

The following form describes 4 roles, which differ in scope, time span, focus, and responsibility level.

Circle the role that best describes you in your current position and which role (if any) you aspire to next.

In determining your current role, consider what you spend 80% of your time doing. While you may spend small amounts of your time doing work associated with almost any role, focusing on where you spend 80% of your time will give you a more accurate fix on the role you currently hold.

ROLE DETERMINATION FORM

Role Definition	Scope
Team Member—(Individual Contributor) • Completes technical tasks or small projects • Primarily works in a self-directed setting, fulfilling goals and strategies of others	Single Subfunctional
Team Leader—(Coach) • Directs the activities of a small team • Either formally manages or coaches the activities of individual contributors • Uses significant levels of influence and collaboration with internal customers • Manages significant project activities and budgets	Single and Multiple Subfunctional/ Functional
Mid-level Manager— (Multiple Team Integrator) • Orchestrates the activities of several teams • Manages significant numbers of people and substantive financial resources • Integrates actively with internal customers that affect business strategies, practices, and processes	Community Relationships, Cross-functional Integration
Executive—(Strategist) • Sets the vision and direction for the function • Motivates the entire team • Delegates authority for major initiatives, but mentors and sponsors key activities of Mid-level Managers/Multiple Team Integrators • Champions significant initiatives with high business impact visibility	External Alliances, Cross-functional Integration

Time Span of Major Activities	Main Focus	Responsibility Level
Ongoing	Team Participation, Technical Skill Mastery	Subfunctional Systems Design and Service
Short and Ongoing	Project Management, Process Improvement, Team Development	Business Partner Problems/Needs, Processes, Subprocesses
Long and Short	Structure/Work Force Design and Change Implementation, Cross-team Communication	Business Partner Problems/Needs, Business/ Cross-functional Integration
Long	Visioning, Strategy Alignment	Whole Business Community Function

If you aspire to any of the leadership roles, the following exercise will help you decide which critical leadership competencies you currently possess and which you need to develop further.

LEADERSHIP COMPETENCY SELF-ASSESSMENT

Complete the following *Leadership Competency Self-assessment Form* to determine what you consider to be your current level of performance in the behaviors critical to your present role and, if any, to the role you aspire to next. Again do a quick run-through. Don't agonize over the details.

Next, check (✔) your top 1 or 2 *leadership competency improvement needs* based on 2 criteria—your *rating scores* and your perception of *importance* or immediate need in your current work and immediate future aspirations.

Then go to the next level of specificity. Look at the observable behaviors listed under each competency. Check your top 2 or 3 *observable behavior improvement needs* again based on the combination of your *rating scores* and perception of *importance* or immediate need.

In the right hand column write a few examples or evidence of why you need to improve these checked behaviors.

Record your synthesized results in the space provided on page 44.

LEADERSHIP COMPETENCY SELF-ASSESSMENT FORM

LEADERSHIP—ALL LEADERS

Performance Management Competency
- Clearly communicates performance standards and expectations (*e.g.*, company or organization vision and values). ____
- Provides ongoing coaching, feedback, and development suggestions to improve individual performance. ____
- Leverages the unique talents of each team member. ____
- Collaboratively generates and tracks professional development goals for team members. ____
- Recognizes and rewards others' accomplishments and ensures that they are visible within the organization. ____ Average ____ Importance ____

Strategic Thinking Competency
- Identifies future business opportunities and obstacles. ____
- Continuously develops ideas for positioning the organization to become an effective long-term competitor. ____
- Makes sound business decisions when faced with complex and contradictory alternatives. ____ Average ____ Importance ____

Key Competencies Enter the number indicating your current level of accomplishment on the line next to each behavior below. *Rating Scale*   0   1 | | | | | 5
                                                                        NA   Very Poor   Excellent

Average Score Sum of scores divided by number of behaviors actually displayed
Check Importance for Success
Comment on pertinent facts and critical incidents that show:
• Key Strengths (*i.e.*, behaviors often displayed)
• Important development needs (*i.e.*, behaviors seldom displayed)

TEAM LEADER—(COACH)

Project and Process Management Competency

• Systematically gathers and analyzes pertinent information to plan a course of actions. ____

• Sets objective standards and develops team goals or objectives that can be measured concretely. ____

• Optimizes the use of time and resources to achieve desired results (*e.g.*, selects and applies proper tools to the task). ____

• Anticipates potential problems and develops contingency plans or process improvements to avoid them. ____

• Monitors and tracks the implementation of plans to ensure desired outcomes. ____   Average ____   Importance ____

Team Leadership and Development Competency

• Personally models the values and work practices expected of the team. ____

• Establishes appropriate team values, incentives, and work practices. ____

• Develops a team with appropriate talents and skills for accomplishing projects. ____   Average ____   Importance ____

MID-LEVEL MANAGER—(MULTIPLE TEAM INTEGRATOR)

Resource Management Competency

• Develops specific action plans and milestones with the team to implement identified strategies. ____

• Specifies critical resource needs required to meet business objectives. ____

• Actively negotiates with key stakeholders and functional counterparts to obtain required resources. ____

• Continuously tracks plans and milestones. ____   Average ____   Importance ____

Cross-team Integration Competency
• Ensures that various functions work together toward a common approach to business development and improvement (*e.g.*, marketing, customer support, etc.) _____
• Builds strong collaborative relationships with business operations to deliver on promises. _____
• Ensures that the market and customer realities are clearly understood by team members. _____
• Takes action to ensure that key strategies, goals, and plans are understood by all team members. _____   Average _____   Importance _____

EXECUTIVE—(STRATEGIST)

Visioning and Alignment Competency
• Creates a vision or picture of the organization and its future that directs and inspires the work force. _____
• Builds buy-in for strategic goals across organization levels and boundaries. _____
• Leverages key relationships and makes the informal and formal networks work. _____
• Clearly articulates the vision and translates it into day-to-day practices. _____   Average _____   Importance _____

Strategic Planning Competency
• Quickly anticipates key marketplace trends, opportunities, and vulnerabilities and positions the company appropriately. _____
• Develops key strategies that add value to customer while outpositioning the competition. _____
• Develops long-term strategic alliances and partnerships that increase the company's competitive advantage. _____   Average _____   Importance _____

LEADERSHIP COMPETENCY IMPROVEMENT NEEDS

If you decided to complete a self-assessment on any of the leadership roles, in the space below record the top 2 or 3 leadership competencies you checked as needing the most immediate improvement.

- _____

- _____

- _____

LEADERSHIP OBSERVABLE BEHAVIOR IMPROVEMENT NEEDS

If you elected to complete a self-assessment on any of the leadership roles, record in the space below the top 2 or 3 leadership observable behaviors you checked as needing the most immediate improvement.

- _____

- _____

- _____

DEVELOPMENTAL EXPERIENCES

When our research looked at how people acquired various critical competencies an interesting pattern emerged. Much learning of the core and leadership competencies (as distinguished from functional/technical skills such as graphic arts or accounting) occurred, not in formal training courses, but through a series of specifically identifiable on-the-job developmental experiences. As most moved through the different career and leadership roles we've described (*e.g.*, team member, team leader, mid-level manager, and executive), each role provided them with a specific set of developmental experiences.

Workbook Appendix A (starting on page 57) contains a detailed description of these experiences and a *Developmental Experiences Self-diagnostic Form*. We put the detailed descriptions of these experiences in Appendix A because they would be of interest only to those who have decided to pursue one or more of the leadership roles we've described.

If you are interested in pursuing a leadership or managerial career path, you can complete the self-assessment form in Appendix A to identify which developmental experiences you have already completed and which you might want to pursue in your current and next, if any, desired career role. If you are not interested in that, you can just move on to page 45.

ENRICHING YOUR CURRENT JOB

Too often people developing career strategies focus only on growth opportunities that might be available in future jobs. However, the successful career strategists we interviewed usually did not focus *solely* on future jobs. They were very proactive about finding ways to fill important competency improvement needs and experience gaps by enriching their current positions. The following exercise will help you explore ways to fill some of the personal growth needs you've recorded in this workbook without changing jobs.

CURRENT JOB ENRICHMENT

EXERCISE

Review the most important competency and observable behavior improvement needs you identified on pages 33 and 34. If you elected to do any of the leadership self-assessments, also review the competency/observable behavior improvement needs you recorded on page 44 and the developmental experience gaps you recorded on page 62. Then complete the following *Current Job Enrichment Form*.

Under each category listed on the next page, note what current job enrichment steps you might take (and when) to fill some of the improvement needs you've identified.

Also note:
- any training you want to negotiate and complete while still in your current job.
- any ideas you have on how to eliminate or delegate some activities from your current job to gain more time for new, enriching activities.

CURRENT JOB ENRICHMENT FORM

Competency and Observable Behavior Improvement Needs

List 1 or 2 job enrichment actions you might take/negotiate within your current job to fill some of the most important *competency* and *observable behavior* improvement needs you recorded on pages 33 and 34 (and on page 44 if you did any leadership competency self-assessments).

1. _____

_____

_____

_____

2. _____

_____

_____

_____

On-the-Job Learning Experiences

List the 1 or 2 most productive and doable job enrichment actions you can take/negotiate to build any needed experiences into your current job (see page 62 if you decided to complete the *Developmental Experiences Self-assessment Form* in Appendix A).

1. _____

_____

_____

_____

2. _____

_____

_____

_____

Training

List any training you want to negotiate while still in your current job. If you don't know specific courses, just list types of training.

_____

_____

_____

_____

Efficiency Possibilities

List any possibilities you can think of for eliminating or delegating some current activities to gain more time for adding enrichment activities to your job.

_____

_____

_____

_____

SUMMARY

Review the *actions* you listed under each of the preceding categories. Look for *overlap* and potential *synergies*. If possible, combine one or more of the actions into a single integrated action. Then, record in the space below a summarized list of the most important integrated actions you want to take. If none of the actions can be combined or integrated, just look at the separate activities you listed under each category and record the most important ones below. If possible, list a tentative date when you want to take each of the actions recorded.

- _____

- _____

- _____

- _____

MARKETING YOURSELF FOR FUTURE JOBS

While many feel they can learn and grow in the directions they choose right in their current jobs for some time, it's still a good idea to:

- Make at least a preliminary hypothesis about if and when you might want to move into a new position (and what type of position it should be).
- Decide what the first steps might be toward that future move.
- Establish at least tentative dates for those first steps.

Even if you are not contemplating any job changes, it's still a good idea to build your network of personal visibility in the career field you've chosen. This increases your credibility and enhances your ability to get your ideas heard and implemented. It also builds a safety net you can fall back on if unexpected changes should make it necessary for you to find a different job. With the above in mind, we suggest you complete the following exercise.

MARKETING PLANNING

EXERCISE

Identify the 3 most important preliminary steps you can take to build your network of personal visibility, and/or to investigate and market yourself for your next position. List tentative dates for each action in the space below.

NEXT-STEP MARKETING ACTIONS
(and tentative dates)

- _____

- _____

- _____

OVERCOMING PREDICTABLE BARRIERS

It's unwise to be surprised by predictable barriers when they occur. It's more useful to identify them in advance and make plans to overcome or avoid them. It's equally useful to identify potential aids in our environments and make plans to increase and enhance these as much as possible. The following exercise will help you do both.

BARRIERS AND AIDS

Think about the career and life planning goals you've recorded in this workbook (*e.g.*, life values priorities, preferred competencies, future job goals, important competency improvement needs, and your marketing plans).

Then use the form starting on the next page to list potential barriers and aids to achieving these goals in your current environment.

Note that this exercise asks you to identify barriers and aids under 3 categories:

- Self
- Organization
- Family/Friends

This is to stimulate your thinking and help make certain you don't overlook important dimensions of your environment.

Your personal aids and barriers list may involve only 1 or 2 of these categories rather than all 3.

BARRIERS AND AIDS FORM

As you review the personal career and life goals you'd like to achieve in the near and longer-range future, what are the most likely barriers and aids (top 3 or 4) that you expect to encounter from yourself, your organization, your family/friends, etc.? List these in the space provided below.

FROM SELF

Barriers	*Aids*
•_____	•_____
_____	_____
•_____	•_____
_____	_____
•_____	•_____
_____	_____
•_____	•_____
_____	_____

FROM ORGANIZATION

Barriers	*Aids*
•_____	•_____
_____	_____
•_____	•_____
_____	_____
•_____	•_____
_____	_____
•_____	•_____
_____	_____

BARRIERS AND AIDS FORM (*Continued*)

FROM FAMILY/FRIENDS

Barriers	*Aids*
• _____	• _____
_____	_____
• _____	• _____
_____	_____
• _____	• _____
_____	_____
• _____	• _____
_____	_____

GETTING STARTED

After you identify potential barriers and aids, you then develop a list of the most important *next-step* actions you can take to overcome the barriers, enhance the aids, and begin implementing your personal career action plans. The following exercise will help you do this.

ACTION PLANNING   EXERCISE

List below the most important *next-step* actions you can take in the next 30, 60, and 90 days to overcome the barriers and enhance the aids to your personal career and life plan.

NEXT-STEP ACTION SUMMARY

Actions to Take Within the Next 30 Days

_____

_____

_____

_____

_____

_____

_____

_____

_____

Actions to Take Within the Next 60 Days

_____

_____

_____

_____

_____

_____

_____

_____

_____

Actions to Take Within the Next 90 Days

Communicating with a New Awareness

Effective communication is especially important if you want to nurture your spiritual as well as material growth and work in more rewarding community with others. To accomplish your career and life planning goals, you need to build understanding and negotiate the backing of others who are in a position to support your pursuits. Use the techniques outlined in the *Your Soul at Work* book Step 4 chapter on "Communicating with a New Awareness."

A Life-Long Process

This completes your workbook entries for now. However, the process this workbook walks you through is lifelong. The exercises, techniques, and self-assessment forms are designed for you to keep on your shelf for periodic updates. We hope you'll use them regularly over time as new challenges and situations occur. We believe they can help guide you on a very hopeful and productive personal life journey through the progressive stages of adult development to ever-higher levels of personal contribution, growth, and satisfaction.

DEVELOPMENTAL EXPERIENCES

Our research shows that much learning and development of the core and leadership competencies (as distinguished from functional/technical skills such as computer programming or accounting) does not occur in formal training courses. Typically, it takes place in real on-the-job situations.

The successful people we interviewed didn't follow any one clear career path, even when they were in the same specialty. There was no sequence of specific jobs or position titles they all moved through to develop credentials for higher level responsibilities. However, independent of whatever position titles they had, as most moved through the career and leadership roles we described earlier (*i.e.*, team member, team leader, mid-level manager, and executive) each role provided them with a set of on-the-job learning experiences that:

- were common to virtually everyone
- were completed in a variety of different sequences
- were consistent, though not identical, with the stages of adult development we outlined earlier (see workbook pages 12 and 13).

With the exception of higher level executive jobs, in today's flatter organizations leadership isn't always reserved for people with formal managerial responsibilities. Often people with no managerial titles or aspirations are thrown temporarily into ad-hoc leadership roles where personal effectiveness necessarily involves influencing the decisions and directions other people take.

As with the competencies, each of the experiences our research identified has a set of activities, which define it and can be used to determine whether or not you've completed the experience. For example, one of the critical learning experiences people need to get in the team leader role is labeled *Consolidation of Leadership Self-image*. This experience includes such things as:

- leading a critical effort in which success or failure will be highly visible
- delivering on a critical customer requirement with limited resources
- positively influencing other teams to collaborate more effectively

Most people can relate to these pragmatic descriptions. For instance, whether we are managers or nonmanagers, most of us can identify with the challenge of leading an effort where success or failure is highly visible, where it's difficult to negotiate the required assistance or resources, and where obtaining needed output from others calls for some very effective influence skills. We've presented our descriptions of both the competencies and the developmental experiences to seasoned professionals at all levels of their organizations' hierarchies. These descriptions have typically generated immediate recognition and credibility across multiple cultures throughout the world.

These descriptions describe the real world, but with somewhat of a twist. While most of us would look at the challenges in some of these experiences as "pains in the neck," our research showed that working through these challenges was often the best way to pick up critically needed skills for career *and* personal growth. The lessons we learn in these experiences not only make us better performers but, properly executed on and off the job, they even make us better, more understanding, and mature human beings.

These experiences don't necessarily occur in the sequence we present in the following pages. Instead, they can occur in a variety of sequences depending on the unique career circumstances of each individual. One job or assignment can give you more than one of the experiences. And all the individual activities that make up a given experience don't have to be picked up on the job. Those we interviewed had picked up many in extracurricular endeavors (*e.g.,* coaching a team or working on a community fund-raising drive).

The successful people we interviewed often negotiated to build these experiences into their current assignments (*i.e.,* deliberately negotiated job enrichment) or they strategized future movement to different job assignments to obtain them. Contrary to much popular belief, movement to a new assignment did not necessarily involve a promotion. Often it involved a lateral or even downward move to obtain a needed experience. With a longer-range goal in mind, many ignored conventional wisdom that a downward move would look bad. They successfully took that risk because they knew intuitively that without filling important experience gaps they would very likely plateau in their growth at or near their current levels of responsibility.

Most of us don't know intuitively what work experiences are critical. We need some guidelines. You can use the following exercise and the self-assessment form starting on Appendix A page 63 to determine which of these key experiences you have already completed and identify any important gaps in your experiences to date. Then you can select one or two experiences you want to negotiate into your work and complete next.

These experience guidelines are general, so don't obsess over them when you complete the exercise.

DEVELOPMENTAL EXPERIENCES SELF-ASSESSMENT

EXERCISE

1. Briefly review the summary list of developmental experiences on pages 60 and 61 but don't make any check marks until you've completed your more detailed self-assessment.

2. Complete the detailed *Developmental Experiences Self-assessment Form* starting on Appendix A page 63 up through your *current* and *next* (if any) desired career role.

3. When you have completed your detailed self-assessment, summarize your results in the format shown on pages 60 and 61 up through your *current* and *next* (if any) desired career role.

4. Review your summary and circle what you believe are your most important 2 to 3 developmental experience gaps (*i.e.*, gaps that are most important for you to fill next).

5. Record these top 2 to 3 experience gaps you want to fill next (*i.e.*, those circled) on page 62.

DEVELOPMENTAL EXPERIENCES SUMMARY

After you have completed the *Developmental Experiences Self-assessment Form* starting on Appendix A page 63, summarize your results on this and the next page. Check (✔) whether you have or have not completed each experience up through your current and next (if any) desired career role. Then circle what you believe are your most important 2 to 3 development experiences gaps (*i.e.*, gaps that are the most important for you to fill next).

EXPERIENCE

Completed the Experience

TEAM MEMBER
(Individual Contributor)

	Yes	No
1. Access to Significant Role Model(s)	☐	☐
2. Stretch Job Assignment	☐	☐
3. Continuous Learning Initiative	☐	☐
4. Significant Technical Success	☐	☐
5. Team Participation	☐	☐
6. Cross-functional Involvement	☐	☐
7. Proactive Problem Resolution	☐	☐
8. Quality Improvement Contribution	☐	☐
9. Exposure to Range of Business Issues	☐	☐
10. Direct Customer Involvement	☐	☐

TEAM LEADER
(Coach)

	Yes	No
1. Consolidation of Leadership Self-image	☐	☐
2. Significant Team Leadership	☐	☐
3. Value-added Customer Involvement	☐	☐
4. Broad Business Involvement	☐	☐
5. Exposure to Global Issues	☐	☐

DEVELOPMENTAL EXPERIENCES SUMMARY
(Continued)

EXPERIENCE	Completed the Experience	

MID-LEVEL MANAGER
(Multiple Team Integrator)

	Yes	No
1. Development of a Leadership Network	☐	☐
2. Partnership and Alliance Development	☐	☐
3. Business/Cross-business Support	☐	☐
4. Product/Service Development Initiative	☐	☐
5. Large-scale Change	☐	☐
6. Turnaround Experience	☐	☐
7. Total Responsibility Assignment	☐	☐
8. High-business Impact Assignment	☐	☐

EXECUTIVE
(Strategist)

	Yes	No
1. Expanded External Network	☐	☐
2. Corporate Leadership Development	☐	☐
3. Community Contribution	☐	☐
4. Work-force Development Experience	☐	☐
5. Culture Change Experience	☐	☐
6. Whole Business Operation Experience	☐	☐
7. Business Strategy Development	☐	☐
8. Strategic Contribution	☐	☐
9. Major International Exposure	☐	☐
10. Industry Leadership	☐	☐

DEVELOPMENTAL EXPERIENCE GAPS

If you elected to complete part or all of the *Developmental Experiences Self-assessment Exercise*, record in the space below the top 2 or 3 experience gaps you identified as those you most need to fill next.

- _____

  _____

  _____

- _____

  _____

  _____

- _____

  _____

  _____

DEVELOPMENTAL EXPERIENCES
SELF-ASSESSMENT FORM

1. Read the bulleted items that describe each experience.
2. Put a check mark (✓) in the box adjacent to those you have completed. Put only one check mark for each numbered experience (*i.e.*, do not check any of the explanatory comments preceded by a dash in some of the experience descriptions).
3. Identify one or two experiences that you have not completed and that would be most important for your competency development and/or your team's success.
4. Note in the space provided what aspect of those one or two most important experiences you want to work on next.

✓ Completed	EXPERIENCE	Comments

TEAM MEMBER
(Individual Contributor)

☐ **1) Access to Significant Role Model(s)**
Develops a personal philosophy and management style based on lessons learned from experience with either of the following types of people:
- An influential mentor or coach (may or may not be direct supervisor)
- A "role model" that creates a lasting impression (may be a positive experience or a negative one that demonstrates what not to emulate)

☐ **2) Stretch Job Assignment**
Performs in a difficult project or assignment that requires:
- Juggling competing priorities
- Making autonomous decisions about priorities
- Solving a difficult problem with team members

3) Continuous Learning Initiative

Learns how to take responsibility for and develop the habits and practices for rapid and continuous learning through activities such as:

- Self-study projects
- Development and tracking of personal learning goals
- Participation in and support for a team learning environment

4) Significant Technical Success

Makes a substantive technical contribution that:

- Requires high personal initiative and ownership
- Yields specific technical results with recognized impact on the organization
- Builds personal visibility

5) Team Participation

Serves as a team member where he/she:

- Makes team strategies and goals a top priority
- Builds consensus for decisions
- Collaborates with others to complete high-impact goals

6) Cross-functional Involvement

Completes significant assignment in another organization function (*e.g.*, marketing, finance, sales etc.) that provides an in-depth understanding of the problems and contributions of other functions to the total business equation

YOUR SOUL AT WORK

☐ **7) Proactive Problem Resolution**

Takes personal initiative to:

– Build a network of contacts with whom to identify and solve product or service problems

– Collaboratively define potential future problems or vulnerabilities in product or service offerings

– Influence counterparts to change policies and practices and improve processes to position product or service offerings better

☐ **8) Quality Improvement Contribution**

Implements a significant quality initiative in which he/she:

– Maps and develops improvement strategies for an important process

– Clarifies the potential value of critical improvements

– Negotiates for appropriate buy-in and resources to implement the changes

☐ **9) Exposure to a Range of Business Issues**

Develops a broad business perspective that results in an understanding of the organization's values, policies, critical business issues, and competitive pressures through assignments that require:

– Meaningful interactions with high-level management and/or

– Direct work involvement with counterparts in other functions

APPENDIX

10) Direct Customer Involvement

Performs in a role where he/she is directly involved with developing a product or service for a customer through such activities as:

– Meeting face-to-face to define problems and opportunities
– Clarifying customer requirements
– Participating in a team effort to deliver products or services to the customer
– Quantifying and tracking the value added in customer terms

TEAM LEADER
(Coach)

1) Consolidation of Leadership Self-image

Performs in an assignment that results in the development of personal confidence as a leader through activities such as:

– Leading a critical effort or project in which success or failure will be highly visible
– Delivering on a critical customer commitment with limited resources
– Presenting to key stakeholders
– Proactively influencing other teams to collaborate more effectively

2) Significant Team Leadership

Performs activities beyond the traditional team leader role by:

- Getting work done through other people and experts
- Translating key strategies into specific plans
- Motivating and aligning team members
- Providing mentoring or facilitating learning opportunities for team members

3) Value-added Customer Involvement

Develops long-term, trusting relationships with customers or internal clients by performing activities such as:

- Establishing credible relationships with key influencers and decision-makers
- Demonstrating "boardroom presence" (major presentations and/or one-on-one meetings)
- Consulting with key customer leaders to develop market/product/service positioning
- Identifying actions that will significantly impact the customer's business operations

4) Broad Business Involvement

Performs in a role that provides exposure to a major business issue or change initiative such as a:

- New system
- Major development effort
- Organizational start-up
- Major reorganization

☐ **5) Exposure to Global Issues**
Develops an in-depth understanding
of the cultural issues related to doing
business in another country or region by:
- Collaborating closely with customers
  from another country around needs
  and requirements
- Considering the competitive factors
  that influence product/service
  positioning (*e.g.*, competitors,
  regulations, etc.)
- Participating in the development of a
  product and/or service-offering
  tailored to a foreign market

MID-LEVEL MANAGER
(Multiple Team Integrator)

☐ **1) Development of a Leadership
Network**
Creates a wide network of personal
contacts through involvement in:
- Special study experiences
- Contacts with professionals inside and
  outside the company (industry
  associations, etc.)

☐ **2) Partnership and Alliance
Development**
Performs in a role in which he/she:
- Develops a supplier relationship with
  another division of the company or an
  outside vendor to improve
  product/service, cost, quality, or
  productivity or…
- Brings a new idea/technology to
  market or…

– Plans and develops a mutually beneficial product/service initiative with customers or internal clients

☐ **3) Business/Cross-business Support**
Leads an organization that supports one or more business units and performs such activities as:
– Establishing and maintaining effective communications with supported business teams
– Establishing continuous learning methodologies and procedures
– Team-building
– Planning and prioritizing the needs of many internal and external customers

☐ **4) Product/Service Development Initiative**
Leads a group responsible for developing or customizing a product or service for an internal or external customer

☐ **5) Large-scale Change**
Oversees and leads the major realignment of corporate practices, processes, and/or services

☐ **6) Turnaround Experience**
Plays a significant role in a situation where the company's reputation is in jeopardy and performs such activities as:
– Assessing a difficult situation
– Rebuilding customer relationships
– Restructuring the team and product/service delivery approach
– Making difficult decisions
– Rebuilding confidence within the team and with the customer

☐ 7) **Total Responsibility Assignment**
Assumes overall responsibility for the direction and operation of a major organization that requires:
– Controlling an entire business operation
– Exercising financial responsibility
– Planning and managing resources
– Motivating and coordinating the direction of large numbers of employees through relationships with functional counterparts

☐ 8) **High-business Impact Assignment**
Performs in a role that requires:
– Negotiating important parts of a partnership that make a significant financial impact on the overall business. For example:
– Developing practices or procedures
– Producing significant improvements in cost, quality, cycle time, or productivity

EXECUTIVE
(Strategist)

☐ 1) **Expanded External Network**
Develops a broad, high-level network of key individuals who can provide objective advice, counsel, and assistance in influencing others (including business and technical leaders from outside the organization) to supply critical information, technical expertise, feedback, and support

2) Corporate Leadership Development

Helps develop future organization leaders through activities such as:

- Mentoring others who have strong potential for future strategic leadership positions
- Modeling critical values and behavior required for excellence
- Coaching existing high-level leaders to help them continue to grow

3) Community Contribution

Promotes the organization's vision and values by taking a lead role in appropriate community organizations and events

4) Work-force Development Experience

Takes the lead in improving the effectiveness of a whole work force by:

- Communicating the critical importance of and leveraging the value of people to the organization
- Championing and providing career and professional development opportunities

5) Culture Change Experience

Provides leadership for the whole organization that produces major shifts in the vision, values, strategies, or practices by activities such as:

- Communicating a vision and the values of the organization
- Developing strategic best practices
- Modeling new, more participative leadership practices

APPENDIX

6) Whole Business Operation Experience

Assumes overall responsibility for a major organizational entity in an assignment (usually an operating management job) that requires:

- Controlling a department or function, or multifunctional operation
- Directing large numbers of employees, multiple products, or processes, with large budgets/resources

7) Business Strategy Development

Performs in positions in which he/she:

- Creates, articulates, and disseminates a vision for organizational excellence
- Develops strategies of overall long-term growth
- Generates strategies for integrating and leveraging sales, development, support, human resources, marketing and finds best practices across the whole organization for competitive advantage

8) Strategic Contribution

Leads an organization toward strategies that improve a business unit's long-term competitive advantage by:

- Creating a vision of future excellence
- Developing and clarifying best practices
- Making decisions with high, long-term impact
- Developing strategies for positioning the organization
- Developing and using business models to generate alternative scenarios

☐ **9) Major International Exposure**
Develops a detailed understanding of business and cultural issues in another country through activities such as:
- Serving a customer in another country
- Integrating practices between international and domestic areas of the organization

☐ **10) Industry Leadership**
Represents the organization in the industry/marketplace by:
- Actively participating in industry symposiums
- Taking leadership positions in industry associations
- Speaking at industry functions
- Publishing articles in industry journals

INVESTIGATIVE INTERVIEW FORM

INTRODUCTION

The following pages will help you conduct and analyze an *Investigative Interview*. We suggest you obtain a larger size master copy of this form from our office (see page 2 of this workbook). Keep one clean master copy of the form and use it to make separate copies for use in each interview you conduct. This form has two parts.

Part I:

Use this part to conduct the five-phase interview. In the *left column* under each phase you will find suggested discussion topics (starter questions) and space to add your own personal questions. The starter questions are not meant to be used verbatim. They are there only to help organize your thoughts and stimulate your thinking. Feel free to change them, rephrase them in your own words, add to them, or use only parts of them depending on your individual situation.

Key words in the **starter questions** are **highlighted** in bold for quick scanning during the interview.

The *right column* provides space for you to take notes on responses to the questions and record other key information (thoughts, insight gained, etc.) during the interview. The back side of each page can also be used for notes if you need more space.

The personal questions you write in the left column should be tailored to determine how well the interviewee's job/career path might meet your own life values and personal criteria for success.

Team Interviews

In some situations several individuals interested in conducting *Investigative Interviews* with the same people have worked together and conducted the interviews as a team. This has been a very positive experience for both the interviewers and the interviewees. The team can delegate various interview questions to different team members.

Part II:

Use this part after the interview to help you analyze the data collected and better determine the match between the interviewee's job/career path and your own life values/personal criteria for success.

PART I
INVESTIGATIVE INTERVIEW FORM

PHASE 1: OPENING
(*Statement of Purpose, Establishing Rapport*)

DISCUSSION TOPICS	NOTES (Complete during the interview)
Introduction **Thank you** for agreeing to talk with me. **Purpose** As you know, I'm **not** here **looking for** any specific **employment opportunities.** My **purpose** is **longer range.** I've **been doing** some fairly extensive **career planning** recently . . . and: • After a lot of analysis I've **concluded a career path similar to yours** would probably be very **productive** and **rewarding** . . . especially for someone **with my** personal **values** and **goals.** (Be prepared to be asked what your values and goals are. This can be a good way to establish rapport and show you have done some real homework. However, keep your response fairly brief since you're there to learn about the interviewee.) • I'm **looking at how** I can **best prepare myself** for a similar career path. • **You've been recommended** (by specific name/names, if possible) as someone who is **highly regarded** in this field . . . and who has a **lot of expertise** I could benefit from hearing. I appreciate your seeing me and I've **done some homework** on the questions to make the **best use of your time.** (This prepares the individual for the fact that you will be using and taking notes.) (Use the above only as a general guideline and **add any other questions/ comments you feel are appropriate** to the specific situation/local environment.)	

PART I
INVESTIGATIVE INTERVIEW FORM
NOTES

PART I
INVESTIGATIVE INTERVIEW FORM

PHASE 2: JOB CONTENT
(Results Expected, Relationships, Key Decisions,
Communications Required, Future Growth Possibilities)

DISCUSSION TOPICS	NOTES (Complete during the interview)

Results Expected
• What are the **most important results** expected from you in this job?
 	
Relationships
• What are the **key relationships**?
  • Superiors?
  • Peers?
  • People who report to you (if any)?
  • Internal and external customers?
  • Suppliers (external vendors and/or internal suppliers whose output you rely on?)
• What does **each expect from you**?
• What do **you expect from them**?
• **What problems do you encounter** and **how** do you resolve them?
• Etc.
 	
Key Decisions
• What are the **most important decisions** you have to make?
• **Who** else is involved in making them with you?
• **Who** has to **approve** them?
• What is your **typical process** or method for making **decisions** and getting them approved?
• Etc.	

PART I
INVESTIGATIVE INTERVIEW FORM

NOTES

PHASE 2: JOB CONTENT (*Continued*)
(Results Expected, Relationships, Key Decisions,
Communications Required, Future Growth Possibilities)

DISCUSSION TOPICS	NOTES (Complete during the interview)

DISCUSSION TOPICS

Communications Required
- What are the **most important communications** required in this job?
  - Upward?
  - Across the organization?
  - Downward?
  - With teams?
  - With customers/clients?
  - Etc.
- What **process or method** do **you use** to assure you are communicating sufficiently?
- Are there any special **cross-functional, cross-business,** or **cross-cultural/ global** communication challenges?

Future Growth Possibilities

What's next?

What sort of **jobs/challenges** would you like to **take on** after this **job**?

What will you have to **do** to **prepare** yourself?

What are your **long-range career goals**?

What else do you want to do before you retire?

Personal Questions

NOTES
(Complete during the interview)

PART I
INVESTIGATIVE INTERVIEW FORM

NOTES

PHASE 3: IMPORTANT QUALIFICATIONS
(Competencies, Experiences, Training)

DISCUSSION TOPICS	NOTES (Complete during the interview)

DISCUSSION TOPICS

Competencies
- What do you see as **the most important competencies** or skills required for success in **this job/career or path**?
  - Technical?
  - Functional?
  - Leadership?
  - Team-oriented?
  - Others?

Experiences
- **Looking back** over your career, are there any particular **experiences** or **challenges** that **stand out** as very **important in preparing you for success** in this work?
  - On the job?
  - Off the job?
  - Hobbies, etc.?

Training
- What type of **training** do you feel is **most important** in order to qualify for a career path like yours?
  - **Degrees or formal certifications** required (and/or merely desired)?
  - **Functional/Technical** training?
  - **Leadership** Training?
  - Etc.?

Personal Questions

PART I
INVESTIGATIVE INTERVIEW FORM

NOTES

PART I
INVESTIGATIVE INTERVIEW FORM

PHASE 4: KEY EVENTS
(Successes, Failures, High and Low Points, Values Met or Missed)

DISCUSSION TOPICS	NOTES
	(Complete during the interview)

DISCUSSION TOPICS

Successes
- What are the **one or two successes** you are **most proud** of (either in this or an earlier job)?
- What was **your personal contribution** to making it successful?
- What **problems/barriers** did you encounter?
- **What** did you **do** to **overcome** the **problems**?

Failures
- What were your **one or two most important failures**?
- **What happened**?
- **What** did you **learn** from them?

High and Low Points
- Were there **any other** particularly **significant high or low points** in your career to date that we haven't talked about?
- **What** did you **learn** from them?

Values Met or Missed
We **all have special values** we want to achieve in life ... things such as prestige, expertness, **achievement, time with family,** service to others ...
- What are the **things you value most**?
- How has this **job**/career path **helped** you **achieve** important **values**?
- Are there any **important values you've had to trade off** for success in this job/career path?
- **Anything** you would **do differently** as you look back?

Personal Questions

PART I
INVESTIGATIVE INTERVIEW FORM

NOTES

PHASE 5: CLOSURE

DISCUSSION TOPICS	NOTES (Complete during the interview)
Missed Questions I've **been asking a lot of questions.** • Is there **anything** you think I **should know** that I **didn't ask about** or we haven't covered? *Thanks and Wrap-up* • **Thank you** very much **for** your **time** and **candor.** • This has really **been very informative.** • I've **learned a great deal** here that **will be very helpful** in my future career planning. • I'm very **grateful to** (specific **name**) **for arranging** this **meeting** with you.	

PART II
INVESTIGATIVE INTERVIEW FORM

Matching Analysis

In this part of the form, you look at the results of your completed *Investigative Interview* and analyze how well the job/career path of the person interviewed does or does not match your personal criteria for success.

1. LIFE VALUES

How well would this job/career path contribute to the achievement of your most important personal *Life Values*? Which values would you achieve and which would be jeopardized (*i.e.*, you would have trouble achieving them)? List below:

Values you would be most likely to achieve	Values that would be jeopardized or that you would have trouble achieving
_____	_____
_____	_____
_____	_____
_____	_____
_____	_____

2. PREFERRED COMPETENCIES

Which of your *Preferred Competencies* would you use and develop in this job/career path? Which would you probably not use and develop? List below:

Motivated Competencies you would use/develop	Preferred Competencies you would probably *not* use/develop
_____	_____
_____	_____
_____	_____
_____	_____
_____	_____

PART II
INVESTIGATIVE INTERVIEW FORM

3. MATCH TO PERSONAL FUTURE JOB CRITERIA

How interested are you in preparing for this job/career path? How well does it match your *personal criteria for success*? Indicate with a circle.

1	2	3	4	5	6	7	8	9	10
Not Interested									**Very Interested**

Different people may interpret the numbers differently but you will probably have a range of ratings, with some of the career paths you investigate being rated much more highly than others. Those career paths you rate highest will be the ones you choose to pursue further while you cross off or eliminate those paths you rate lowest.

4. PERSONAL STRENGTHS AND WEAKNESSES

If you have a strong interest in the job/career path represented by the person you spoke to in this particular interview, what current competency strengths can you bring to the work and what new competencies (or skills) would you have to develop? Also, what experiences do you already have that will make you most marketable for the job, and what critical experience gaps would you have to fill? List these in the space provided for each below.

Competencies Consider all competency types (*i.e.*, core, leadership, and functional/technical competencies).

Strengths What are your current *competency strengths* that would be most marketable in pursuing this future job/career path?

_____

_____

Weaknesses What are your most important *competency weaknesses* (*i.e.*, gaps) that would have to be filled to better prepare you for this job/career path? Again, consider all competency types.

_____

_____

PART II
INVESTIGATIVE INTERVIEW FORM

Experiences Consider the *Developmental Experiences* identified in our research and any other important *Functional/Technical* experiences this interview identified as important.

Strengths What *experience strengths* do you already have that would make you most marketable on this job/career path?

_____

_____

_____

_____

Weaknesses What are your most important *experience weaknesses* (*i.e.*, gaps) that would have to be filled to better prepare you for this job career path?

_____

_____

_____

_____

5. TRAINING

What training did this interview show you might need to get if you want to pursue this job/career path? If you don't know the titles and locations of specific courses, just list the type and content of training you need.

_____

_____

_____

_____

_____